The Land Between the Rivers

John Paul Poston

Best Wishes,
Paul Poston

Blue Ridge Publishing

GREENVILLE, SOUTH CAROLINA • BELFAST, NORTHERN IRELAND

The Land Between the Rivers
Copyright © 1999 John Paul Poston

All Rights Reserved
o part of this book may be reproduced, store in a retrieval system, or transmitted in any form or by any means—electronic, mechanical, 1otocopy, recording, or otherwise—without written permission of the publisher, except for brief quotation in written reviews.

Published by
Emerald House Group, Inc.
Blue Ridge Publishing
427 Wade Hampton Blvd.
Greenville, SC 29609 USA

and

Ambassador Productions
Ardenlee Ave.
Belfast, Northern Ireland

www.emeraldhouse.com

Dedicated

To the Memory of My Parents:

Father-Mack Kenzie Poston 1888-1954
Mother-Carrie Yulee Greenwood Poston 1894-1948

who were the builders as stated in I Corinthians 3:10:

"According to the commission of God given to me, like a skilled master builder I laid a foundation, and another man is building upon it. Let each man take care how he builds upon it."

My Gift to My Children and Grandchildren

John Wayne Poston 1951
Leta Anne Poston Cook 1954
Stanley Ray Poston 1956

John Steven Poston 1983
Brian Kristopher Poston 1985
Emily Anne Cook 1986
Harrison Paul Cook 1989
and any additions

Who are the Present and Future Builders
on that Foundation.
A challenge to the heirs:

You are who you are because they were who they were.

Don't take that heritage lightly as you have been fitted to be the best that you can be. Go out into the world and use what you have been given for His glory and the betterment of mankind.

Acknowledgments

There is no way this book could have been written without the help of my dear wife, Leta. I wish to acknowledge and thank her for her tireless efforts in editing, typing, and getting the manuscript ready for printing.

I would also like to acknowledge and thank my son, Wayne, for the time, energy and expenses incurred while scanning and getting the manuscript ready for printing.

My daughter, Anne, and son, Stan, spent an inordinate amount of time and effort editing the manuscript and making suggestions. And for this I would like to acknowledge and thank them.

A project such as this book has to have input from a lot of people. I especially want to express thanks to my son, Stan, for drawing the map of the area where I grew up. Also, my children, Wayne, Anne, and Stan, for always wanting me to tell them stories about the "olden times." They continued to help during the writing by making suggestions and editing the manuscript.

My brothers and sisters, David, Jerry, Rowena McPhatter, and Virginia Chinnes, contributed greatly by jogging my memory and helping locate some of the pictures. I am grateful to my niece, Carol Poole, for encouraging me to write this book and for her help in locating some of the pictures.

I would like to recognize and thank my former daughter-in-law, Kris Stafford, for painting the art work on the book cover. The children in the picture are my children and grandchildren.

CONTENTS
Reminisce
Introduction

1.	"The Land Between The Rivers"...................	2
2.	Poston, The Town	3
3.	Some Tenants of The Land	6
4.	"Ca-hoot" Farming.................................	9
5.	Initiation to the Social Mores of "The Land Between the Rivers"................	12
6.	"Aunt" Mariah's Billy Goat......................	15
7.	"The Big Move".....................................	17
8.	My First Memories of Christmas and Santa Claus....................................	23
9.	My First Trip to Johnsonville....................	26
10.	My First Day at School...........................	28
11.	My First Trip to Myrtle Beach...................	30
12.	A 1924 Model T Touring Car...................	34
13.	A Mule Named Jack...............................	39
14.	Preacher to the Possum...........................	41
15.	1931 Hoover Cart.................................	43
16.	A Wooden People.................................	44
17.	Spared By God's Grace and Pee Wee's Barking..	45
18.	Dad's Last Fishing Trip with Mr. Joe King	47
19.	Trinity School.......................................	50
20.	Trinity Methodist Church	55
21.	Our Move to "Powell's Corner"..................	58
22.	Mud Pies...	61
23.	Catching Wild Hogs	63
24.	Shad Fishing on the "Mighty" Pee Dee..........	65
25.	"The Dumb Bull"	68
26.	Our First Radio	73
27.	A Tobacco Barn Raising	77
28.	Betty and Rhodie, The Ultimate in Mule Power..	79
29.	We Fired the Ice Man	83
30.	A New Car......Wow!!!...........................	86
31.	The Move from "Powell's Corner" to "The Backwoods"..	88
32.	I'll Never Forget My Friend Christmas...........	95

33.	Rover, My Best Friend............................	100
34.	My Parents' "Do-Good" Rules.....................	103
35.	Things That I Remember About Dad..............	107
36.	Things That I Remember About Mom............	116
37.	Grandma Greenwood...............................	125
38.	Grandpa Greenwood	129
39.	Uncle "Bubba"	131
40.	Uncle Furman "Pum"...............................	136
41.	Aunt Alma	140
42.	Grandma Poston......................................	142
43.	Uncle Zack...	146
44.	Aunt "Culia"...	152
45.	"The Well Digger"....................................	154
46.	"The Wild Man"	157
47.	Lost in The Pee Dee River Swamp................	159
48.	The Infamous Squirrel Hunt........................	161
49.	B. L. Poston, An Institution........................	164
50.	Johnsonville High School...........................	168
51.	Sex and Sexuality.....................................	174
52.	We Raised Our Boys to be Men....................	182
53.	Bits of Humor...	184
54.	Local Tobacco Customs.............................	193
55.	Common Illnesses and Their Cures................	196
56.	Different Foods We Ate.............................	199
57.	Colloquial Dialect....................................	208
58.	Local Superstitions...................................	212
59.	Ghosts?... or Haunts?... or What?.................	214
60.	They Say It Really Happened......................	220
61.	A Tap on the Shoulder..............................	225
62.	The Onslaught of World War Two	231
63.	Answering My Country's Call.....................	242
64.	Forever..	263
65.	Parables of Life	291
66.	Family History..	302

Map of portion of Florence County, South Carolina

Different Places we lived in the "Land Between the Rivers" from 1921 to 1955

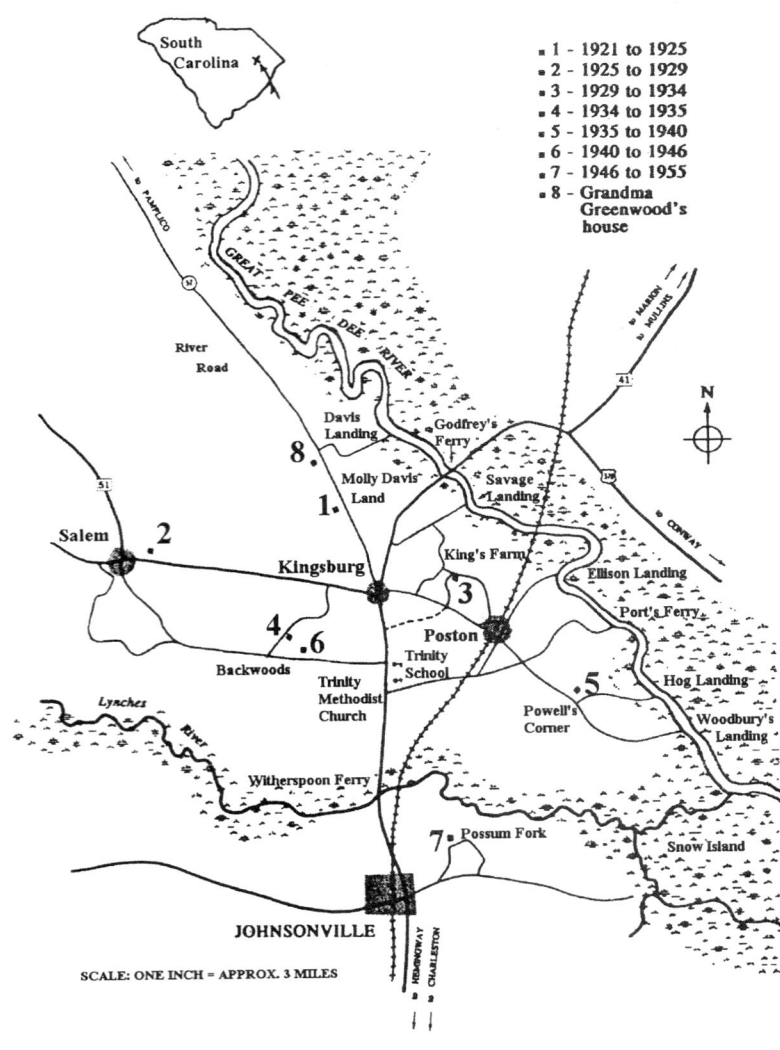

REMINISCE

Take me back to the land where I whiled away my youth,
To an area ingrained with honor and truth;
Let me see the old oaks all drooping with grace,
And gray Spanish moss hanging like lace.

Back to a land where the Swamp Fox aspired,
To secure the freedom from an evil empire;
Where the men were strong and the women clever,
As they lived on "The Land Between the Rivers."

Let me live in a house where there's nothing but love,
A feeling inspired from the heavens above;
Let me wake in the morning by the dawn's new light,
To start my day ere the sun gets bright.

Take me back to the time when cotton was king,
Before I ever heard of that weevil thing.
Where growing tobacco was a tedious chore,
Though life was simple, it was never a bore.

Let me follow my mule as I till the land,
The journey is long toward becoming a man;
Back to a school where the three R's flourished,
A Bible was welcomed and a prayer was nourished.

A time when discipline was not all gab
'cause all it took was "I'll tell your Dad."
Take me back to the church atop the hill,
Where families were large and the pews were filled.

Let me roam the woods and ponder a spell,
With my dog at my side wishing me well;
With worms for bait and a bamboo pole,
Let me head once again for the old fishing hole.

On my back in the dark let me gaze at the stars,
Hoping to see Big Dipper, or maybe Venus, or Mars;
Let me awake in the night to hear once again,
The lonesome whistle of a far-off freight train.

Let me reacquaint myself to my friends of old,
In a land where your neighbor was truer than gold;
To an area where lawyers were surely not needed,
As a promise and a handshake were constantly heeded.

While I pause and recall the past with a nod,
I'm reminded that in the midst was Almighty God,
The observer may see that I get excited and quiver,
When I reminisce my life on "The Land Between the Rivers."

Written by John Paul Poston

INTRODUCTION

The Land Between the Rivers is the title I have given to this book because this is the area where I grew up—between the Lynches and Great Pee Dee Rivers. The insistence of my children and grandchildren prompted me to write how it was in (what they call) "the olden days."

I have attempted to write this in my own words and have tried to explain each event as I perceived it at the particular time that it occurred. It has been my endeavor to be as factual as possible, but, as we all know, perspectives change with the passing of time and age. I have ventured to portray each incident through the eyes, ears, heart, mind, and aspirations of a young growing boy.

The period in time that I have written about was the 1920's, 1930's, and 1940's. Each decade was different as it had its own unique problems. The Twenties were years of "boom and burst," but there were many bank failures beginning toward the end of the decade. The Thirties were years of deep economic crises. The Forties were years of the "awesome" World War II.

Technology has advanced so rapidly since 1950! It may be difficult for my young readers to comprehend life as it was lived during those years.

It is my hope that the reader will recognize that I grew up with an older generation who had survived the Civil War; I actually knew some people who had been slaves. The memories retold to me about that strife, the Charleston Earthquake of 1888 (the Big Shake), the Spanish American War, the sinking of the Titanic, and World War I will encircle my mind's eye forever.

The family that I am addressing is the Mack Poston Family. This is the 7th and 8th generation of Postons since John Poston emigrated from England in 1703. The area where it all happened was in and around a town named Poston, which is located between the Great Pee Dee and Lynches Rivers in Florence County, South Carolina.

Chapter 1

"THE LAND BETWEEN THE RIVERS"

Francis Marion, The Swamp Fox, roamed the dense forest of "The Land Between the Rivers" during the late 1700's. While strolling the area, he crafted his strategy to defend his troops and to launch his surprise attacks on the British army.

Snow Island was selected for Marion's hide-a-way encampment. This island is across Lynches River from "The Land Between the Rivers." Once his hidden camp was in place, he had to devise a plan of defense to the north of his fortress.

Port's Ferry crossed the Pee Dee River about four miles north of where the black waters of Lynches River flowed into the yellow waters of the "Majestic" Pee Dee. Marion fortified this crossing, and then he fortified Witherspoon Ferry, which crossed Lynches River about five miles west of the area where the two rivers joined.

It was at Witherspoon Ferry that Marion accepted command of the Williamsburg Militia. These extra troops strengthened the units under his command. Marion now initiated a scouting system that ran from Port's Ferry to Witherspoon Ferry so that he could be forewarned of the invading British troops. The British were never able to penetrate the ingenious scheme of the "master warrior."

In my mind no piece of land on the continent of North America played a more vital role in the defeat of the British than "The Land Between The Rivers." As a boy, I used to sit on the banks of the Pee Dee at Port's Ferry and beg the river to tell me about what went on there. I simply knew that the river remembered what went on, but it just kept rolling along.

I could feel that my hero, the Great Swamp Fox, had been there and the results of his sacrifices were still there. In my love for his patriotism, I tossed pebbles in the swift running water and dedicated them to Marion and his men.

When I walked through the woods and spotted a huge oak tree, I just stood and admired it. My thoughts meandered: perhaps Marion passed that tree ...... did he lean his gun against it? ...... maybe he sat by it to rest ....

Chapter 2

POSTON, THE TOWN

The defeat of the British by the Revolutionary Army was a time of jubilation for many people in all the colonies. But sadly to say, the people who lived in "The Land Between The Rivers" just drifted along and forgot about the significance of their role in the new gained freedom.

Throughout the 1800's, the Pee Dee maintained its dominance as the transportation conveyance system for that part of the state. During this period a river port named Ellison (located about two miles north of Port's Ferry) developed and prospered. This port became one of the main ports between Georgetown and Cheraw.

The primary exports were cotton, tobacco, corn, and lumber. The main imports were rice, indigo, manufactured goods and essentials needed for day-to-day existence. During the mid-1800's Ellison gradually evolved into the Town of Poston...due to the influx of Postons who came up the river and settled in the area.

In the beginning Poston was in the Marion District. The river was a difficult barrier between Poston and the county seat. Progress for the town came very slowly, but with the help of a few prominent leaders such as Andrew Poston, Poston did begin to grow.

By 1860 some of the leaders had become influential and wealthy. People in the area contributed to and participated in the Civil War of 1861-1865. In searching the history we found no Postons who owned slaves, and we certainly hope this was true.

The year of 1888 brought some political changes for Poston and the surrounding area. Florence County was formed from parts of Marion, Williamsburg, Darlington, and Clarendon Counties. It became a county by an act of the State Legislature at twelve o'clock midnight December 23, 1888.

Senator L. S. Bigham, an ancestor to the Bigham family who was murdered in 1921, was a driving force in creating this county. Of course, Andrew Poston, John Woodberry and other citizens of the area were instrumental in the political process.

This change should have produced some real advantages for

this area by not having the river as a barrier. There were very few advantages for being in Florence county for many years. The swamps along the Pee Dee between Florence and Poston were more difficult to cross than the river had been to get to Marion.

A very positive event happened for Poston in 1914 with the coming of the railroad. This occurrence diminished the importance of the Great Pee Dee as a transportation line forever. A railroad line was then run from Poston to Florence, which connected Kingsburg and Pamplico. Now Poston had a direct link to the county seat, so political representation did improve.

Poston became an active center and brought in people who worked with the railroad. Much to the surprise of a lot of people, the railroad company became interested in building a union repair shop at Poston because of its proximity to other central lines.

People of the town were aroused and fought the plan because they believed this would create too much soot and smoke; they also feared it would bring in some undesirable people.

Another obstacle was that one of the prominent citizens wouldn't sell the land needed to build the shop on. The company built the shop in Andrews. In retrospect we can see that Poston was the loser in this situation.

In its heyday Poston boasted a hotel, several restaurants, a number of boarding houses, a cotton gin, a blacksmith shop, a gristmill, and several large general stores. There were a number of impressive homes in the area.

The Seaboard Railroad Company had six railroad lines running through the town. The main street was extra wide, which was apparently designed with the future in mind. Many people really thought that Poston would become a large city, but that was not to be.

Poston began its decline from prominence during the late stages of World War I. The death of one of the founding fathers, Andrew Poston, in 1916 was a jolt that the community probably never overcame.

Andrew had two sons, Charles and Louin, from his first marriage who were left to manage his vast wealth. Each of them died untimely deaths at a young age. This evidently left a leadership void that was never filled.

There were other prominent families in the community such as the Warren Powell's and the John Woodberry's, who either moved away or died, and this increased the leadership void. The Powells and the Woodberrys owned most of what was known as "Powell's Corner."

The fact that Poston did not get the Railroad Repair Shop, which eventually was put in Andrews, hurt the future of the town. The decline of the railroad's importance for freight and passenger service really put the nails in the town's coffin. As the activity of the railroad abated, those persons employed by the railroad moved away.

Poston relied also on a very strong farming interest in the area. The method of farming changed over the years to more machinery and less laborers. Those people who used to be on the farms around Poston were required to move away to find employment.

Today Poston consists of a single railroad line running through it, a paved road, and a few houses. This is a sad omen to progress in reverse.

Chapter 3

SOME TENANTS OF THE LAND

On a cold wintry night before daylight on Christmas morning December 25, 1888 a baby boy was born. This event took place in the Blossom section of the newly formed Florence County. This was in an area where the land was nestled between two great rivers, Pee Dee and Lynches.

This baby was named Mack Kenzie Poston. The proud parents, Edward P. and Emily Creel Poston, probably didn't realize at the time that they had brought forth a son who would become very special in the lives of a lot of people. It is quite possible that Mack was the first person to be born in "one day old" Florence County.

Six years later on a warm starlit night on August 25, 1894 a child was born to John Travis and Adelia Ann Marsh Greenwood. This beautiful baby girl was named Carrie Yulee Greenwood. This blessed event occurred in the Savage section near Kingsburg. John and Adelia could not have envisioned that they had brought forth one of God's saints.

These two babies grew up in separate areas of "The Land Between The Rivers." By chance or by celestial design, Mack met Yulee eighteen years later. A friendship and love developed between the two. They were married a year later on December 25, 1913 (Mack's 25th birthday). Mack was a farmer, so they lived on various farms in the Savage area for years to come.

This young couple worked hard and were just ordinary "dirt" farmers, except for one unique difference: what they let their lives stand for. They had a special relationship with their God, which never wavered. This life-style was taught to their children.

The union between Mack and Yulee produced ten children.

Merrill Willard	November 17, 1914
Lance Edward	December 15, 1916
Daltrum Holmes (Bunkus)	May 30, 1919
Nellie Yulee	October 7, 1921
Rowena Byrd	November 27, 1923
John Paul	August 20, 1926
David Milton	November 1, 1928
Max Lefay	November 16, 1931
Virginia Ann (Sis)	November 18, 1933
Jerry Travis	July 1, 1937

The writer of this book is Paul, the sixth child born into this family. The writing is an effort to recall various experiences of a large family growing up during a very depressed economy.

In writing this book, I have emphasized the strong family structures that my parents commanded. Both parents had a deep faith in their Lord, which sustained them through some very arduous crises.

The first years of the marriage of my parents were good years. By 1924 they were able to buy a Model T Ford for cash. Serious economic problems for the family began in November of 1924. At this time the bank in Johnsonville went bankrupt and closed its doors. Dad was caught by surprise and ended-up losing everything.

Many people could not have endured this terrible dilemma. But, Dad's faith in God, faith in himself, and love for his family gave him the strength needed to survive some troublesome times.

He lived with the philosophy that he had been "bent very badly but he was never broken." He was left with no money, but he had his honor, his integrity, his health, and his faith in God, which reinforced his sagging spirits.

Yulee died in 1948 from burn-out, and Mack died in 1954 from cancer. Their deaths were like their lives -- a calm assurance of life hereafter.

Before their deaths, they had done well enough to quit sharecropping; they had bought and paid for a nice farm. They had come a long way and now lived in a house that they could call their own.

Hard work, faith in God, love of land, love of country, love of family, and astuteness had paid-off. They never saw any of their children become involved with alcohol, drugs, or a crime worse than a speeding ticket.

Each child accepted Christ at an early age. Chosen professions for their children were: ministers, farmers, housewives, secretaries, corporate executives, factory workers, politicians, communication professionals, and store owners.

My family endured many hardships during the depression, but we were fortunate in many ways. First we lived in this great country of opportunities. Second, we had parents who stood like the "Rock of Gibraltar" through any storm. With faith to move mountains, we were able to pull ourselves out of many destitute situations.

Chapter 4

"CA-HOOT" FARMING

Following the Stock Market Crash of 1929, the economic condition of our county was crucial. We had to begin our lives as sharecroppers on a tobacco farm; there seemed to be no other way to survive. During the depression years, many families lost their farms and many of those families depended on sharecropping for survival. Landlords furnished the land, fertilizer, seed, a house (or an excuse for one) to live in, and advance money to buy the necessities until the crops were made and sold.

When the crops were harvested and sold, and after all the advances were taken out, the net proceeds were divided equally between the landlord and the sharecropper. The sharecropper furnished all the labor, the mules or horses, the feed for the mules or horses, and all the tools and farming implements required for the job. There was an old adage about sharecropping that was widely heard during this era. It was said that this arrangement was farming on "ca-hoots"...the landlord got the money and the sharecropper got the "ca-hoots."

Work for the sharecropper never ended. In the summer he had to "gather" tobacco and put it into barns. In the winter he had to cut the wood needed to supply the heat for the curing of the tobacco. In January the seed beds had to be planted and covered with a protective canvas so the plants would grow large enough to be transplanted in the fields by late April and May.

The tobacco usually grew fast and would be ready for "gathering" in late June. Harvesting or "gathering" (as it was called then) of tobacco was done very scientifically. Leaves of tobacco plants ripen a few at a time, beginning on the bottom of the stalk. Every week a few leaves had to be "cropped" off. There were usually five or six "gatherings" over a period of five or six weeks. This process was normally completed by the first or second week of August. The ripened leaves were "cropped" off the stalk and placed in what was called a drag (similar to a sled). The leaves had to be straight and untangled. The drag was then pulled to the barn by a mule, and the driver was usually a boy ten to twelve years old.

When the drag arrived at the barn, the tobacco was taken out and put on a bench with all the stems running in the same direction. The leaves were put in bunches of four or five by "handers" (usually teenage girls) and handed to "stringers" (usually women). The "stringer" strung these bundles with twine on a stick about five feet long. These sticks of green tobacco weighed about fifty pounds and had to be handled carefully to keep from damaging the tobacco or breaking the twine.

The sticks were then hung in a barn on tier-poles. A twenty foot barn had tier-poles which were four feet apart creating five divisions called rooms. The tier-poles were stacked at two foot intervals extending to the top of the barn and were eight or nine poles high. The sticks of tobacco were placed on the tier-poles about eight inches apart. A barn would hold several hundred sticks.

When the barn was full of green tobacco, a fire was built in the two furnaces to cure it out. It usually took about a week (running at a temperature up to 210 degrees F) to cure all the sap out of the leaves and stems. During the harvesting season the sharecropper had to "gather" tobacco all day and then sit up at night to fire the furnaces to cure the tobacco. Farmers worked continuously seven days a week.

The harvesting season was usually over by mid-August, and then it was time to prepare the cured tobacco for marketing. Every leaf of the tobacco had to be carefully examined and separated by quality and color. Next each quality level was tied in small bundles of about a quarter pound each. Next, there was the process called "sticking-up," where the bundles of tobacco were put on sticks about four feet long. The tobacco was then taken to the market on these sticks.

Markets in the local area were at Pamplico, Lake City, and Mullins. Tobacco was hauled by mule and wagon or Model T trucks. Transportation improved in the late thirties with the use of Chevrolet, Dodge and Ford trucks. This phase of the operation was usually completed by the end of September. During the depression a farmer made about 750 pounds of tobacco per acre and his crop usually sold for 15 to 20 cents per pound. Lack of adequate fertilizer kept production low.

October was the month to pick cotton. Most of the schools

halted classes during the time cotton picking was going on. One year during the depression our school ran only seven months. When the cotton was all picked, ginned, and sold, there should have been some time for the sharecroppers to rest, but there was no rest. It was time to prepare and plant the seed beds, clear the fields for next year's tobacco crop, and chop wood for next year's tobacco curing. You can see why it was said that "a sharecropper's work was never done."

The sharecropping system had a lot of shortcomings. One of these was the bookkeeping system. Most sharecroppers lacked formal education and had to depend on the honesty of the landlord for his rightful share of the earnings. Sharecroppers were lucky if they "broke even." Most of the sharecroppers never accumulated anything. Many lost hope of ever regaining their independence and lived their lives numbed by a day-to-day existence.

As I think back on the life of a sharecropper, I am reminded of the song, "Sixteen Tons." There is a line that states, "Sixteen tons, and what do you get? Another day older and deeper in debt." Very often the sharecropper moved before the crop was harvested and sold. Sometimes he became disenchanted because he just couldn't see anything better in his future. Occasionally he had a fuss with the landlord, who ran him off. There were very few written contracts.

Toward the end of the depression some landlords began renting some of their land and even selling some through the Farm Home Administration and the Federal Land Bank. The Government at this time enacted production controls and price supports. The National Recovery Act and President Roosevelt's New Deal helped many sharecroppers begin a better life. Farming today is done mostly by large corporations that have adequate funds to provide for mechanization and automation, thus making sharecropping obsolete.

Chapter 5

INITIATION TO THE SOCIAL MORES OF "THE LAND BETWEEN THE RIVERS"

The first thing that I can really remember as a habitant of "The Land Between the Rivers" happened one cold wintry night in January 1929. We were living in a house near Salem. The yard had several large trees and was surrounded by large fields of corn, cotton and tobacco. My Dad was a revenuer during the days of prohibition. A revenuer was a term used to describe a government officer who was hired to control the illegal manufacture and use of alcohol.

Several days before this eventful night Dad found an active liquor still making moonshine whiskey. Well, Dad and several other revenue officers dismantled the still in sections and brought the sections to be stored in our barn until the still could be completely destroyed. This turned out to be not only a breathtaking mistake but a regrettable one.

Somehow the owners of the still learned that the still was in our barn, and apparently they knew that my Dad was not home on this particular night. Dad had gone to a Masonic Lodge meeting, and as I learned later, very few things kept Dad away from his "Lodge"... he was there every time there was a meeting.

A short time after Dad left, strange things began to happen. Mom was busy getting the small children ready to be tucked in for the night. We started hearing loud noises. There were people outside the house talking loudly... yelling and cursing. Suddenly loud blasts sliced through the darkness. We quickly learned these blasts were coming from shotguns and rifles.

We were hushed by our Mother and made to lie down on the floor or on the beds as buck shot and bullets shattered our windows and splintered the walls. The fire in the fireplace was doused with water and the lamps were blown out. It was so quiet in the house that I couldn't hear anyone breathe. I was in a bed that had a high wooden headboard.

A bullet came through the wall and hit the headboard over

my head with a thunderous blast. There was not a single pane of glass in the windows that was left unbroken. We were scared "out of our wits," but no one was physically harmed. I realized later that this was my initiation into the land of living, breathing mortals, who are indeed less than perfect inhabitants of this hallowed land.

It was quite apparent that these moonshiners did not like having their still put out of business. Not bothering to break the lock off the barn door, they just tore the door off the barn to get to their still. They killed the dog, let the mules out of their stalls, let the cows out, and let the hogs out ...that is, those hogs that they elected not to kill.

This particular still was never recovered, nor were these moonshiners ever brought to justice. Dad continued as a revenuer for a couple of years. He did it for two reasons. First, he had an intense hatred for liquor and what it would do to a person. Second, he did it for the few dollars that he received from it to help feed his family.

When the revenuers discovered a still and the still operators were caught, there was a trial. I can remember a number of times when these trials were held at our home. The judge, sheriff, deputies, and anyone else involved would come to the house for the trial, and Mom would prepare dinner for them. The defendants were not fed. Sometimes the trials lasted all day and most of the officials would take a long nap during the middle of the day.

Dad's strong attitude against alcohol caused problems with his friends and neighbors and even with some family members. He had no tolerance or sympathy with its use whatsoever. He had been this way since his spiritual conversion experience, and he never changed as long as he lived. The end to his work as a revenuer came when he found the "Big One."

The "Big One" was a huge still operated commercially by a man from Poston. This man's name is being intentionally omitted because he was never named, tried, or brought to justice. When Dad went to the sheriff with the evidence of the still that he had found, the sheriff wouldn't press charges. He asked Dad to "go slow" and sort of "forget this one."

Dad told him that he would have no part of that kind of law. He further said that he would have absolutely nothing to do with people or a system that would go around hunting and tearing up stills of the small moonshiners while leaving the big bootleggers untouched. The small moonshiners were making a little liquor to drink while the big bootleggers were making liquor to sell for huge profits.

I can still see Dad as he reached for his badge and gun and handed them to the sheriff. I will never forget that scene as long as I live. It made me proud to see my Dad put truth, honor, and principle above all else.

I have often wondered what the world would be like if everyone was that unwavering about what he believed in. I am grateful that I am an heir to such a sound and uncompromising philosophy on life.

Chapter 6

"AUNT" MARIAH'S BILLY GOAT

"Aunt" Mariah was a black lady who lived about four hundred yards from the house that we lived in at Salem, South Carolina. Her husband had passed away and her children were all grown and with families of their own. She was a very fine lady, who left an indelible impression on all who knew her, especially the children in our family. Her Christian love and compassion left their marks on each of us.

"Aunt" Mariah was generous with what she had and there was one delicious treat we could count on when we visited her...baked sweet potatoes. If you have never had a potato baked in the fireplace on a bed of hot coals, then you've never really had a good baked potato.

A lot of different animals were kept at "Aunt" Mariah's place; it was somewhat like a zoo. She had a mule, cow, hogs, sheep, a goat, turkeys, guineas, chickens, bantam chickens, pigeons, dogs, and cats.

The ruler of this menagerie kingdom was a big, white billy goat. He was huge, with horns that almost wrapped around his head. He was probably only about two feet tall, but to my young eyes he seemed twice that size. If you happened to cross his path, he would let you know right off and without any uncertainty who was boss. His reputation was known throughout the area, particularly by the children.

One day Dad, Mom, and the older children went to the Joe King farm in Kingsburg to clean a house for us to move to. This left Rowena, David and me at home to be watched by "Aunt" Mariah. When she stayed with us, she always cooked, washed clothes, and "straightened-up" the house.

Sometime during this particular morning, she started a big fire under the wash pot, which was the usual process for boiling the clothes. We were playing with the fire around the pot and really aggravating "Aunt" Mariah. I think she was praying for something to happen to get our attention away from the fire. Shortly thereafter her prayers were answered.

"Aunt" Mariah's billy goat got out of his pen and came over to our house. We thought he came to visit us, but we found out when he got there that he had other things on his mind. He started running after us. He was chasing us everywhere until the only place we could escape was under the house. We were screaming and crying as we scrambled under the house, which was mercifully too low for him to get under.

For anyone who has never been butted by a goat, I can tell you nothing is harder than a goat head. When a goat butts you, you feel like you've been hit by a freight train. "Old Billy" got down on his knees and looked at us and twisted his head as if to say, "I'll get you later." But, he didn't make a sound. We were terrified!

"Aunt" Mariah finally persuaded him to get up, and she tied him to a tree until she could carry him back home. She gathered up the poor little hysterical children, changed our clothes, and put us to bed to get us calmed down. I'm sure "Old Billy" was lonesome after this episode because none of us children ever went near him again.

Chapter 7

"THE BIG MOVE"

As the decade of the twenties began to close, life for most farmers continued to regress. Dad was renting a farm in the Salem area at the time and had experienced several pretty bad years. Things just would not come together for him. Even in childhood he had endured tough times. When he was a boy, his own father had lost everything that he owned due to illness and poor crop years.

It was customary for a farmer to borrow money on the future yield of his crops to pay for the expenses of growing the next crop. When the crops were sold, all debts were paid.

During the autumn of 1924, Dad's struggles really began when he sold his tobacco and put the money in the Farmers and Merchant Bank of Johnsonville. Several of the local banks had become insolvent, but the banker assured Dad that the Farmers and Merchant Bank was solid and would remain solvent.

Confident that his money was safe, Dad wrote checks to the people he owed. On the very next day after the deposit was made, the bank declared insolvency and closed its doors. All the outstanding checks were worthless. Dad simply lost everything he had that was of any value. I can remember hearing him say, "I had ninety-six cents in my pocket."

From all reports the next few weeks were critical times at our house. There were no provisions for buying even bare essentials like food and clothing. Dad somehow kept his composure, his dignity, his reputation, and most of all his faith in his Lord. He went to his creditors and they agreed to work with him. They sealed the agreement with a handshake and a promise to pay.

The next several years were difficult. Despite Dad's determination and daily struggle to earn a living, he just didn't make any progress. He realized something had to change. His creditors were getting anxious. He reached a point where he couldn't borrow money for fertilizer or get advances to live on until the crops were gathered and sold.

Determined to overcome this desperate situation, he decided

to begin sharecropping. This decision changed our lifestyle for many years to come, but every debt was paid-in-full by the time the depression was over.

The first step in becoming a sharecropper was to find a landowner who would agree to sharecrop his farm.

Mr. Joe King of Kingsburg was a very prosperous and successful landowner. He had several thousand acres and at least twelve sharecropper families farming for him at the time, as well as other laborers. Dad talked with him and they made an agreement for us to move and to work a two-horse farm. Mr. King agreed to advance living expenses on the future crop in exchange for our labor (see contract). This eased our situation a bit.

We moved into a sharecropper's house, which was by no means a mansion. But it was shelter for us and we were grateful.

Cleaning a house before you moved into it was always a big ordeal. There were several things you had to do before you could actually move into a house. The primary chore was ridding the house of cinches (bedbugs), lice, fleas, and roaches. There were no disinfectants at this time and the only effective means of eradicating these pests was by scrubbing with homemade lye soap, Red Devil lye, and scalding hot water.

Scrub brushes were made by boring holes into a board eight inches wide and eighteen inches long and nailing a handle about five feet long to the board. Then corn shucks were stuffed into the holes to form a rough brush. After preparing the brushes, big wash pots were filled with water and lye and heated with firewood to a boiling temperature. Gourds were used as dippers to toss this hot water onto the walls, ceilings, and floors. Then the walls were scrubbed with the shuck brushes. Finally, the house was rinsed off with clear hot water.

There was no need to worry about taking the paint off of the walls or floor because none of the houses were painted.

After a house was cleaned this way, you waited a day or two until the house was completely dry. I remember the clean, fresh smell of the house after having such a thorough scalding. In early January of 1929 the house was ready, so plans were made for the "Big Move." We moved during one of the worst flu epidemics on record. Our Grandpa Greenwood died during this awful scourge.

On the designated moving day several neighbors and friends came with their mules and wagons. Everyone pitched right in to help us move. Some of the neighbors loaded their wagons with furniture, some loaded kitchenware, some loaded corn, some loaded hay, some loaded chickens, some loaded pigs, and some loaded farm tools. With all the wagons packed and loaded, the "Move" was ready to begin.

The mule train pulled out with the cows tied behind the wagons, where they had to walk along as fast as the mules. Merrill, Lance, and "Bunkus," the three older boys, had to go with the wagons, but the rest of us, Nellie, Rowena, David and I, fared better....almost. We traveled in our 1924 Model T three-door touring car. It was a cold day, so the curtains were put on. We carried blankets to wrap up in because there were no heaters in cars in those days.

The distance between our old house and the new house was about eight miles, so we should have made the trip in about thirty minutes. Of course, that didn't happen. The Model T did not have a gas gauge. So, about half way between Salem and Kingsburg, the car started sputtering and coughing. Dad didn't have to stop the car as it did that on its own. He found a stick, stuck it in the tank and.... you guessed it....the tank was empty.

Dad took a spare can and walked to Kingsburg where he bought gas and walked back to the car. By the time we got the car started, the mule train had caught up with us. The whole procession began again. Of course, we left them and arrived at the new house about an hour ahead of the mule train. So we had to wait for them. When the mule train finally arrived, everyone really got busy. The rush was on to get the cook stove set up so food could be cooked and beds put up so we'd have a place to sleep. With careful planning and everyone's hard work, everything was in place by nightfall.

The new house had a kitchen, dining room, three bedrooms, and a path to the outhouse. Two of the bedrooms had fireplaces, so we had to sit, read, and study in the bedrooms. There were seven of us children so needless to say we were crowded. One of the bedrooms had three beds in it. The smaller children (me being one of them) slept three to the bed to ease the need of having so many beds.

There were many superstitions during those days. One of them was that when you moved to a new house, on the first night a ghost or somebody would try to put a scare on you. I really think (if that happened to us that first night) no one knew a thing about it as we were all so tired from the move that we just passed out.

The house had glass windows, but it did not have screens. Some of the rooms were sealed with finished lumber but some of them just had the outside boards. The floors had cracks in them so wide that you could see the chickens walking around under the house. The house was extremely cold in winter, but somehow we all survived. People had no choice but to adjust to the rough conditions. Layers of quilts were piled on the beds to keep us from getting too cold at night, and everyone from grown-ups to babies wore "long-handled" underwear.

The next summer the family had further hardships to endure. There was a serious epidemic of malaria and most of the family contacted it. At times there were not enough well members to take care of the sick ones. Malaria was said to be spread by mosquitoes, so we were prime targets as we had no screens to keep them out of the house.

The mosquitoes bothered us more at night when we were trying to sleep. There was no cure for malaria and a person had to try to "hang-on" and "wear it out." Some deaths occurred in the area and for several days it looked like we were going to lose Lance, but somehow we all survived.

Sharecropper's Contract between Dad and Mr. King in 1928

"Memorandum of agreement" State of South Carolina
County of Florence –

This agreement made and entered into this the 20th day of November 1928 between J. W. King Landlord hereinafter designated as party of the 1st part and M. L. Poston Tenant hereinafter known as party of the 2nd part is an agreement for farming a so-called share crop, for the year 1929 on the farm of party of 1st part known as the Mike Cain Farm, containing 35 acres more or less. The Party of the 1st part agrees to furnish Land and Fertilizer in sufficient quantities to produce the best results – approximately 800# 1010 lbs per Tobacco per acre. 400 lbs per acre for cotton and 100 lbs acre, or it equivalent for corn. The said J. W. King agrees to furnish in cash and provisions $200.⁰⁰ Two Hundred Dollars. Starting about Feb 1st – 1929 – and furnishing $25.⁰⁰ per month.

M. L. Poston, party of the 2nd part, agrees to plant, cultivate harvest and get ready for market the crops grown on said farm, planting about (8) eight acres in Tobacco – about (10) ten acres in cotton – about (3) three acres in Hay feed and the balance in corn. Party of 2nd part agrees to furnish teams, tools and feed for teams. Be it further agreed that when Party of the 1st part shall have been paid his advances – that the proceeds from the sale of the balance of the crops shall be divided half-and-half between the two parties. Furthermore it is agreed that Mr King and M. L. Poston shall raise hogs on shares of one half and one half – each furnishing the same number of Brood sows, boars, shoats, pigs, or their equivalent in hogs. The same feeding the hogs – the two parties furnishing equally in all same – Witness: E. Holiday J. W. King   Landlord
Witness: D. H. Haskins   M. L. Poston Tenant

Notice of Bank Foreclosure

FARMERS & MERCHANTS BANK
ESTABLISHED 1912
JOHNSONVILLE, S. C.

Nov. 17th, 1924.

To Our Depositors and Customers:-

As most of you are aware, owing to a protracted RUN we were forced to close our doors for the benefit of all parties concerned on Oct. 31st. While it is true that conditions in this section, and throughout our territory are the worst from a financial standpoint that they have been since this bank was established, still with normal withdrawals and deposits the bank was in position to continue its normal operations, but owing to the above conditions, and to some false rumors that got in circulation, and the fact that three banks had closed in this immediate territory during the past two years the RUN developed into such form that we did not think it fair to the folks that had always stood by the bank, and that were not here, to attempt to try and stem the tide further and endanger the future of the DEPOSITORS and Creditors of the bank for a benefit of the parties that were giving us the trouble, therefore, after careful consideration we decided to Suspend Business for a period of thirty days in which we could have a thorough audit of the bank, an understanding with our DEPOSITORS and Creditors and reach some agreement as to the future of the bank.

We had a thorough audit of the bank made, the finding of which was as we had expected, it shows that as a going concern the losses are not estimated to reach over $20,000.00, and should not exceed $10,000.00; or in other words, a disinterested committee after passing on our assets does not figure that as a going concern that our capital stock is in danger, and agrees with the directors that it is possible to save $10,000.00 of the $20,000.00 Surplus with careful attention and a good crop year. However, they agree with us, that if it is necessary for the bank to go into liquidation that it will take at least three normal years to liquidate. With these facts in mind we called a meeting of all DEPOSITORS and with half of them in dollars present, about 95% agreed that they would leave their deposits on deposit with this bank on certificate of deposit, one half payable Nov. 1st, 1925, the balance payable Nov. 1st, 1926, with interest at 5% per annum payable annually. We are asking that 85% of our depositors sign this agreement in order that we may know that they are with us, and in order that we will not be bothered with any further RUNS on our Deposits. The local people are responding very nicely. However, this is a big job, and we want to hear from every one concerned as quickly as possible as we are anxious to open the bank for business as quickly as possible; therefore, we ask that if you have not already done so, that you sign the enclosed blank and return it at once, stating how much of your deposit you will agree to leave under this plan, the certificates to be dated Nov. 1st, this year.

If you want to see the bank go on, and if you want a banking connection in Johnsonville, this is the surest way to get it as well as the quickest, and possibly the only way; therefore, we ask you if you have not already signed up to do so at once.

Yours very truly,

E. M. HUSBANDS, President.

LETTER TO DEPOSITORS

Chapter 8

MY FIRST MEMORIES OF CHRISTMAS AND SANTA CLAUS

Christmas of 1929 is the first memory that I have of Christmas and Santa Claus. In January we had moved from Salem to Mr. Joe King's farm and shortly thereafter Grandpa Greenwood died. So, I'm sure everyone was trying to think of something to brighten our outlook.

All the older children started talking about what Santa Claus was going to bring them. I didn't know what they were talking about, but you can bet I soon joined in.

As I remember, Nellie did most of the decorating. She cut a pine tree that was about five feet high and put it in an old butter churn that had been filled with dirt to hold the tree upright. She popped corn, laced it together on twine with a needle, and put the garland all around the tree. All during the year she had saved pieces of chewing gum wrapper tinfoil which she then wrapped around sweet gum balls. This made pretty silver balls to hang on the tree. This tree business really puzzled me. I couldn't understand why Santa wanted us to have a tree.

Nellie and some of the older children went out in the woods and found some holly with red berries. Sprigs of this holly were put on the mantle, the windows, and over the doors. Naturally I noticed the decorating preparations and tried to join in the fun. And, I'm sure I got in the way at every opportunity.

There were some other big things going on unannounced that I wasn't aware of. Mom had been baking cakes and pies for the holiday season. This was all so new to me; I just couldn't take all of it in. I remember hearing them talk about the different kinds of cakes and pies that Mom had cooked such as fruit, nut, raisin, coconut layer, chocolate layer, Lady Baltimore and several others. I think she had baked about seventeen cakes and about that many pies.

Dad had been making his Christmas preparations too. He had been stalking wild turkeys for several days and had bagged a big gobbler a few days before Christmas. Baked wild turkey would be a part of the menu for Christmas dinner.

Christmas Eve finally came and there was a lot of excitement in the air. The older children (the ones who could read) were busy reading every Christmas story they could find to the smaller children. The one that I remember most vividly was "Twas the night before Christmas." Nellie tried to teach us some Christmas songs and the most unforgettable one went something like this:

> "Johnny wants a pair of skates,
> Suzy wants a dolly,
> Nellie wants a story book
> she thinks dolls are folly'
> as for me my little brain
> it isn't very bright,
> so choose for me Old Santa Claus
> what you think is right."

This song seemed so sad. Here is this little person who wasn't so bright and was unselfishly concerned only about his or her brother and sister. It did humble me and made me think more of others. It caused me to look beyond our personal problems and to realize that a lot of other people were hurting too.

At last it was Christmas Eve and time for each of us to write a letter to Santa. These letters were put in individual boxes with our names on them. These boxes were shoe boxes that had been saved for this specific purpose. There were seven children at that time, so seven letters were written and seven boxes set. One of the older children had to write my letter and the following is the basic content of my letter:

Dear Santa,
I am a little boy three and a half years old. My name is Paul. I have tried to be a good boy this year. Hope you have a good trip with your reindeer tonight. Please leave me a spinning top that hums, a cap, an apple, an orange, and some candy.
Love,
Paul

All the other letters were similar to mine. When they were all written and the boxes set, we went to bed. The older children had trouble sleeping as they were so excited, but I just fell asleep immediately. Our parents let the older children get up at two A.M., but I didn't get up until the usual time. The older children built a fire in the fireplace and got the house warm. Then they played with their toys, ate their fruit and shot firecrackers until daylight. When I got up, I found out from those who could read that Santa had written me a letter which read as follows:

> *Dear Paul,*
> *I am out of caps, but I'll leave you a bugle.*
> *Love,*
> *Santa*

The bugle was a pleasant surprise and I was thrilled to have it. There was a lot of excitement in the air and firecrackers were shot all day and into the night. I soon learned that Christmas dinner was a very special occasion. I found out that it was the one day a year that there was plenty of the best food that was available.

During the next week there was a lot of visiting back and forth between families of the brothers and sisters of Mom and Dad. My first memorable Christmas was a special season, but our parents did not let us forget that the reason we celebrated Christmas was the birth of The Christ Child, our Lord and Savior.

Chapter 9

MY FIRST TRIP TO JOHNSONVILLE

Johnsonville was a sleepy little town of perhaps a hundred people and a half dozen stores. It was about five miles from where we lived on Mr. Joe King's farm. My Dad and Mr. Benny Mims, a neighbor, and several other men usually got together on Saturday morning and drove a two-horse wagon to Johnsonville to get groceries.

I always wanted to go on this trip to get groceries, but Dad would just tell me that I couldn't go and that was the law for me. When Dad wasn't around, Mr. Benny would go into an explanation as to why I couldn't go. He said, "There are some really bad policemen in Johnsonville who will pick up little boys and put them in jail and never let them out."

Mr. Benny was a World War I veteran who was married to my mother's first cousin. He was a good neighbor and I believed him when he said a policeman would get me. Mr. Benny was also the neighborhood barber. He cut hair at his house on Saturday for ten cents per person.

Finally it was time for my trip to Johnsonville when I was about five and a half years old. You must remember that I had never been away from "the Land between the Rivers." It happened unexpectedly and I wasn't really prepared for it.

My grandmother sent Uncle Jessie, Mom's youngest brother, to our house to get me and bring me to her house for a visit. Uncle Jessie was her youngest child, and all the other Greenwoods thought he was Grandma's favorite.....and he probably was. He was single at the time and had one of the prettiest 1931 Model A convertibles any of us had ever seen. It even had a rumble seat, which was a seat that was built in the trunk of one-seated cars.

After Uncle Jessie picked me up and we started to Grandma's, he decided he had to go by Johnsonville. This did not set well at all with me because I hadn't forgotten about the bad policemen in that town. I also dreaded crossing the big wooden bridge over Lynches River. At this bridge, the river was probably no wider than one hundred and fifty feet, but to me, it might as well have been the ocean.

When we got to Johnsonville, Uncle Jessie pulled over in front of the Eaddy's Drug Store and parked the car. The streets weren't paved, and since there were no side walks, he parked in the sand in front of the store. There was no way that I was going into that store with him. As soon as he got out and went in the store, I slid down and hid under the dash of the car.

For anyone who doesn't know, a Model A doesn't have any insulation between the motor and the floor boards. It was not unusual for temperatures to climb to over one hundred degrees right after the car had stopped. To make it worse, I rolled the car windows up to keep the police out.

Someone came by and asked me what I was doing. I told him that I was hiding from the police, and then I asked him if he was one. This kindly man assured me that he wasn't a policeman and went into the drug store to tell Uncle Jessie about my plight.

Uncle Jessie, the befriended stranger, and one of the Eaddy brothers came out to check on me. I was absolutely washed down with sweat, soot, grease, and dirt. They took me out, fanned and cooled me and told me repeatedly that the police would do me no harm; they said that they were good men who tried to help little boys.

After I regained some composure, the Eaddy man bought and gave me my first ice cream cone. This trip turned out to be an enjoyable venture, as I rid myself of the fear of policemen and sharpened my craving for ice cream.

Chapter 10

MY FIRST DAY AT SCHOOL

My first day at school was a real emotional experience for me. I had never been away from home, except to Johnsonville on that one occasion that I mentioned before and to Grandma Greenwood's house which was only a few miles from home. My exposure to people other than the family and the Greenwoods was limited to people visiting us and people passing by the house on the way to the store.

I had learned the ABC's and how to spell and even write my name by asking and listening to the older children. Even with my lack of exposure to the outside world, I was probably as prepared for school as most of the other children.

In early September, the time finally came to go to school. I had just turned six on August 20, 1932. Mom woke me up and told me that I had to get up and go to school. Nellie, my eleven year old sister, was assigned the duty of looking after me. The walk to school was about three miles. About half of that distance was through the woods and, of course, there was a log about twenty feet long across a branch of water that we had to cross. We also had to pass St. Mark Church, a church attended by black people, and a Black Lodge Hall, which was supposed to be haunted.

My legs were so short; it didn't seem like we were ever going to get to school. It was almost nine o'clock before we finally got there. After that first day, we made it more quickly because the teacher said we would be marked tardy if we were late again.

The schoolhouse was so big to my young eyes. There were three classrooms downstairs with a wide hall. There was one classroom upstairs and a big auditorium. My world seemed to have suddenly gotten so big!

The school yard was full of children. It seemed to me that all of them were running, skipping, hopping, laughing, talking, yelling or squealing. It was frightening to someone who had been so protected. The noise came to a halt when the bell rang. We were lined up like soldiers by grades on the outside of the building; then we marched into the classrooms. The principal rang a bell when it was time to take-up and let-out school and for recess.

In the school yard there was a sliding board. I had never seen a sliding board, much less slid down one. The big children played with the small children on the board, pushing them down the board and catching them at the bottom to keep them from getting hurt. I was having great fun until the short pants I was wearing got caught on a snag. They were split almost in half. I think I showed all my "credentials" the rest of the day. All of the activities amazed me... classes, meetings in the auditorium and especially recess. All of this was more than I'd ever seen.

The first grade teacher had to teach the first and second grades, so the most important thing the first graders had to learn on that first day was to be quiet. My teacher was Miss Smith, a pretty blonde, and I fell in love with her that very first day.

Miss Smith did take enough time with us first graders to show us how to draw an apple and a rooster. When we finally got home late that evening, Mom asked me what I had learned. I told her, "I learned how to write a apple and a rooster." That revelation of my new found knowledge and the way I explained it was never forgotten by my family. Members of my family kept reminding me that at the very best I knew how to write an apple and a rooster.

Chapter 11

MY FIRST TRIP TO MYRTLE BEACH

In the fall of 1932 a group of farmers who were farming on Mr. Joe King's farm decided that they were going to Myrtle Beach. None of these families had been on a vacation in years. They decided that it would be good to get away for one day and have a big picnic. This trip would take place after they finished selling tobacco.

Mr. King was approached for permission to drive his red Model T Truck, and he readily agreed to let them use it. The truck was a farm truck and didn't even have a cab. The bed was probably six feet wide, nine feet long, and had sides that were probably four feet high. I couldn't see over the sides of this truck when I stood up, so to a six year old boy, it was an enormous truck. Dad was the designated driver; he normally kept the truck and drove it for Mr. King.

By the last Saturday in September everyone planning to go to the beach had finished selling his tobacco, and plans were finalized for the trip. The people who were going on this adventure were: Mr. Benny Mims and his wife, Daisy; Mr. Edward Eaddy and his wife, Florrie; Mr. Lucian Powell and Mr. Raleigh Powell; Mr. Ryan Altman, his wife, Vera, and children, Willie May, Carl, and Dalton; from our family—Dad, Mom, Merrill, Lance, "Bunkus," Nellie, and Paul (me). Daisy, Florrie, Vera, Lucian, and Raleigh were brothers and sisters and were Mom's first cousins.

Mom didn't go on this trip to the beach and I just couldn't understand why she didn't want to go. However, on October 16 we had a new brother, Max, in our home. After I learned about the stork deal, I figured out why Mom didn't go with us.

The Saturday finally came for us to go on our trip. The time had to be on Saturday when there was no other work scheduled for us to do. A total of seventeen people made up this party, which attempted to fit into a little Model T truck.

There was no way to get all of these people into the back of the truck. If we had gotten them in, the front of the truck would have tilted up in the air. Dad positioned the people as follows: one sitting out on each of the two front fenders, one standing on each of the two running boards, one sitting beside the driver, and eleven in the truck bed. The women and small children were assigned to the truck bed.

We children were not very enthused when we learned that we had to get up, dress, eat breakfast, and leave before daylight, but we wouldn't miss this trip for anything. Those of us in the back had quilts to cover up with and a lot of us took naps off and on during the trip. It was at times a very bumpy ride. None of the roads between home and the beach were paved. Driving on some of the roads was like driving over a washboard.

We got to the Great Pee Dee River before daylight where we had to stop and pay the toll for the bridge. The area where the toll-keeper worked was lit up and there was a big draw bar to keep you from going through until you paid. This thing was awesome! It was scary for me as I had not been away from "The Land Between the Rivers" but once before and that was my trip to Johnsonville.

The normal toll for a car was ten cents, but for this truck loaded with all these people, the toll was raised to twenty-five cents. We paid the toll and went on through arriving at Potato Bed Ferry on the Little Pee Dee River just about daylight. The ferry was on the other side of the river, so we had to wait for it to come over to our side to pick us up. Well, here went another twenty-five cents toll.

It was real scary driving on to the ferry because it was so bumpy. A cable spanning the length of the river controlled and pulled the ferry, which I thought was a real engineering feat. There was so much for me to take in! In probably thirty minutes we made it across.

It was now daylight and I could see the inky darkness of the Little Pee Dee. It was the blackest water I had ever seen.

Everyone had packed a lot of food, so we kept snacking along the way. The older people kept telling me how big the ocean was and how I wouldn't be able to see across. I sort of suspected when we got there that I was going to be able to see England and France, and it was going to be the first time anyone had done this. I thought that if my eyesight was good enough to see the moon and the stars, that surely it was good enough to see England.

After we crossed the ferry, I went to sleep and didn't know anything that happened for a while. Just before we got to the beach, Florrie Eaddy woke me up and said, "Paul, wake up! We are going to see a really big mud hole soon."

I don't know how long it took to get there, but it had to be three and a half to four hours. Model T's were notorious for running hot. We had to stop several times to get water for the truck because the water boiled out and the truck got hot. The truck had no gauges so there was no way of telling when it was getting hot until you smelled it and the water was boiling out.

We finally arrived at the beach and stopped the truck. I couldn't see anything, of course, because I couldn't see over the sides of the truck bed. Dad let the tailgate down and we spilled out of the truck.

I got my first view of the ocean. No, I couldn't see England or France. That big ocean really messed me up. It was supposed to run straight out, but it rose up to the sky and shut out all the other countries. I have to say I was disappointed. I had anticipated seeing all the way across the ocean.

We parked the truck just outside a wooden pavilion that had a boardwalk out in front that extended down the beach for a short distance. There were several real big houses along the beach and a number of small houses. There was one big hotel that was the biggest building I had ever seen. It was called the "Million Dollar Hotel" because that's what it cost to build it. The name was later changed to the "Ocean Forest Hotel." There were no sidewalks and all the streets had oyster shells scattered on them.

Lots of people were walking barefooted up and down the strand. Some of the people were wading and splashing around. A few of them were trying to swim. They had on what they called "bathing suits." They were the ugliest things I had ever seen. They covered the entire body down to the knees and out almost to the elbows. Most of them were black and white stripes with the stripes running around like a zebra.

The swimmers all looked like convicts. Merrill was the only one of our family who had a bathing suit. He had borrowed it from Uncle Mack Greenwood, Mom's brother. It was ugly and scratchy because it was made of wool.

We spread all our food out and had a real feast. The only thing we had to drink was Myrtle Beach water, and believe me, it was terrible. I thought it tasted like fish.

We had to pack up and leave about two-thirty because

everyone knew that it would take us a long time to get back home. Also, we didn't want to be so late into the night.

The trip back home was a reverse of the one going to the beach. Once again we experienced the ferry, the toll bridge and the "washboard" roads. Every time we stopped and got ready to start again, someone had to crank the truck with the hand crank. At times you would think it wasn't going to start, but it would finally come back to life. The "cranker" was always hot, sweaty, and out of breath by the time the truck started-up. It was dark when we got home and all of us were worn out, but the memory of that day at the beach will remain with me forever.

Chapter 12

A 1924 MODEL T TOURING CAR

The decade of the twenties ushered in much excitement and enthusiasm. So much was going on! Most of the people in lower Florence County could not comprehend all of the changes. There were many newsworthy events to read about. The nation had just come out of World War I, and there were many unsatisfied veterans trying to get pensions.

Baseball was a hot topic. The Chicago White Sox team was accused of throwing the world series in 1919. The incomparable Shoeless Joe Jackson was one of the nine players who was banned from playing baseball for the rest of his life. He grew up in Greenville, South Carolina. Babe Ruth was sold to the Yankees in 1920. Boxing was a big craze. One of the highlights in this sport was when Gene Tunney beat Jack Dempsey in the tenth round in the 1926 Championship.

The country was still talking about the sinking of the great ship, the Titanic, in 1912. Approximately 1590 people perished when the ship hit an iceberg and sank on its maiden voyage. There was excitement in the air about the growth of the airline industry and Charles Lindbergh's non-stop flight over the Atlantic in 1927.

In our very own state, Charleston dance mania began in 1925. Dancing has never been the same since this crazy dance was developed in Charleston. Some other dances created about this same time were the fox trot, the shimmy, and the black bottom.

Automobiles were becoming more and more popular. Everyone was buying them. I am sure Dad was not financially able to buy one, but he couldn't resist the temptation any longer. In the fall of 1924 he went to Lake City and bought a 1924 Model T Touring car. It had been shipped from Detroit by rail in a wooden crate. He watched in amazement as they uncrated it.

As the dealer mechanics uncrated and assembled the car, they explained the different features to Dad. When it was ready to go, Dad was given a test drive, and with this brief on-the-job driver training, he drove it home.

This car cost four hundred and thirty-six dollars. It was a beauty! It was black with a convertible top. When the top was up, it had two rear windows about eight inches square, which sort of set it apart from other cars. It had only three working doors.... one on the passenger side in the front and two in the back. The driver had to climb over a solid panel where a door normally would be expected. The solid door was designed to protect a lever that provided the three necessary functions of high gear, clutch, and hand brake.

There were three pedals on the floor. The left one was low gear, the middle one was reverse, and the right one was the brake. This car had a starter button which was optional at extra cost. It also had a crank that hung idle in the front of the car under the radiator, and when the starter wouldn't start the car, you had to engage the crank into the engine and give it a turn.

The car had two levers on the steering wheel: the one on the left adjusted the spark of the coils which were under the dash, and the one on the right controlled the speed of the vehicle. It had a battery and a magneto. A magneto is an alternator with permanent magnets which are used to generate current for the ignition. You cranked the car up on battery, and when it was running, you switched it over to the magneto.

The tire sizes were 30 by 3 1\2 on the front and 30 by 3 1\2 oversize on the back. Some cars had a spare tire, but that was one of the options Dad didn't take. When there was a flat tire, he would take the tire off and come home on the rim.

This particular car would run between thirty-five and forty miles an hour when everything was adjusted just right. Even though it had a starter, it still had to be cranked with the hand crank quite often. Sometimes while hand cranking, it would kick and sprain your arm or even break it. Merrill had more bad luck on the hand crank than anyone else, primarily because he did most of the cranking. It wasn't unusual to see him going around with his arm in a sling.

The tires were the weakest parts of the car. After running for a few hundred miles, they would rim cut and go flat. Two of the options that came with this car were storm curtains and black woolen coverlets. When it rained or was cold, the curtains were put up, making the temperature inside a little more comfortable.

The car was driven until 1930 when the economy worsened

and we couldn't afford gas or parts to keep it operating. It was then pushed under a shelter and forgotten.

In the fall of 1937 after the economy had improved somewhat, the body was cut off and it was made into a little truck. It actually started back up fairly easy and ran quite well. We used it for hauling tobacco to the market and other hauling that had to be done. It was sold in 1940 for twenty-five dollars and a thousand tobacco sticks.

I hated to see our Model T go. I had learned to drive on this car and used it to go to the gristmill on Saturdays.

I didn't have a driver's license, as I was too young to get one. However, it wasn't unusual to drive without a license back then as there was only one highway patrolman in the whole county, and your chances of getting caught were very slim. When you became 14 years old, all you had to do to get a license was go to the Highway Department at Florence and buy one for fifty cents. Your name, address, age, sex and color were stamped on a little copper plate and you hung it on the key chain.

Dad's registration for 1924 Model T.

1924 Model T - exactly like the Model T owned by my Dad. This car is owned by Mr. James Jeter of Greenville, S.C., and it runs great after 72 years

Certificate of Title for Dad's Model T

South Carolina State Highway Department Motor Vehicle Division

NUMBER 124722

CERTIFICATE OF TITLE OF MOTOR VEHICLE

In pursuance of the provisions of an Act of the General Assembly of the State of South Carolina, approved the 21st day of March, A.D. 1924, (Statutes at Large, Volume XXIII, page 1013) the State Highway Commission does hereby certify:

That application has been made for an official Certificate of Title in the name and to cover that certain motor vehicle, as is set forth, and described in said application, as follows:

MAKE & TYPE	MOTOR NUMBER	SERIAL NUMBER	WEIGHT OR TONNAGE	DATE OF ISSUANCE
FORD TOUR.	8431293 T 1924		9.05	MAY 6, 1925

M. K. POSTON, 124722
KINGSBURG, FLOR. CO., S. C.

That according to the application hereinabove referred to, the liens or encumbrances upon said motor vehicle are as follows:

AMOUNT	CHARACTER	DATE DUE	IN WHOSE FAVOR OR TO WHOM DUE	ADDRESS

That the State Highway Commission is satisfied that the above applicant is the owner of said motor vehicle hereinabove described, or otherwise entitled to have the same registered in his, her, their, its name, and therefore the said State Highway Commission does hereby issue this Certificate of Title so said applicant upon information believed to be reliable, but said Commission in no wise warrants or guarantees the above applicant's title to the motor vehicle hereinabove described.

This Certificate of Title is good for the life of the motor vehicle for which it is issued so long as the same is owned, or held by the original holder hereof.

In witness whereof the South Carolina State Highway Commission at Columbia, has caused these presents to be signed, numbered, dated and issued over the signature of its Secretary or thereunto authorized agents, authenticated by the seal prescribed for this purpose.

W. W. Goodman
SUPERVISOR MOTOR VEHICLE DIVISION
STATE HIGHWAY DEPARTMENT

L. H. Thomas
SECRETARY STATE HIGHWAY COMMISSION

Chapter 13

A MULE NAMED JACK

In 1923 my parents were living on the huge Molly Davis plantation near Kingsburg. Dad was farming on a small section which consisted of approximately twenty-five acres. When Merrill reached the age of nine, Dad thought he was about ready to start plowing. With the additional plow hand, Dad figured he could till more land and would need another mule.

Mules were expensive at this time; they were really the most valuable thing a farmer had if he didn't own land. In 1923 good mules were selling for $200 to $250 each, which would be about $15,000 today.

Dad did a lot of shopping and finally decided on what he thought was a bargain. He bought a jenny mule for $100. A jenny is really a female donkey or an ass and not a real mule. A real work mule is a cross between a male jackass and a mare horse.

The advantages of a donkey are that they are sure-footed, they don't require a lot of food, and the quality of feed doesn't have to be as good as that of horses and mules. The disadvantages are numerous, but the worst one is that they are pathetically stubborn. They are also light, weak, and very hard to train.

Dad named this fellow Jack, which turned out to be an appropriate name. Well, Jack was as slow as he wanted to be. He figured out that when he worked along side the regular mule, if he lagged behind, the other mule would have to do all the work.

Up in the morning when the temperature got a little warm, Jack would lie down in the field. He would lie there until dinner time, if you didn't make him get up. Lance was about seven years old at the time, and his job was to take a piece of wire with a sharp point and follow along and jab Jack when he either balked or laid down. This went on everyday. He would not work all day without causing problems.

Dad tried every way he could think of to get rid of Old Jack. He tried selling him, but nobody would give him anything for him. Then he tried trading him, but no one would agree to trade at any price. When Dad had really had it with this jackass, he said that he was just going to give him away.

Finally, "Uncle" Dan Davis, a black gentlemen, agreed to take him. So, at last "Old Troublemaker Jack" was gone. "Uncle" Dan picked him up and took him to his house, which was about two miles south of Poston. We thought we could just forget "Old Jack." But, not for long!

On the third morning after his departure, we heard a noise out at the stables and saw Jack trying to tear his way back in. He had torn out of "Uncle" Dan's stable and had come back home. "Uncle" Dan came back and got him. He actually kept him for a few weeks, but Jack was so sorry and contrary that finally "Uncle" Dan just turned him loose.

The next day, guess who showed up at our place? Yes, our friend Jack was on the scene again. Dad had to start trying to get rid of him once more. This time he found a gentleman at Bazen Cross Roads by the name of "Uncle" Tom Brown, who agreed to take him. We never saw Jack again, but we always hoped that he had "turned over a new leaf." I am sure that no animal had ever caused the anxiety and frustration that Jack had.

Jack taught Dad a good lesson, and for the rest of his life, he kept the best mules that were available no matter how much they cost.

Chapter 14

PREACHER TO THE POSSUM

During the depression Methodist preachers had tough times. All preachers may have had difficult times, but I am only familiar with Methodist, as that's what we were. There was very little money available to give to the church, and since preachers got only a small portion of that, they were often in need of the vital necessities of life.

Once a year usually close to Thanksgiving, the people of the church gave the preacher a "pounding." Everyone brought something to the church to give to the preacher. This event was called a "pounding" because the things given to him were such things as a pound of butter, rice, sugar, meat, flour, grits, etc. These contributions would last for a while, but then the preacher and his family would again get hungry.

Our preacher usually worked out a schedule for visiting someone everyday for a meal and for whatever that someone might give him in lieu of money. I remember very vividly when the preacher and his family had meals with us.

It was known quite well that Methodist preachers loved fried chicken. So Mom usually tried to have fried chicken when they came to eat at our house. In those days adults were always served first and by the time the children were served, the choice of chicken pieces was limited to wings, feet, livers, and gizzards, and yes, even the feet were cooked.

Preachers usually had a garden and kept chickens, a milk cow, and hogs to help feed their family. When the preacher visited, you always gave him something to take home. He expected it and society expected it. You gave him vegetables out of the garden, corn out of the barn, potatoes out of the dirt banks where they were kept, or you caught a couple of chickens from the yard.

Sometimes you gave him a turkey or a pig or whatever you had. You wanted to, and you were expected to share what you had with him. If you gave him chickens, he would tie their feet together so they couldn't get away. If you gave him a pig, he would tie all four feet together, put him in his car and take off. His car was usually old and most of the time the back seat had been taken out to facilitate the transportation of these gifts.

In the early thirties, Reverend Johnson was our preacher. It seemed to me that he visited us pretty often. On one occasion we had run out of almost anything that we could give him. We did, however, have a big fat possum in the possum cage.

We had a wire cage specifically built to keep possums in. Dad would catch the possums and put them in this cage. Then they were fed for several weeks to get them "cleaned out" and to get rid of some of the wild taste. Well, as stated earlier, we had run out of anything to give to the preacher except for the fat possum in the cage. So, preparations were started to give the possum to the preacher.

Dad had to build a small box to put him in so the preacher could carry him home. Rowena saw what was going on and got very excited. She ran to me exclaiming, "Paul, Daddy gave the preacher to the possum!" Needless to say, we never let her forget that statement.

When the Reverend Johnson heard about it, he used that statement as a sermon topic. The giving of a big fat possum back then was a sacrificial gift. Live possums were a treat for most, but they were very hard to transport. The next time we saw Preacher Johnson he commented about how good that possum was. We were proud that he had enjoyed it, and we felt that we had shared from our poverty as the widow did out of her mite as found in the Bible. (Mark 12:42-44).

Chapter 15
1931 HOOVER CART

When Herbert Hoover was elected as our president in 1928, he promised better days for everyone. He said, "There will be two chickens in every pot and two cars in every garage." The country was in a robust mood and it seemed that the sky was the limit.

Then the Stock Market crashed in 1929, and everything was all downhill for the rest of the Hoover administration. He initiated and got Congress to pass several programs that should have helped, but the depression was world-wide and so deep that nothing seemed to help. With each passing day of his administration, things got progressively worse.

The "two chickens in every pot and two cars in every garage" did not happen, but the ingenuity of our people could not be denied. Most of the cars owned at the time had been permanently parked. There was simply not enough money to buy gas, tires, or repair parts to keep them running. So, off came two wheels, an axle, springs, and a cushioned seat. These parts were converted into a two-wheeled, one-horse cart which quickly became known as a Hoover Cart.

This cart was very comfortably built with pneumatic tires, springs, and a cushioned seat. Usually a step from an old buggy was installed to facilitate getting in and out. It had a place for your feet which was similar to the front floorboard of a car. It was necessary to have a good, fast, smooth horse if you wanted to travel with any speed.

The only problem here was that almost everyone had mules. The mules filled in okay, but they were not known for fast racing speeds. It was a common sight to see an entire family driving a Hoover cart to church with children hanging on the sides. Horses that pulled the carts were tied to trees at Trinity Church during the worship service.

We personally didn't have a Hoover cart, but Mr. King did; his cart was used to take their son, Billy, back and forth to Trinity School. Quite often as we were walking to school, we were picked up and taken to school. This was a real treat. The cart was not a pretty sight; it was an everyday reminder of just how bad things really were.

Chapter 16

A WOODEN PEOPLE

Patience is just not one of the virtues that I was born with. There has never been enough time to do everything I have wanted to do. I've always tried to find a faster way to do things. I even tried to speed up the process of eating at a very young age.

About the time I was learning to read, Mom noticed how fast I was eating. She talked to me almost every meal about the big mouthfuls I was taking and how fast I was chewing and eating. I tried to explain that I was speeding-up the process of eating, but she didn't buy that at all.

One of the books that I was beginning to read was Pinocchio, the wooden puppet who turned into a real live boy. This story fascinated me. I wanted to look like Pinocchio, to act like Pinocchio, and to be Pinocchio. I went through a period of make believe... pretending that I really was Pinocchio. This was my defense to Mom on my fast eating habit. I told her, "Fast eating will not hurt me because I am a wooden people." The serious thing about it was that I really believed that I was different and couldn't be hurt.

The statement that I was a wooden people stayed alive for a long time at my house. The rest of the family just wouldn't let me forget it. When I was cold, someone would say, "Wooden people don't get cold." When I was tired, someone would say, "Wooden people don't get tired." When I went in the army in later years, one of my sisters even had the audacity to say, "Well, Paul, we are not going to worry about you because bullets won't hurt wooden people." This time, for some reason, it wasn't very funny.

Chapter 17

SPARED BY GOD'S GRACE AND PEE WEE'S BARKING

Our dogs were always kept outside the house—all of the dogs except Pee Wee. Pee Wee was a little white rat terrier that Grandma Greenwood had given us. This little dog was different and special. She was so little; we were afraid that if we left her outside, she would freeze or something would get her. So she became a house dog. She was like a toy that everyone petted and played with.

In the late fall of 1933, after the weather became too cold to go barefooted, Dad bought a pair of shoes for each of us. These shoes were supposed to last until the next spring when the weather became warm enough to go barefooted again. The shoes that were bought for me were two-toned-tan, high-tops. I thought they were the prettiest shoes I had ever seen. I liked them so much; I just wanted to look at them and not wear them. It was the first pair of non-black shoes that I had ever had.

On this particular night I sat in front of the big fire that was blazing in the fireplace. I took my new shoes off. I sat there for a while admiring them and then put them in the corner of the room near the hearth. Dad was away at a Masonic meeting in Charleston. The three older boys went to their bedroom, which was a room built out of part of the front porch. Mom and the smaller children went to bed in the room that had the fireplace.

Sometime during the night, Pee Wee started barking and raising cane like she was trying to get someone's attention. She finally succeeded in waking Mom, but by this time the room was already full of smoke. All of us who were in the room were coughing and gasping for air.

Sometime during the night a log had rolled out of the fireplace and onto the floor. My new shoes were burned beyond recognition. We managed to put the fire out with the available water, but the house was a mess with smoke and soot on everything.

Being seven years old, I was not phased by the seriousness of this life-threatening crisis. My only concern was the loss of my new two-toned-tan, high-top shoes. It was several days before I could get a new pair of shoes so I could go back to school. And wouldn't you know! The replacement was the kind of shoes I had always worn ... they were black.

Mom, Dad and the older children understood the gravity of what had happened, and they were appreciative and thankful that our lives had been spared. After this experience, Pee Wee was even more special to each family member. She had earned her keep for as long she lived.

Chapter 18

DAD'S LAST FISHING TRIP WITH MR. JOE KING

Mr. Joe King had a resort cottage at Murrell's Inlet, South Carolina. Once a year when all the crops were harvested and sold, he would invite his male sharecroppers to a fishing outing. These excursions ordinarily lasted for three or four days and usually from eight to ten of his sharecroppers accepted the invitation.

These trips were made in December or January when the weather was cold enough to keep the fish from spoiling. On many of these excursions the fish catch was plentiful. Traveling to Murrell's Inlet was in Mr. King's 1930 or 1931 Chevrolet four-door car and in his Model T truck. Mr. King drove the Chevrolet and Dad drove the Model T. Those riding in the Model T really had to wrap up to keep from freezing.

The particular fishing trip that I am writing about happened either in December of 1932 or January of 1933. Dad and Mr. King had always gotten along well and they seemed to respect each other. There were, however, two distinct differences between them: Dad was a teetotaler who would have absolutely nothing to do with alcohol, and he was not bashful about expressing his view on the subject. Whereas, Mr. King was known to be a frequent partaker and he wasn't bashful about his views either.

Most of the other sharecroppers who were on the trip were not teetotalers, but they were not normally open about taking a drink. On this particular outing the booze started flowing and things got out of control. Several of the fellows got in pretty bad shape. A few of them got in terrible shape, and one got completely out of it and became bedridden for a while.

Dad was embarrassed to be involved in what he considered a real mess. He thought of it as an affront to what he believed in and what he had tried to let his life stand for.

The friction between Dad and Mr. King started building as the sobering process began. The hangovers must have been awesome. Things were said that could never be retracted or forgiven, and relationships were destroyed forever.

Dad said some things about their conduct that offended Mr. King. Mr. King told Dad, "You weren't invited as an equal and you're in no position to say the things you're saying." Dad told us what Mr. King had said to him. This was just like taking a knife and cutting Dad's heart out. He lived twenty years after this incident, but he never really got over it.

We stayed on Mr. King's place through the rest of 1933 as Dad had already started planting the tobacco beds and turning over the land for the new crops. Dad and Mr. King just endured each other the rest of the year. It was a strained and difficult relationship.

In the fall we moved to "The Backwoods" on a farm owned by Mrs. Molly Johnson, who was Mr. King's aunt. The problems should have been over now that we had severed our relationship with Mr. King, but that was not the case. Feuding went on for years to come. The grudge between them resurfaced over and over at every opportunity.

A real serious problem arose in 1935 or 1936 when Mr. King decided to run for school trustee of Trinity District 35. Dad didn't think too highly of this at all. He set out to line up opposition to Mr. King's election. The heat was on and that was all the community talked about. Both sides lined up their votes and the turnout was tremendous. It was said to be the most hotly contested election ever for District 35. The vote was close, but Mr. King won. He was popular and had the loyalty vote of his sharecroppers.

There were several re-election campaigns afterward and the results were always the same. The results were always close, but Mr. King came out ahead of anyone running against him. You would think that after a few years things would have gotten back to normal, but that wasn't the case.

The trustees hired an agriculture teacher from Johnsonville as principal of the Trinity Grammar School. He had no grade school educational experience, which created rumors that he was hired to help Mr. King do his farming.

One of the former principals of this school told my Dad as he was leaving, that he was instructed by the trustees of the school to not have anything to do with Mack Poston or he would get into trouble. Well, this principal did associate with my Dad. He hunted and fished with him and even went to the same church. After he resigned under duress, he said that he felt Dad was the best friend he had.

The situation affected the relationship of every teacher of the school and all school-age children in our family. It was difficult for the teachers as well as the children. At the end of my sixth grade year, over half of the class flunked. Of course, most of these children were in the "opposing group." I, needless to say, was one of those children. Later, during the summer, some souls were evidently searched and a decision was made to promote us to the seventh grade.

There were several reasons for this change of heart, but the main one was that the line-up of those who had passed and those who had failed was so obvious that it was quite apparent what had happened. Another reason could have been that the seventh grade would have been almost completely wiped out. One teacher was dismissed as the result of this apparent cover-up.

It was difficult to be a good student in this atmosphere. When I was in the fifth grade, I was subjected to a little dose of these politics. One particular day I (barefooted as usual and wearing my outgrown overalls) was quietly studying in my seat. My feet did not touch the floor so my right foot was swinging back and forth. I didn't even realize that my foot was moving.

The teacher slipped up back of me with a whip and cut loose on my bare right foot and leg with several whacks. It scared the daylights out of me and it just added to the intimidation I already felt. I did not dare tell my parents, knowing full well that I would get another whipping at home because "little boys shouldn't swing their legs while studying at school."

The feuding, back-biting, and distrust ran deep. The school problems of that period were blamed on all the infighting. The feelings did not go away until our family moved to the Johnsonville district and Mr. King died an untimely death in the early 1940's.

It has not been my attempt to lay blame on either side. Mr. King was a well-respected farmer and businessman. He was one of the few landlords who had written contracts with his sharecroppers. He helped a lot of people during the deep depression of the thirties. A number of these people looked at him with respect similar to that of President Franklin D. Roosevelt.

Mr. King and Dad were both strong-minded people. Neither was willing to forgive or forget once this wound was opened. Dad had such a strong conviction against the use of alcohol that he never wavered in opposition to those who used or condoned it.

Chapter 19

TRINITY SCHOOL

Trinity School was always an impressive building in my young eyes. It was probably built in the late teens or early 1920's. The building was massive for no more classrooms than it had. There were four classrooms, three downstairs and one upstairs. The classrooms were about forty by forty feet and the ceilings were at least fifteen feet high. The hall was probably twenty-four feet wide. The bottom stairs were extremely wide and divided at the first landing into two stairways—one on the left and the other on the right leading to the second floor.

The auditorium probably seated two hundred and fifty people. There was a stage, and there were dressing rooms behind the stage. The floors were all made of pine and, for those of us who went barefooted, the splinters were awful. Oil was put on the floor to try to keep down dust and reduce splinters. This floor oil created a real problem trying to clean it off the bottom of your feet at night.

The school had huge windows on all sides, so the lighting was good. Each classroom had a big potbellied stove. In the early thirties we burned wood, but by the mid-thirties we were burning coal. The male students had to build fires in the mornings, and sometimes we had the flues red hot to the ceiling. I don't see how we kept from burning the building down.

We didn't get electric lights until 1936 or 1937. The building was painted white with some green trim. It was built about three feet off the ground, so one of the main play areas for little boys was in the sand under the schoolhouse. This was also a very good place to hide. The school ground was fenced in with an expensive fence, but the fence was continuously torn down at the boys toilet and in the corner near the highway where the artesian flowing well was located.

There was a six-seater boys' toilet on the far, right-hand corner of the school ground. The girls' toilet was on the far left hand corner, which I suppose was also a six-seater. That area was totally off-limits for boys, so I can't verify what was in that toilet.

Cleanliness in the boys' toilet was very poor as the aim of

little boys is bad, so there was never a dry seat. Another big problem was the shortage of Sears, Roebuck and Co. catalogs, which was the main supply of toilet paper. The toilet was the main place where the older boys "hung out." Here they would discuss various subjects, but the most frequent subject was sex.

Some of the older boys were beginning to smoke, so they hid out in the toilet and did their smoking. They always had lookouts watching for the principal. If he caught one of the boys smoking or smelled smoke on his breath, that boy received a good thrashing with a substantial whip. During this period girls just did not smoke so it was absolutely unheard of for a girl to get in trouble for smoking. There was always a clean path going to both toilets.

Grass in the school yard sometimes got about knee high before it was cut. There were lots of sandspurs that played havoc with the bare feet of many of the children. There were no lawn mowers at this time, so the school hired a farmer to cut the grass with a mowing machine pulled by mules. Normally this machine was used to cut grain and hay to be used as feed for the livestock.

There was an artesian flowing well that had a good flow of water, and this water was so cool. Water came out of four pipes so that four children could drink at the same time. The water overflow dropped into a brick tank that overflowed into a ditch. We always had a ditch to play in, so getting wet feet was a common occurrence.

The school yard had very limited athletic equipment. There were three seesaws, two "acting bars," four swings, one sliding board, and two basketball goals. The game played most by the boys was baseball, and usually there were several games going on at the same time. This was possible because the boys made their own equipment.

Some of the more skillful boys would cut a small hickory or ash tree and hew it down to where it looked something like a bat; then they dried it in front of the fireplace. These bats didn't look so great compared to professional bats, but they served the purpose.

To make a ball, you took a rock about the size of a golf ball and wound tobacco twine over the rock until it reached the size of a baseball. When the ball was big enough, you then laced and wove the twine so it would not unravel when it was hit. These balls and bats weren't very pretty, but we enjoyed many a game with this crude equipment.

Another real popular game that we played at school was shooting marbles. According to school rules, you could play only for fun because, if you were caught playing for keeps, you would get a whipping.

We had two recesses: one that lasted for thirty minutes and one that lasted for an hour. During this time you went to the toilet, went to the drinking fountain, ate the lunch you brought from home, and then you played whatever you wished for the rest of the time.

There was usually about one hundred and fifty children. The number of teachers was three and four depending on the decision of the trustees, which I am sure was influenced by the amount of money available. When we had three teachers, the first and second grades were in one room, the third, fourth, and fifth grades were in one room, and the sixth and seventh grades were in another. When we had four teachers, the first grade was in one room and the other classrooms had two grades for each teacher. It was very difficult to learn in classes where there were three grades in one room …. but somehow we did it.

The teachers usually boarded in Poston with Mrs. Owens Poston, Mrs. Lawrence Creel, Mrs. Hern, or Mrs. Minnie Smith. Transportation had to be arranged for the teachers because none of the teachers (except the principal) ever had a car. The only car ever parked at the school was that of the principal. So, you can see, parking was never a problem at Trinity.

In 1936 or 1937 a house was built on the school ground and this was large enough to house the principal, his family, and all other teachers. All the teachers except the principal had to be single and female with no exceptions. At no time were any local teachers hired on a permanent basis. The teachers came in and became a part of the community; they attended the local churches but could not get into politics on their own.

The makeup of the student body was mostly sharecroppers' children. A large portion of the land was owned by landlords, who lived out of the county. Mr. Joe King was the largest landlord who lived in the area. There were a few farmers, who owned small farms and had been fortunate enough not to lose them due to the poor economic conditions.

Family size usually ran from four to twelve children with about half of the children from each family attending school at a given time. Some of the people who lived in Poston worked with the railroad and their children dressed better and had better lunches than the sharecroppers' children. Some of the sharecroppers were so poor that their children didn't bring lunches. The government started a program of giving food to the poorer children, and the teachers had to decide who would receive this food.

Trinity was located about ten to twelve miles from the Bigham Place, where there was a mass murder in 1921. An entire family was wiped out except an accused brother, Edmund, who afterwards served over thirty-nine years in the penitentiary in Columbia, South Carolina for these murders. There was still a lot of talk about the murders in school and in the community.

Edmund's sister had adopted two little McCracken boys, who were also killed by the murderer. The half-brothers and sisters of these little boys went to Trinity. The oldest one was one of my best pals, and we had a lot of fun together.

Once one of the McCracken boys was expelled from school. It wasn't long before his Dad brought him back to school and told the principal that he wasn't going to expel him. Mr. McCracken was mad and said that he had two little boys killed and he just wasn't going to let people run over the rest of his children. The principal backed down and let the boy stay in school. When Mr. McCracken left, we were all relieved as we thought he was carrying a gun in his pocket.

Trinity School was really the hub or core of the whole community. Many activities were held at the school and most of them were about the school. There were a lot of good teachers, who left indelible memories on the minds of the young people from the community. Some of these teachers were: Mr. Floyd, Mr. Sanders, Mr. Jordan, Miss Smith, Miss Carter, Miss Graham, Miss Shuler, Miss Roberts and Miss Petilla. I am sure the community was enriched as a result of having these people live and teach at Trinity.

A COW UPSTAIRS?!!!!!

What in the world would a cow be doing upstairs at Trinity School? How could it have gotten up there? Would anybody put a young mama cow upstairs in a schoolhouse?

Somehow one morning when we got to school, there was a lot of excitement as there was a lot of lowing and hoof sounds on the second floor. When a cow gets excited, her bowel movements are like she's had a great big dose of castor oil. The classroom and the auditorium were a mess as it was splattered everywhere. It took a while for us to figure out what to do.

First we had to catch the cow. Then we blindfolded her, and several people tried calming her down and slowly backed her down the stairs. When we got her downstairs and took the blindfold off, she ran wildly trying to find her calf.

The cleanup was a real chore, and the older boys had to do it; but even these cleaning chores they liked better than studying. The culprit or culprits who performed this dastardly deed were never apprehended. This crime has never been solved.

Chapter 20

TRINITY METHODIST CHURCH

Trinity Methodist Church was organized about 1850 and has been an active viable church since that time. I heard that Francis Asbury, a pioneer Methodist Minister (1745-1816), stopped there once when he came up the Pee Dee River and landed at Ports Ferry.

It would be safe to say that Trinity Church was second to Trinity School in being at the center of what went on in the community. This church always and still does have strong leadership. In the twenties and thirties, it was one of a four-church charge with Johnsonville, Prospect and Vox, and at that time, it wasn't the largest but it was one of the most vital.

The people at Trinity always made a difference. They were caring, concerned, and compassionate people. Even though most of them weren't wealthy in my early days, they shared what they had with the less fortunate.

During the late thirties when the Methodist Episcopal Church North and the Methodist Episcopal Church South merged, a lot of churches split off. This was because of the fear of integration, as Blacks were already integrated into the northern churches. Trinity remained a strong force in the newly-formed Methodist church.

Church services were always in the afternoon, starting at 2:00 P.M. except on the fourth Sunday, and on that day services started at 10:00 A.M. Sunday School usually lasted about an hour and the preaching service lasted a long time.

The preachers would get wound up and go on and on. It was not unusual for one of them to preach for an hour. We never got to sing the third stanza of any song, and many times the last song was cut out of the service. Most of the time it was about five o'clock before we got out.

It was quite normal for children and some adults to get up and go to the toilet during the service. This toilet was a two-hole one in the woods behind the church with a path leading to it. In the summer you had to really watch for snakes because they were everywhere. Sometimes, they got in the toilets.

Trinity was blessed with two good musicians: Mrs. Mattie

Woodberry and Mrs. Ina Richardson. One of them was always at church, and I don't ever remember not having the piano played at a service. There was an active choir, which did a real good job.

There were always teachers for the children's classes. The dedication of these teachers to show us how Christ would handle different situations has been a beacon for me throughout my life, and I am sure has been to many others. My Dad was the Sunday School superintendent all the years we attended Trinity. And, of course, he was always an inspiration to me whether at church or at home.

Trinity usually had a revival in the spring of every year. Some of the time it would last two weeks and sometimes one week. Preaching was always done by visiting preachers, and usually the attendance was very good. All of the preachers were different; they had different backgrounds and education, but most of the time they had the same message. They preached Christ's love, but they also stressed the urgency of repenting and turning to Christ before it was too late.

One of the preachers, Rev. Henderson, opened a window one night, dangled his leg out, and preached to the people in the graveyard. This made a lasting impression on me. The visiting preacher stayed with our regular preacher, but he ate every dinner and supper with different congregation families.

Always there seemed to be people getting converted at these revivals. I had a heart-warming experience during a revival in 1937 when I was eleven years old. I joined the church and have been an active Methodist since that time. Though I have strayed, the spirit that was present that Sunday morning always leads me back to that altar.

My first memory of the church was that it had only a sanctuary and no Sunday School rooms. The sanctuary had a big heater and you tried to sit as close as possible to the heater to keep warm. Then you would get all cozy and warm, and I well remember some people had trouble staying awake during the sermon.

The biggest problem that we had was getting to and from church. Our Model T was parked due to not having money to run it, and we lived about three miles from the church. In the early thirties people either walked or drove their mules and wagons -- only a few drove cars.

Mr. Luther Richardson had a school bus, which he drove on

Sundays to take people back and forth to church. This turned out to be the main transportation. At times he picked up two loads on each Sunday. At first he had a Model T bus and then a 1933 or 1934 Chevrolet bus. The bodies on both of these buses (inside and outside) were homemade. As the economy improved, more and more people bought cars and drove them to church.

The people who I remember as the stalwarts of the church were the families of the Luther Richardsons, the Fred Richardsons, the Durham Richardsons, the Douglas Furcheses, the Bernie Postons, the Ira Perrys, the Les Perrys, the Clarence Woodberrys, the Lawrence Creels, the Wilton Eaddys, the Walker Powells, the Louis Rogers, the Walt Richardsons, the Durant Hughes, the Connie Hughes, the Buck Rawlins, the Lourie Postons, the Houston Taylors, the Willie Richardsons, the Morris Munns, the Owens Postons, the Liston Postons, the Louie Postons, the Ray Postons, the John Gregg Woodberrys, the Dr. J. W. Johnson family, Mr. Billy Johnson, the Mack Postons, and many others.

All of these people influenced my life and helped to mold me into the person I have become. It is with a sense of humbleness and pride that I remember these people, and I thank them for being there when I needed them. I have tried to carry with me and share with others what they shared with me during those critical character building years.

Chapter 21

OUR MOVE TO "POWELL'S CORNER"

The late twenties and early thirties brought many changes in laws, politics, lifestyles, and the economy. The 1929 Stock Market Crash devastated the entire nation. The boll weevil also came in the twenties and destroyed the cotton farmers livelihood. Up to this time farmers had prospered and made cotton the king of all farm crops. The whole nation was at a standstill; unemployment reached astronomical heights, and bread lines began and continued for several years.

Gangsterism peaked and then began to wane as the F.B.I. became more effective in dealing with the situation. During 1934 the infamous Bonnie and Clyde were gunned down in a police ambush at Shreveport, Louisiana. These feared desperadoes had menaced the Southwest for over four years and had caused twelve deaths. The notorious John Dillinger was gunned down in Chicago by the renowned F.B.I. agent Melvin Purvis from Florence, South Carolina. Dillinger robbed numerous banks and caused 16 deaths. "Pretty Boy" Floyd was also wiped out by Agent Purvis. He was described as the most dangerous man alive and was involved in numerous bank robberies and murders. George "Baby Face" Nelson, listed as the nations Number 1 outlaw, was found dead. He tried to avenge his partners, Dillinger and "Pretty Boy," in a shoot-out with the police. He used machine guns and killed several policemen. Ma Barker and her son Fred were gunned down by the F.B.I. in Florida. Charles Lindbergh's baby was kidnapped and killed. Richard Hauptman was later captured and convicted of the crime.

On the political scene, Franklin D. Roosevelt was elected president of our country. At his inauguration he said, "The only thing we have to fear is fear itself." He declared a bank holiday and closed the banks for a week to try to stabilize the industry.

The National Recovery Act (N.R.A.) program began in 1933. That same year the Civilian Conservation Corps (C.C.C.) came into being and hundreds of thousands of young men were put to work. In 1933 prohibition came to an end with the repeal of the 18th Amendment. This happened after Utah, the 36th state, ratified the 21st

Amendment.

The most serious change for the world came in 1933 when Adolph Hitler was named Chancellor of Germany and was granted dictatorial powers. Later in 1934 he was made president, which changed the course of the whole world forever.

Radio was becoming more popular each day as people sacrificed their food budget in order to purchase a radio. Radios were used in our area mostly for news and hillbilly music.

As the economy slowly improved, more people began to buy cars. Some new cars were bought, but the majority of cars bought were used cars that were brought from up north and driven or pulled to the south. These were mostly Model A Fords that had set up during the worst part of the depression and were in good condition. Black Model A's were popping up everywhere just like ants in a hill. The Model A's had to be well built in order to withstand the ruts and rocks on the rough dirt roads.

After sharecropping with Mr. Joe King for five years and Mrs. Mollie Johnson for one year, Mr. Pete Cornwell, who owned the Woodberry farm, contacted Dad about moving to his farm. Mr. Cornwell was a railroad engineer for the Seaboard Airline Railways. He needed to relocate to Savannah, Georgia as most of his runs were out of Savannah. Mr. Cornwell was looking for a sharecropper, but he was also looking for a caretaker for the farm and the beautiful home. Dad and Mr. Cornwell made an agreement and we moved in December of 1934 to his farm.

This move was a joyous one for the whole family. Everyone was so excited; we couldn't sleep at night. It seemed at last something good was about to happen to the Poston Family.

This two-story house had nine rooms and was painted inside and out. It had four fireplaces downstairs with flues for two heaters upstairs. There was running water from an artesian well in the kitchen and on the back porch. Porches extended around three sides of the house. Glass windows were in every room, and the house was tight and warm compared to what we had gotten used to.

But the greatest thing was that there were so many bedrooms! Now everyone could have some privacy by age and sex. We even had a guest room! Dad went to Florence to buy a load of furniture for the guest room and the living room. We all thought (and I still believe) that getting to move there was the answer to a lot of prayers.

The yard was fenced in and had four large magnolia trees in the front. A winding walkway bordered by a hedge led to the house. There were pecan, pear, peach, and plum trees. There were grape vines and a lot of flowering trees and vines. The original owner had equipped the house with many amenities including carbide lights. Many of these pipes and fixtures were still intact. It was a dream home, and we felt that we were more than blessed to have the opportunity to live in it.

The farm was a five hundred and fifty acre tract which was fenced and cross-fenced. There were about one hundred and forty acres under cultivation with the rest in forest. This was what was called a four-horse farm.

We already had two mules, so we had to buy two more. This meant that we had a mule for Merrill, Lance, "Bunk," and one for a black man, Roosevelt Ellison, who was hired as a laborer to help. The farm was well equipped with various tools, a tool house, a blacksmith shop, an old commissary, and much more. We planted twenty-five acres of tobacco, twenty-five acres of cotton, and about fifty acres of corn.

There was a field called the "bay field," which had about twenty-five acres in it; this field was planted with peanuts, corn, and beans just for the animals to graze on in the fall. Because it was a bigger farm, there was more income, which helped at a time when it was really needed; but, it also meant a lot of hard work for everyone. The abundant woodland acres afforded opportunities for all who liked to hunt. Living and farming here was the first step out of the dismal situation we had gotten into. It was a notch above regular sharecropping and really helped us to start building the groundwork to step-up to something better in the future.

We stayed here for five years and most of us felt that this was where we really grew up. When any member of the family recalls the various places we lived, this place always ranked over all the others. It was a time when not only the young children were growing up but the older ones were leaving home. Merrill got married and moved out to sharecrop with Mr. Joe King. Lance got married and moved to Pamplico to work in a grocery store for Mr. Bob Cox. "Bunk" joined the navy. The farm was too big for us after the three older boys left home. So after the place was sold, Dad decided to rent a smaller farm in the "Backwoods" from Mr. Henry Holliday.

Chapter 22

MUD PIES

It was a custom at Trinity School for the children to draw names and exchange gifts at Christmas. In December of 1935, I was in the fourth grade, and there was a lot of excitement as Christmas drew near. The day came when we were going to draw names and there was a lot of anxiety.

A little girl in my class told a friend of mine that she hoped Paul Poston didn't get her name. He asked her why, and she said, "If he gets my name, all he could give me would be mud pies." Though I was only nine years old, this hurt me deeply. It really cut my heart to pieces and scattered it to the winds. It spoiled this normally festive occasion for me this year and for many more to come.

As I know now, children can be cruel, but they are the product of what they are taught at home. This hurt healed slowly and was something that I have never forgotten. This incident changed my life as it helped to put a drive in me that has never calmed down... even after retirement.

We weren't any worse off than fifty percent of the people, but it just seemed like this little girl now made things a lot worse. It was enough that we knew how bad things were, but it was even more humiliating to know that others perceived how things were for us. I did not tell my parents or family about this because I did not want them to feel the hurt that I was experiencing. In fact, this is the first revelation of this incident. I couldn't sleep at night because I was thinking and planning what I could do to better our lot in life.

I had to do something financially productive, so I started selling The Woman's Home Companion, Collier, Red Book, and The Grit paper. A dear little lady at Poston had a scheme whereby she would get a magazine and state that if she liked it she would pay me next week. The problem was she never liked it but always wanted to examine another. It took me (at nine years old) several weeks to figure out what was going on. She was reading the magazine at a poor little boy's expense, and to top it off, she was from a family of means.

Shortly after that experience I got a job feeding hogs for Mr.

Pete Cornwell for one dollar a week. This lasted for over a year. I killed squirrels and sold them for ten cents each. I did a lot of fishing and sold them for whatever I could get for them. Any day that I could get work on a neighbor's farm...that is ...when Dad could spare me, I worked for thirty, forty, or fifty cents per day.

My friend Christmas, a black man who lived on the farm with us, and I did a lot of possum and coon hunting. We ate the meat and sold the hides. We picked up several dollars from selling hides as a good coon hide would bring about three dollars and a possum hide from fifty cents to one dollar.

At the age of fourteen I got a job at Bernie Poston's store. I worked whenever Dad could spare me from the farm and on Saturday all day and Sunday evenings. My pay was one dollar and fifty cents a day. After the "mud pies'" episode, I was never broke. I could have bought this little girl a nice Christmas gift anytime I drew her name.

This experience taught me that you have to choose your words very carefully with children because one word may affect them for the rest of their natural lives. I certainly hope that the incident about "mud pies" made me a more thoughtful, considerate, and loving parent and grandparent.

Chapter 23
CATCHING WILD HOGS

From 1935 to 1940 we lived in "Powell's Corner" on a farm known as the Woodberry Farm. This farm contained over four hundred acres of fairly dense forest land. The farm was situated in a corner formed by Lynches River running into the Pee Dee River. The adjoining farm was known as the "Old Powell Farm" consisting of over a thousand acres.

Mr. W. W. Montgomery, a Philadelphia lawyer, owned this farm, which he posted and turned into a haven for wildlife. Deer, turkeys, squirrels, birds, wildcats, and a few bears were spotted, but wild hogs were numerous and became a real nuisance. If these hogs were not controlled, they would eat the corn crop from the time it was planted until it was harvested. Catching them served several purposes: it helped the corn yield, it gave us additional meat to eat, and it gave us some needed income by selling some of these hogs.

During our stay in "Powell's Corner" we caught a lot of wild hogs, but there were still a lot of them in the area when we moved away. Handling these vicious animals was dangerous and required experience and skill, which we developed quickly from necessity. Wild hogs will normally run from a person unless they get hemmed in or caught; then they get vicious and will cut a person to bits with their tusks.

There were three methods of catching these hogs. One method was to stalk them and shoot to kill when the opportunity arose. This was used very seldom and then as a last resort. The second method was to catch them with dogs. We used this method on several occasions. A black man, "Uncle" Henry Eaddy, had several dogs trained specifically to catch hogs, and Dad got him to help on the roundup several times. This was dangerous business even for the dogs. Once we had a fine bulldog named Jim who got his throat cut by a big hog.

I remember on one of the roundups Dad got a little excited while trying to tie a hog up and swallowed a big chew of tobacco. It made him sick and that finished his wild hog roundup for that day.

The third and most practical way to round them up was to build a camouflaged pen with a trapdoor. When we used this method, we scattered acorns and corn around the pen and inside to get the hogs used to feeding around that area. When we got conditions right for a catch, we took an ear of corn and tied it to the end of a piece of wire.

The next step was to take the other end of the wire and tie it to the top of a trapdoor. The ear of corn was then taken to the far corner of the pen and hooked under a prong. The wire was tightly drawn to hold the trapdoor open. When the hog tried to get the ear of corn, it became unlatched and the trapdoor closed.

This pen had to be very sturdy and at least five feet high because these hogs would go under, through, or over just an ordinary fence. Some of these hogs were so wild they wouldn't eat for weeks. On one series of roundups like this, we caught seventeen hogs, which was probably the most successful roundup we ever had. The usual number caught was four to six.

These experiences taught me valuable survival lessons at an early age. I learned that you had to know your adversary, know his capabilities, and quickly discern his intent. These experiences greatly enhanced my ability to cope with future situations, particularly those I encountered while serving in the U. S. Army during World War II. I also learned an alertness that heightened my ability to organize, supervise, and follow-up during my working career over the next forty-five years.

Chapter 24

SHAD FISHING ON THE "MIGHTY" PEE DEE

Roe shad routinely swam up the Pee Dee River from January through May. The best runs were usually in the cooler months of February and March.

The American shad is somewhat like salmon in that it lives in the Atlantic Ocean and swims upstream in fresh water to spawn. A shad weighs from three to six pounds. The meat is a little oily but has an excellent taste. The main aversion to shad is that they are very bony. Shad roe is very good especially when scrambled with chicken eggs. It is considered the best substitute for the roe of sturgeons, which is used in making caviar.

The main reason people seined for shad during the depression was to feed hungry people. Seining for shad is extremely hard work and it is also dangerous on the treacherous Pee Dee River. Also, during January, February and March the weather gets extremely cold, and especially so on the water. I have seen my Dad's fingers crack open from exposure while shad fishing.

Shad fishing with a bow and net is definitely for the tough, hale, and hardy. Dad's fishing equipment consisted of only a big log boat, a bow with a net, and paddles. The log boat was about twenty feet long and was hewed out of a cypress log. The boat was about thirty inches wide so it definitely came from a big tree. It weighed about four hundred pounds and was not only solid and heavy but very tricky to paddle. It could easily turn over—just like a log in the water.

Fishing was done by two people—one person paddled and the other held the bow. The paddler was always in the back of the boat and the bowman in the middle. The paddler guided the boat as the swift current carried them downstream as fast as they wanted to go; they usually drifted downstream for one to two miles.

The bow was about twenty feet from the tip to the cross at the handle and about twelve feet wide at the widest point. It had a string running through the net and the bowman kept the string wrapped around his finger so he could feel when a shad struck the net. When he felt a strike, he dipped the bow out as fast as possible to try to keep the fish from getting away.

After drifting as far down the river as they wanted to go, the fishermen had the task of paddling back upstream against the current. Both of the men had to paddle to get the boat to buck the swift current. Usually the other fishermen kept a big fire burning at the boat landing, and each time the two fishermen made it back to the boat landing, they rested and tried to get warm.

This downstream/upstream cycle was repeated over and over. I've seen them do this all day without a strike, but I've seen other days when they caught two or three shad each time they went downstream. I went with them a number of times when I was growing up, but my main job was to keep the fire going.

When I was about sixteen, I finally got Dad to agree to let me try my hand as a bowman. The problem was (at sixteen and weighing only about one hundred and twenty pounds) that I was just not heavy or strong enough to do the job.

As we drifted downstream, I thought I had a strike and dipped the net out but nothing was in it. Then after a few minutes I had a good strong strike, but I wasn't strong enough to dip the net out fast enough to prevent the shad from getting away. This was a tough experience and this one episode convinced me that I never wanted to go back shad fishing as the bowman.

I did go back as a paddler and saw my Dad catch several nice shad. He just had a natural talent for figuring out the areas in the river where the shad would most likely come upstream. He knew exactly when to dip the net after he had a strike. He was strong and made it look so easy, but I knew firsthand that it was a strenuous job. Dad always looked so pleased when he landed a big shad. He never said anything, but I could sense the inner exhilaration that he was experiencing. It was a triumph for him. He knew he had just won a battle and had caught food that all of his family would enjoy.

As I grew older and stronger I went back a number of times as a paddler for Dad. He always seemed to approve of my paddling and this made me proud. I always did my best to win his approval on whatever he had me doing. Fishing with him was always serious business. There was no fooling around...just hard work because being with him was always a learning and growing experience.

These experiences gave me a base to build my life on. These outings gave me some quality time with Dad that I would not have had otherwise. Being with him in times of his pleasure pointed out to me that he was the same person in every setting. I saw that his values didn't change: whether teaching a Sunday school class, fighting a forest fire, worrying about the drought on his crops, trying to endure the boll weevil, or just having fun fishing for roe shad. His consistency of demeanor caused me to want to follow in his footsteps. It is not my intent to try to portray him as faultless (he had some flaws), but as his young son, I couldn't see them.

Chapter 25

"THE DUMB BULL"

One Saturday night in the spring of 1936 an unusual event occurred that affected our lives for several weeks to follow. The night air was brisk and the moon was in its fourth quarter, so the night was extremely dark. It was still too cool for snakes to be crawling. The quietness of the darkness was interrupted occasionally by the screeching and hooting of owls and other night birds.

There was no worry about mad dogs, as rabies usually wasn't a problem until the hot summer months. A bear had been spotted in the area, but this wasn't a great concern. This just seemed to be a night destined for something to happen. There seemed to be a sense of restlessness in the air.

Dad had gone to Bernie Poston's store to get groceries that we needed for the next week. Merrill, my oldest brother, was off dating his future wife, Nellie. Lance, my nineteen year old brother, "Bunkus," my sixteen year old brother, and Joseph Furches, a visiting friend, were itching to do something exciting.

Lance, the usual leader of mischief, decided that they should make a "dumb bull." "Bunkus" and Joseph were baffled until Lance explained what it was and what it did. They became very excited and enthusiastically agreed to help him build this mysterious thing. The three of them discussed with Mom what they were up to. She cautioned them about the possibility of someone getting hurt, but they nevertheless continued with their plan.

"What is a dumb bull?" That was my first question when I heard them discussing it. Lance and "Bunkus" explained it to me as they began to create it. They took a nail keg and knocked out both ends. Then they took a piece of a cowhide (this was from a cow that we had butchered earlier) and stretched it over one end of the keg as tight as possible. A small hole was bored in the center of the cowhide.

The next step was to pull a string about three feet long through the hole. A knot was tied on the string on the inside so the string wouldn't pull out. The string was heavily waxed with beeswax. When they set the keg on the ground and pulled the waxed string, it made the most awful sound that had ever been heard in that part of the country.

The equipment was now complete and we started moving about so the terrible noise could be heard from different locations. "Uncle" Jessie Ellison and two of his grandchildren, Daisy Bell and Bo, lived in the house across a swamp in the "Crappy" field. "Aunt" Sara Eaddy lived down the road about three hundred yards from us with the back of her house facing "Booger" swamp. "Aunt" Sara lived with five of her daughters who ranged from ten years to teenage years. The decision was made to start in "Booger" swamp between "Uncle" Jessie's and "Aunt" Sara's houses.

When we started pulling the string and changing the rhythm and the beat, it sounded monstrous. The quietness of the night was shattered when the dogs in the community started barking and howling, the cattle were lowing, and the mules even began braying. A lion, tiger, or bear never sounded as ferocious and dangerous as "Old Dummy" did.

We could hear the pounding of the hammer at "Uncle" Jessie's house up on the hill. We were to learn Sunday morning that he not only closed all the wooden doors and windows but he nailed them tightly. In the process of nailing the doors and windows, Bo was holding a torch for light so he could see how to drive the nails. Some tar from the torch dropped on "Uncle" Jessie's head and burned his head in several places.

We came out of the swamp and worked our way down a ditch in front of "Aunt" Sara's house. After hearing the noise from the "dumb bull," John Henry and his wife left their house and ran like a streak to "Aunt" Sara's house. This was a distance of about two hundred yards.

About this same time a man by the name of Lassies Cooper was returning from Poston to his home, which was on Mr. Montgomery's place. He was about even with our house when he hollered out, "John Hen-reee, John Hen-reee, did you hear that?" John Henry stuck his head out of the window and yelled, "Lassie's, I sho' did." (This was going on at a distance of two to three hundred yards.) Lassie's called, "What did it sound like, John Henry?" John Henry yelled back, "I don't know but I believe it's the devil."

About that time we cut down on the string and Lassie's yelled out, "Close the door and open the window 'cause I'm coming in." We could hear the women and children screaming and crying. The dogs all around were still having a fit. Dad came home and he told us to stop, so things did settle down for a while.

The next morning was a new day; the sun came up brightly, so everyone got up with the idea of finding out just what really went on last night. Uncle Jessie found a track in a ditch where two dog feet had come together, so he was sure something big had been through the night before. Dad normally wouldn't go along with any foolishness, but he reluctantly went along and agreed with Uncle Jessie that the track indicated that probably a big tiger was on the prowl.

A lot of preparations were made all day Sunday for the probability of the return of the monster Sunday night. People borrowed gun shells, rifle bullets, axes, pitch forks and anything that would help protect them from this unearthly creature.

By Sunday night everyone was prepared for this monster's return visit, and there was so much tension that very few people got any sleep. Uncle Jessie thought he heard something outside his house, so he opened the window just wide enough to stick the barrel of his gun out and let go with two or three rounds. This just increased the anxieties of the other people.

No one heard any beastly sounds all Sunday night. Monday morning they all hoped that it had moved on across Lynches River to Snow Island or across the Pee Dee River into the swamps of Marion County. Nothing happened Monday night or Tuesday night. So things were gradually settling down to a normal routine again.

Wednesday night the peaceful hopes of everyone were shattered as the "thing" struck again. This time it was behind Dutchman Altman's house, a neighbor who lived about a half mile from our house toward the town of Poston. Dutchman had two little boys named Gordon and Lenair. They were about six and four years old.

During this period about every family had a milk cow, and it was a practice that you milked the cow early in the morning and late in the evening. You milked the milk out of three udders and left one udder for the calf. The calf was then left with the cow for about thirty minutes to nurse and then they were separated until the next milking time.

Dutchman had milked his cow earlier, so now he had to go

out to the barn to separate his cow and calf. By this time it had really gotten dark. Gordon and Lenair wanted to go with him, so they followed along behind him. Dutchman hadn't cleaned the growth of weeds and brush around his barn; he just had a narrow path to get to the barn.

Lance and "Bunkus" thought it was about time for a little more excitement, so they had slipped around behind Dutchman's barn and they were waiting for him to come to separate his cow and calf. About the time Dutchman reached for the fence gate, "Old Dummy" squalled out. It was said that he jumped several feet high. He seemed to start running in several directions at the same time. Then he apparently realized that he couldn't leave his little boys out there to be devoured by this treacherous sounding monster, so he grabbed one son under each arm and tore off toward the house. When they got to the house, his wife was at the door coaching them to come on in.

On Thursday morning Dad was gone, so the boys thought it was time to have a little more fun. This time the fun involved our smokehouse, which was a small building in the yard where pork meat was salted down, cured and smoked. The building was about twelve feet wide and sixteen feet long and had no windows. It was built very sturdy with a heavy door to prevent the meat from being stolen.

"Bunkus" was supposed to be at school, but this day he did not go. However, the folks on the farm didn't know it. So, Merrill and Lance locked "Bunkus" up in the smokehouse with the "dumb bull." Then they leaked the word to the neighbors that they had captured the beast in the smokehouse. They were careful to explain that the door to the smokehouse had been left open, and when they heard the noise, they ran and closed the door. They said that they didn't have a chance to see what the "thing" was.

The curious people came, and they were cautious and well protected with their shotguns. They crept up near the smokehouse and listened. "Bunkus" pulled the string on "Old Dummy" and hit the walls like he was tearing out. Everyone took off running in all directions.

Now all the neighbors realized that they had to come up with a plan to get rid of this monster; it had already created too much anxiety for the community. Uncle Jessie wanted to take some buckshot and just shoot up the smokehouse, but my brothers convinced him that the shot would not penetrate the thick walls with enough velocity to kill that "holy terror."

We had several sticks of dynamite left when we were blowing up stumps, and one of the fellows wanted to take that dynamite and blow up the smokehouse. Merrill and Lance had to talk him out of that. Then someone came up with the master plan of just setting fire to the building. They talked him out of this plan saying that our home and several other buildings might burn.

Merrill and Lance convinced the others to just wait until Dad got back, and he would come up with a way to destroy the creature. When things settled down and the people agreed to go back to work, the unforgivable happened. When no one was looking, the "thing" tore a couple of boards off and got away. "Bunkus" was really glad to get out of the situation. When Dad did get back and heard what happened, he would not let us use the "dumb bull" again for fear of someone getting hurt.

Eddie Hughes, Lance's friend, borrowed it one night and tried it out near the house of Ariah Davis, which was about a half mile from our house toward Poston. Eddie pulled the string on the "dumb bull" a time or two and Ariah pulled the trigger on his shotgun. Eddie had to lie on the ground in the woods until Ariah ran out of shells. Then he got up and ran like a streak of lightning for safety.

Eddie kept the "dumb bull" a few more days. He slipped behind Doward Perry's house and set up behind Doward's haystack. He was in a squatting position just pulling away on the string when Doward eased down to the haystack. With his shotgun poking out, Doward said, "Stick 'um up!" Eddie just fell back on his back with his hands and feet flopping in the air. He was so stunned that momentarily he just lay there. When he did get a grip on things, he got up and disappeared into the night. He forgot the "dumb bull," and needless to say "the cat was out of the bag," and that was the end of the "dumb bull."

Chapter 26
OUR FIRST RADIO

Italian inventor Marconi proved the possibility of broadcasting radio signals in 1895. By 1920 Stations KDKA of Pittsburgh and WWJ of Detroit made the first regular broadcasts in the United States. After 1920 stations mushroomed all over the country in the bigger cities. Aerials began popping up on a lot of houses as the growth of home radios was over a million a year.

This invention did not affect our immediate family for seventeen years after the first two stations went on the air. We heard people talk about them, heard them discuss the programs, and saw the aerials going up at homes all around us. However, we knew we couldn't afford one of these new inventions as we didn't have the money. In the mid-thirties the price for a radio was $100 which would be something over $3000.00 in today's market.

In February of 1937 our lives made a big change as a whole new world opened up to us with the purchase of a radio. During the thirties radios became more and more popular, but there was a problem in the rural areas because there was no electricity.

The power problem was solved with big expensive dry cell batteries. Batteries normally lasted 800 to 1000 hours or a period of four to five months. The people who had radios were talking so much about what they were hearing until the peer pressure was building up on Dad something awful—to get a radio! Everywhere we went, whether it was school, church, or the store, conversations were about Amos and Andy, Fibber McGee and Molly, Lum and Abner, the Grand Ole Opry, and on and on.

The older children got all caught up in the chatter that was going around so they began to put pressure on Dad to get a radio. Financially we really weren't in position to buy a radio. There were so many other things we needed much worse such as shoes and warm clothes. We still did not have adequate transportation. We rode the school bus to church, but everywhere else that we went, we had to either walk, drive the mule and wagon, or ride Merrill's bicycle.

The desire to get in on the hottest fad of the thirties outweighed logic and finally Dad buckled to the pressure. He would never buy anything without really checking it out, so the search was on for the best buy in a radio. He checked with people who had radios and he checked with various stores that sold radios.

After a few weeks of looking, he decided to buy a big console Silvertone from Sears, Roebuck and Company in Florence. The big beauty cost sixty-nine dollars and forty-six cents with the batteries included. The batteries consisted of one big A dry cell that weighed about twenty-five pounds and three B dry cell batteries that weighed about ten pounds each. A set of batteries cost about seventeen dollars.

Dad was so proud of this radio. He thought it would be heard and seen better if he put it up on a stand; so he built a special stand about twelve inches high and covered it with a pretty piece of cloth. This did make the radio really stand out -- at least we thought so.

Since we didn't have anyone who knew how to hook it up, Mr. Hern from Poston came and hooked it up for us. Two cypress poles were cut and put up that were taller than our two-story house. The wire for the aerial was strung between the tops of the two poles down to the radio. No lightning arrestors or anything like that were used. The reception was excellent; we could receive from stations in Florence, Columbia, Charlotte, Raleigh, Nashville, Cincinnati, and New Orleans. This was really something we just couldn't believe.

The radio was put in the living room because it was felt that we would be doing a lot of entertaining with people coming to listen to the radio. This turned out to be true as we did have a tremendous amount of visitors coming and sitting to listen to what was going on in other parts of the world other than our world around Poston.

The preacher came by several times a week and neighbors often dropped by to chat and listen to the radio. The older children who were dating would double-date with someone who had a car and usually come by on Friday and Sunday nights.

The big night though was Saturday night listening to the Grand Ole Opry. We would build a big fire in the fireplace and several neighbor families would come to listen to the Grand Ole Opry. The main entertainers that they wanted to hear were Uncle Dave Macon, Roy Acuff, Hank Williams, Grandpa Jones, Ernest Tubb, Minnie Pearl, and others. This would go on until about twelve o'clock midnight, and then everyone had to get to bed so they could get up the next day to go to church.

Black families also came by to listen to the radio to see what everyone was so excited about. They were amazed at this "thing" and just couldn't seem to take it all in. For one person in particular named Harley Davis, this "thing" was beyond his comprehension. He called it a "talking box." He would go over and look behind it and just laugh with excitement. He thought we had some person in the box. He wanted to believe us, but he still had a little distrust. He would keep going back over and searching behind the radio for someone that had to be in it. It took some persuasion to get him to believe that the signals were being sent through the air and the radio was picking them up.

The radio was one of the highlights of the otherwise dull and depressing thirties. It opened up new worlds of comedy, song, different ways of life, and current news. Our small world of Poston and community suddenly expanded. The radio probably turned out to be one of our best investments and was certainly our most enjoyable.

A Bill of Sale for our First Radio

SEARS, ROEBUCK AND CO.
ATLANTA, GA.

ACCOUNT NO. ARB375937   DATE 3-8-37 Feb 25, 1937 gm

PLEASE MENTION ACCOUNT NUMBER WHEN WRITING OR SENDING PAYMENTS

M. K. Poston
Poston
S.C.

KINDLY NOTIFY US IF YOU CHANGE YOUR ADDRESS, GIVING NEW and OLD ADDRESS

div 57	1	radio with batteries	69	46
		Deposit	30	00
		Balance due us	39	46
		Payment 2-25-37	10	00
		Balance Due us	29	46

TERMS: $ 5.00 Monthly
Next Payment Due:
12-27-37 (Past Due)

Please see that payments reach us on or before the above date each month.
WE DO NOT SEND ADVANCE NOTICES

You may make the payments personally at any of our Retail Stores.
The safest way to send money is by check or money order.
If it is necessary to send cash, your letter should be registered.

THIS STATEMENT IS SENT YOU FOR YOUR INFORMATION AND TO PROVIDE YOU WITH A MEANS OF RECORDING YOUR PAYMENTS. SEE REVERSE SIDE.

F 2206 Rev. 6-25-36

Chapter 27

A TOBACCO BARN RAISING

In l937 we needed another tobacco barn due to increased yields and increased acreage of tobacco. Dad and Mr. Cornwell decided to build a twenty-foot log barn on a hill in the middle of the "Crappy" field. This field consisted of about forty acres of loamy soil that was across a swamp from the house we lived in. We children named it "Booger" swamp. I always thought the swamp had ghosts in it but, thank goodness, none ever got me.

The first thing that was done on the barn was the cutting of the logs. Dad went through the woods and marked the pine trees that he wanted cut. Merrill and Lance cut the trees and "Bunkus" and Roosevelt Ellison peeled off the bark.

The logs were then hauled to the site where the barn was going to be built. All other preparations were made such as buying the bricks for the furnaces, the tin for the roof, and the lumber, nails and other supplies that would be needed. Now the stage was set for the barn raising.

The day came and all the neighbors gathered to build the barn. Dad already had the foundation laid, so they started right into notching the logs. There were crews bringing the logs and putting them in place. There were "notchers" on each corner because all four corners had to go up at the same time. There were people to relieve the "notchers" so that there would be no delays in this process. Dad had a measuring stick and he went from corner to corner so he could tell the "notchers" whether they had to notch more or less. This was done so the building would be level.

When the logs got about six feet high, it was time to start adding what was called tier-poles. The tier-poles were put there to hang the tobacco on. The poles were put at intervals of four feet so there would be what we called five rooms in a twenty foot barn. There was a crew to notch these tier-poles and put them in because they didn't want to delay the corner "notchers." After the first tier-poles were put in, more tier-poles were added at intervals of about two feet on up to the top of the barn.

All of these people came and worked like trojans, and they

did not receive one cent of money. They did it because of friendship and for the fellowship and food. Also, it was expected that Dad would help them if they built a barn.

At noon everybody stopped work and a feast was spread before them. This feast was prepared by my Mother. There was chicken and rice, barbecue, fried chicken, different vegetables, biscuits, corn bread, cakes and pies, coffee and lemonade. Everyone ate until they could eat no more; then they rested and some even took naps. On the farm you always took a two hour break in the middle of the day.

By night all the logs were in place and the workers had begun to nail the slats over the cracks between the logs. The next day the group came back; some worked on getting all the cracks closed, some mixed clay and water and dabbed the clay in the cracks between the logs from the inside. Another crew worked on getting the top on the barn.

At noon they stopped and had another feast. In the afternoon they completed the dabbing, finished the roof, and made a shelter. All was complete except the furnaces and flues. None of these people were brick masons, so Dad hired Mr. Luther Richardson to make the furnaces. This routine was repeated over and over as various neighbors built barns.

This particular barn turned out to be an exceptionally well-built barn. Dad wouldn't have had it any other way as anything he did had to be done well. He came up with some ideas on ventilation which really helped to get the heat to rise in the barn when the leaf was green.

At about the time I became a teenager I had to start helping cure tobacco at night. I always dreaded with a passion staying at this barn at night by myself. There was an old house right by the barn, and I could hear all kinds of noises when I was curing tobacco by myself. I just knew that the old house was haunted and full of ghosts.

I was scared but thought it would be unmanly to admit this feeling to anyone. So, I just quietly endured it, but I still believe there were ghosts in that old house. I believe there were ghosts in the swamp between our house and the barn too. I never saw one, but for some reason I felt they were around and at times this fear made my hair stand straight-up on my head.

Chapter 28

"BETTY AND RHODIE", THE ULTIMATE IN MULE POWER

Before the popularity of tractors on the farm, the main focus of farmers was mules and horses. A farmer took great pride in his team or teams of mules or horses. Some farmers liked horses better and some liked mules better; it was mostly a matter of preference.

Horses generally were a little stronger, but mules had smaller feet, were more sure-footed, were not as high strung, and adapted well to different situations. In the tobacco section of Florence County more mules were used than horses.

When farmers gathered at the country stores to do their bragging, the conversation may have started out with how many pounds of tobacco they produced to the acre, how many bales of cotton they had picked, or how many pigs the old sow had farrowed. However, sometime before the bragging session was over, they always got around to bragging about how strong, how obedient, or how fast their mules or horses were. During the thirties the popularity of the buggy had waned and racing speed was not a priority; thus, mules became more popular than horses.

In 1937 Dad decided that he needed one bigger pair of mules. Some of the soil in "Powell's Corner" was hard clay and it was tough on small mules to plow in it. He felt that if he had a big pair of mules to work the heavier land, the smaller pair could handle the lighter land. So, he shopped around until he found the pair he wanted.

These mules were a cross between draft horses and apparently well-bred jackasses. They were big and tall, probably weighed fifteen hundred pounds each. One was a beautiful roan color with a black stripe down her back, and the other one was totally black. We named the roan colored one Betty and the black one Rhodie.

These mules were about seven years old and very wild. They were definitely untrained; they had never been bridled with bits in their mouths. They had been bred and raised on a vast range in Tennessee, and they had not come in contact with people very often. Dad paid seven hundred and fifty dollars for them and this was one of the highest prices paid for mules in this area during that era. It would be equivalent to about twenty-five thousand dollars today.

These mules lived-up to the price paid for them. They broke fairly easy, were strong, tough, and would adjust to do whatever was needed to be done. They could pull a disc harrow all day and not slow down. If they needed to walk slow while siding small plants to prevent covering the plants up, they would slow down and walk at the speed you wanted them to. If you wanted a team to pull a tobacco transplanter at a slow and consistent speed, these mules could do it.

When you let them walk at their normal gait, it was faster than most mules, so you could get a lot done in a day. Overall, Rhodie was the better of the two mules. She was stronger, sturdier, more placid, and just adapted to every situation better than Betty.

Roosevelt Ellison was given Betty to work and Lance was given Rhodie. Roosevelt wanted Betty because she was more high-spirited. He said that he had never broken and worked a mule that he couldn't ride. He didn't know it then, but he had just been given a mule to work that he would never ride.

She worked well for him and adjusted to all situations. Apparently though she made up her mind that he was not going to ride her, and he was never able to stay on her back. They had a number of rounds, but she always came out the winner. At noon Lance, Merrill, and "Bunk" would come to dinner riding their mule, but here would come Roosevelt, walking and leading his mule.

Merrill got married in 1938, Lance went to work for Bob Cox in Pamplico in 1939, "Bunkus" joined the Navy in 1939, and Roosevelt had moved in 1938. A big shift was taking place in who worked which mule.

Samuel Christmas Brown moved with us in 1939, so when working double, he worked Betty and Rhodie. Herbert Brown moved with us that same year and he worked the other pair of mules named Sue and Jane when working double. When working single, Christmas got Rhodie, Herbert had Sue, Dad had Jane, and guess who got Betty to work! You are right! At the age of thirteen I was given this big, high-spirited, high-stepping animal to work. After I followed her all day, I was truly ready for the bed at night.

Over the next several years, Betty and I spent a lot of time together (she doing the work and me just mostly following and trying to keep up with her). I became very fond of her and I really believed that she liked me. After we got to know each other and used to each other, we talked about me riding her; but, she was wary still and I was understandably cautious, so we put off my riding her for a while.

I kept working with her and finally I built up enough confidence to try to ride her. So, I began riding her regularly. She was never overjoyed about having me on her back and always walked cautiously while I was up there. Dad never liked for me to ride her. He constantly cautioned me but he did say, "Mules just look out for children."

One day when I was coming home for dinner, something spooked Betty and she ran out from under me. I hurt a little physically but my pride was hurt considerably.

Then one Friday afternoon Christmas and I were backplowing corn and wanted to finish so we could go fishing on Saturday morning. We were pushing the mules, and as things would be, I hit an underground stump and broke a dixie plow point. I took the traces loose, put them across the hames, and crawled on Betty's back. We started out to the house to get a plow point.

I began to push her as we really did want to finish so we could go fishing the next morning. Betty was trotting along pretty well, and about the time we got to the top of a long, red clay hill, Betty decided that she just wasn't going to put up with all this junk. She started bucking and jumping and was determined that I wasn't going to stay on top of her. Christmas said that the last time he saw me I was as "high as the pine trees."

When Betty threw me off, one of my legs got caught in one of the plow lines and the other knee hit the hard clay road. It busted my knee and luckily my other leg became untangled. When she successfully got rid of me, she jumped the ditch, stopped, turned around and looked at me.

I got up and hobbled over to her; I took her by the bridle and led her back across the ditch. We talked a while; I patted her and crawled back up on her because I knew that if I didn't get back on her right then, I'd never ride her again.

For several weeks I limped around the house and Dad wanted to know what was wrong. I told him that I'd bruised my knee, but I didn't tell him how because I knew that he'd make me stop riding her. Oh, by the way, we did finish back plowing the corn and went fishing that Saturday morning.

When I went in the Army, David inherited Betty. They got along good, but I don't believe David ever rode her. To my knowledge, I'm the only person that ever rode her.

Dad kept these mules until they were eighteen or nineteen years old, which was getting up in years for mules. Rhodie was still in good shape, but Betty was beginning to have some arthritis in her front legs. This turned out to be the best investment in mules that Dad ever made as they did excellent work for about twelve years. These mules were so beautiful and such high steppers! They got a lot of attention everywhere we took them. They were our objects of great pride and they always "did us proud."

Chapter 29

WE FIRED THE ICE MAN

In the summer of 1936 our lives were changed and would never be the same again. The economy had already improved to the point that we could afford a twenty-five cent block of ice twice a week.

To keep the ice from melting right away, a hole was dug in the smokehouse and a washtub was placed in the hole; then sawdust was filled in around the tub. A lot of heavy woolen cloths were then put on top of the ice to insulate and keep the cold ice from melting too fast.

Ice was used to keep milk cool. Milk was put in glass jars and set in a tub near the ice. Then the ice and milk were covered with woolen cloths. This procedure kept the milk from souring for about forty-eight hours. Without the ice, milk would sour overnight.

The other important use of ice was to chip it up and put in glasses of ice tea for dinner. This was the most refreshing drink that had come along in a long time—that was in reach of the poor. After working all morning in the heat, nothing "hit-the-spot" like ice tea. It was talked about all morning as we worked. We just couldn't wait to get to the house to get a glass of that tingly delicious ice tea.

In the summer of 1937 things really improved for us in the cooling department. A Mr. Petway out of Florence was selling refrigerators that burned kerosene. The name of this refrigerator was Servel. It was the forerunner of modern refrigerators and looked similar to those sold today.

Mr. Petway would take one or two refrigerators, put them on a pickup truck, and peddle them from door to door. When he got to our house, he ate dinner and spent the day with us; but, he didn't make any headway with Dad, as the price of the refrigerator was about two hundred and fifty dollars. Well, we just couldn't afford it!

Mr. Petway finally left our house late that evening, but he was back early the next morning. He started on Dad again, and finally he got Dad to agree to let him leave the refrigerator for a week to see how we would like it. At the end of the week Dad still wouldn't buy it, but he did agree to let him leave it for a while longer. After about a month, of course there was no way we could live without it, so Dad finally broke down and made arrangements to pay for it over a long period of time.

This new machine had shelves to put food and milk on, a vegetable tray, and it made its own ice, which was frozen in trays. Milk would keep from souring for several days and was so cool to drink. The refrigerator was powered by burning kerosene. It burned about five gallons a week, and the cost was fifteen cents a gallon; so, it wasn't cheap.

The "thing" had no moving parts; it had a burner, a generator, a separator, a condenser, an evaporator, and an absorber. The heat from the kerosene burner went to the generator. The tank contained a strong solution of ammonia gas dissolved in water. The heat caused the solution to boil, thus causing the ammonia vapor and solution to rise to the separator, which removed the liquid. The hot gases continued to rise to the condenser, where it was cooled and liquidized. The water was separated from the ammonia, so the liquid was almost pure ammonia. The liquid ammonia flowed through a tube into the evaporator or freezing unit, where it vaporized with hydrogen gas. The hydrogen equalized the pressure between the condenser and the evaporator. The vapor absorbed heat and produced refrigeration. This cycle went on and on and produced ice and a good cool place to store food.

The preparation for meals and the preserving of food was changed forever. We had twelve in family, so this was a tremendous help to Mom as she went about her normal chores of cooking, canning, washing, and taking care of the family.

There were a few things that were important to the proper operation of the unit: the refrigerator had to be level, the wicks had to be kept trimmed, pure kerosene had to be used, and the refrigerator had to be defrosted regularly. "Bunkus" was assigned the job of keeping the "machine" running until he went in the navy in 1939, and then I got the assignment.

At thirteen I was really challenged to keep it going until I learned all of its little quirks. I mastered this assignment and "the beat went on" as this invention changed our lifestyle forever. We didn't have to buy ice anymore on a regular basis except when the refrigerator broke down. The ice truck came from Florence, and it continued to pass our house going to other customers. However, when the refrigerator broke down, we had to run out and flag him down to get ice. But, we had fired the ice man!

Chapter 30

A NEW CAR.....WOW!!!!

By 1938 the economy was somewhat better and a lot of people were buying cars. Throughout the early thirties people had bragged about their teams of mules. As times got better in the late thirties, this particular bragging waned. The love affair with the car was generating like hot fever. Gradually, bragging about cars replaced bragging about mules. Peer pressure to keep up with the Joneses was something awful. Salesmen for several years had tried unsuccessfully to sell Dad a car, but this was about to change.

In September of 1938 Lucus Bigelow, Dad's nephew, brought a 1938 Chevrolet to our house. He spent the day and stayed until Dad agreed to buy the car. The car sold for eight-hundred and fifty dollars. The model was about to change, so it was discounted. They took off all the options such as heater, radio, big horn, and Lucus gave up his commission. Lucus was selling cars for Hyman Motors of Pamplico.

With all the reductions the price of the car was seven-hundred and forty-five dollars. We really weren't financially able to buy this car, but the older children put such pressure on Dad that finally he gave in and bought it. Paying for it over the next several years strained our existence even though the economy had improved.

The new Chevrolet was a beauty. It was a Master Deluxe Town Sedan with two seats and two doors. The dark green exterior was accented by yellow trim and the upholstery was a plush velour. The only options above standard equipment were a clock and a cigarette lighter.

The standard size for tires for the late thirties was 600x16 inches. This time we even had a spare tire. The engine was a straight six-cylinder with overhead cams and was rated at eighty-five horse power. Young boys liked to brag about how fast their car would run.

Ford cars were really the fastest cars, but you couldn't get any of us Chevrolet owners to admit it. Fords had V8 engines and would fly, but they had mechanical brakes which sometimes failed. It wasn't unusual to see the front of a Ford bashed in because it wouldn't stop and had run into something. The car we had would run about ninety miles per hour—when it was properly tuned.

"Old Faithful" (as it was called in later years) turned out to be a much needed investment. It served as transportation for all of us and it pulled a trailer to haul tobacco to the market. The tires lasted about fifteen thousand miles. The motor had to be overhauled at forty-five thousand miles and again about every fifteen thousand miles after that. The transmission had to be overhauled at fifty thousand miles and then every twenty-five thousand miles after that.

This car lasted until 1950, when it was sold to Christmas Brown for two hundred and fifty dollars. He totaled it in a wreck shortly after he got it. We all felt like we had lost a good friend.

The demolished car was parked behind the Shell Station in Johnsonville. We went to the station just like we were going to a funeral. We looked at it, touched it, and grieved a little because it was like a part of the family for twelve years. After all, this car had gone through seven drivers in the family and numerous other people had driven it to carry Dad different places. Dad never did drive it; he drove the Model T but he never attempted to drive this car—none of us ever knew why.

There were no paved roads in those days except the streets in Florence, Lake City, Pamplico, and Johnsonville. It was impossible to keep a car clean or keep the rattles out of it. The roads were dominated by the white male drivers during this era. There was no place where the white male ego was more intense than on the road behind the steering wheel of a car.

It was considered a "No No'" for a female or black male driver to pass a white male driver on the road. I have seen fist fights erupt because of blacks passing whites on the highway. Roads were very dusty and men just didn't want someone to pass them and fill their car up with dust. All the windows would be down, and the dust would just cover you up.

Women drivers were very cautious, and they drove really slow. They wouldn't take chances in passing other cars, and if you got behind one, you were usually held up for a while. This caused a lot of fussing and complaining by the male drivers. However, this slow and cautious driving by the women had a very definite advantage when they traded their cars in. Car salesmen would advertise these cars as "driven by a little old lady," and they sold for a premium.

Chapter 31

THE MOVE FROM "POWELL'S CORNER" TO "THE BACKWOODS"

The tempo of life for many people began to pick up during the late thirties. With the wide use of radios, the increased number of automobiles, the improved speed of railroads, and the growing popularity of telephones, all of life's activities became faster. The news media became active around the world, and consequently the size of the world began to shrink.

In 1935 the National Recovery Act (NRA) was replaced by the Works Progress Administration (WPA) and thousands of people were put to work building highways, schools, parks, etc. The program did a lot of good as more money was put into circulation; but, like most government programs, it was abused and the title WPA became a laughing stock of the country.

The government became more active in all of our lives, and the Social Security Act came into being in 1935. Then, later in 1938 the first Minimum Wage Act was passed and set at forty cents an hour. Franklin D. Roosevelt's popularity grew and in 1936 he was reelected as President of the United States by a big landslide.

Our interest in world and national affairs increased by leaps and bounds. Will Rogers, the famous entertainer, was killed in an airplane crash while flying over Alaska in 1935. In 1936 King George V of England died and was succeeded by King Edward VIII, who later during the same year abdicated the throne and married an American divorcee.

The Hindenburg, a dirigible filled with hydrogen, blew up and burned in New Jersey killing 36 people in 1937. This German dirigible was the largest airship ever built. It was 803 feet long and had flown thirty-six times across the Atlantic, but this big tragedy ended airship service.

Joe Louis, the boxer who later held the world heavy weight championship longer than anyone, became the world champion in 1937 by knocking out Jimmy Braddock. Amelia Earhart, the famous female flyer, was lost at sea that same year. The movie that has become a legend, <u>Snow White and the Seven Dwarfs</u>, was made in

1937 and shown in 1938. It was the first fully animated movie. The Wizard of Oz, an all-time favorite, premiered in 1939. Also in 1939 the forever renowned movie, Gone With the Wind, starring Clark Gable and Vivian Leigh, opened with enthusiastic applause in Atlanta. Though it would be years before most of us would see these movies, there was still a lot of talk and excitement about them.

At the same time all of these national events were taking place, life on the farm was also changing. Sharecroppers were finding factory jobs and moving to the cities. Some of the small landowners were selling their land and moving away. Large landowners were still buying all the land that they could get at cheap prices.

By the end of the decade our family size had shrunk. Merrill had gotten married and moved out, Lance had gotten married and moved, and "Bunkus" had joined the Navy. I was thirteen and the oldest male child left at home; so a tremendous responsibility was placed on me.

The "Powell's Corner" farm had really gotten too big for us. In 1939 the Woodberry farm in "Powell's Corner," where we had lived for five years, was sold to a Mr. Willoby from Scranton. This fine farm and tract of land of five hundred and fifty acres sold for six thousand and five hundred dollars or about twelve dollars per acre. The beautiful two-story house and numerous outbuildings were included in the sale. The timber was cruised about thirty years later and valued at over a half-million dollars.

Dad understood that Mr. Luther Richardson was going to buy the place. Since Mr. Luther was a brother-in-law to Mr. Pete Cornwell, who was selling the place, Dad made no effort to try to buy it; he didn't want to upset Mr. Luther. For some reason the purchase by Mr. Luther fell through, and it was sold to Mr. Willoby before Dad knew what had taken place. Mr. Willoby and Dad became good friends and Mr. Willoby asked Dad to stay on and sharecrop with him. This was a tough decision because we had grown very fond of this fine farm and beautiful house.

Sometime earlier Mr. Joe Holliday of Gallivant's Ferry, while in his last days here on earth, had sent for Dad to come to see him. When Dad was young, his Dad was sick for a long period of time. He had some poor crop years, and due to indebtedness to Mr. Joe Holliday, he foreclosed on the mortgage. This meant that they lost everything, and at that time Dad told Mr. Holliday that if he had any heart at all that he would give them time to work it out.

While visiting Mr. Holliday in those last days, they reminisced about things that had happened in years gone by. Mr. Holliday told Dad that he had instructed his boys to help Dad in anyway they could to help him get back on his feet.

So, at the opportune time, after the Woodberry place was sold, Dad went and talked to Mr. Henry Holliday, one of Mr. Joe's sons, about what farms he may have to rent. Mr. Henry had a nice little farm in "The Backwoods." This farm had about fifty acres of cleared land and a new six-room house. This house was built out of green lumber but had never been sealed. He told Dad that he would rent it to him for a little over two hundred dollars a year. So.... needless to say, Dad took it without any hesitation.

The move to this house was the roughest part of the whole change. We had gotten used to having a nice, fairly-warm house, and here we were back in a house that had cracks in the walls so big that you could see the moon and stars at night. The green boards used for the floor had shrunk and left cracks so big you could see the chickens walking around underneath the floor. When the wind blew, you could feel the breeze and, believe me, in the dead of winter we were cold.

I took what little money I had and could scrape up and bought some screen wire and some boards. I made some screen doors and windows and put them up. For a fourteen year old boy, making a screen door was a big undertaking. The doors didn't look all that great, but they kept the flies and mosquitoes out.

Dad took the floor boards up and tightened all of them. "Bunkus" was in the Navy, so he sent home enough money to buy sheet-rock to seal the house. It wasn't too long before we had the house livable. We had water problems with a thirty foot deep open well that kept caving in and going dry, but I'll cover this in another chapter.

The first major problem that we ran into, other than the house, was the mule stables. When the Hollidays built the stables, they didn't build them for mules the size of Betty and Rhodie. They had built them for much smaller mules.

On the day that we moved, after we were through with the mules, Christmas and I went to put the mules up. Can you believe that we couldn't get either of the mules to even try to go in the stables? We pulled and whipped, but those two mules decided that there was no way they were going in those little stables.

Well, what do you do with two big mules and no place for them to stay? We had to hook them back up to the wagon and drive them back to "Powell's Corner," which was about five miles. We left them down there for several weeks until the stables could be enlarged and a fence put up. Everyday we had to go back and feed them; if the car wasn't available, we had to walk. We did more walking than we did riding.

The land on the new farm was heavy and would get hard as a rock after a rain. Having the big mules was a real asset as pulling a disc harrow in this land was hard even for them.

The depression was near the end, and rumors of war were beginning to be heard. Prices for farm products were getting higher, so there was more money in circulation. There was a demand for products other than tobacco and cotton. We planted pimento pepper, hot pepper, highland rice, sweet potatoes, etc.

We were thrilled at the end of each year when all we had to do was pay the rent; now we didn't have to share everything with the landlord. This was the beginning of our turn-a-round. It was the start of a better life for all of us. President Roosevelt talked about the "New Deal." Well, this certainly was the "New Deal" for us. It gave Dad a chance to start saving a little money every year. Even though we started accumulating a little money, our lifestyle didn't change as we continued to live very conservatively.

When the time was right and Dad had enough money for the down payment on a farm, he bought the Old Eaddy Place in "Possum Fork" on the Johnsonville side of Lynches River. He purchased this farm in 1946, and it was a good little farm. The house wasn't the greatest, but it was home and it was ours.

The economy improved during the war and for a number of years after the war. Dad was a good tobacco farmer and things really began turning around for him. By the time of his death in 1954, he had paid for the farm, had bought another larger farm, and had paid about half of the cost of the new farm.

All these accomplishments were the result of faith in God, faith in self, a lot of sacrifices, a lot of hard work, and the end of the depression. You might note that I didn't write about our move from

"The Backwoods" to "Possum Fork." Well, that's because I was in the Army and out of the country at that time.

Jerry, Virginia "Sis", and Paul's best friend Rover
on steps of home in Powell's Corner - taken about 1938.

Jerry with many kittens in the Backwoods - 1943.
Note house with dog-trot back porch and no underpinning.

Family

Max, David, and Paul in the Backwoods - ready for church - 1943.
Note our 1938 Chevrolet

Mom and "Bunkus" in the Backwoods. "Bunk" was home from the war - 1945.

Merrill's 1931 Model A with rumble seat.
Pictured are Rowena, Max, David, Bobby, "Sis", Jerry, and Nellie - Taken about 1944.

Chapter 32

I'LL NEVER FORGET MY FRIEND CHRISTMAS

In 1939 Merrill, Lance, and "Bunkus" had left home, leaving me at the age of thirteen as the oldest boy in the family. At this age I had the major responsibility of feeding four mules, several cows, and about fifty hogs, plus all the other farm chores that were required. I also had the big responsibility of supplying wood to cook and heat with.

A lot of wood was needed to cook three meals a day for a family of nine people and to keep us warm in winter. I had to go out in the woods and chop down trees; then, the felled trees had to be cut into pieces small enough to go in the stove. In order to get the wood to the house, I had to either carry it in a burlap bag (we called it a "croaker bag") across my shoulder or hook-up a pair of mules to the wagon to haul it to the house. All of these major responsibilities were just thrust on me overnight, and I was hardly prepared for them.

Samuel Christmas Brown had been farming with Mr. Joy, but he helped us gather tobacco during the summer. Mr. Joy decided to retire that year and move to Johnsonville, so Dad got Samuel Christmas to come and farm with us.

Samuel Christmas was born on Christmas day, so Christmas became a part of his name. He registered for the Draft during World War II as Samuel Christmas Brown and that forever attached Christmas as his name. He was known as Christmas by everyone who knew him. He agreed to come to work for something like seventy-five cents a day and three acres of tobacco on shares.

Christmas was married to the former Susie Woodberry. They had two children, Prince and Loudottie. Prince was probably four years old and Loudottie was only a few months old when they came to farm with us. As I remember, Prince was well adjusted, but Loudottie did a lot of hollering when Susie had to work. She just wanted to be held and didn't want her mother to leave her.

Christmas was born in the Black Mingo section of Williamsburg County, and he had a dialect different from the dialect in lower Florence County. For arm he would say "am" and for car he would say "kha." Most all of the R's were left out except the R in R. C. Cola and that was pronounced as "Aror C. Cola."

Christmas was tall, probably 6'3", and very slim; he probably weighed one hundred fifty pounds. He walked on his toes and had the smoothest walking gait of any person that I have ever seen. He just floated along. You could have put a bucket of water on his head while he was walking and none of it would have spilled. Christmas worked at a very slow and deliberate pace. Every movement counted, and he could accomplish much more than the average person.

Since Dad did not drive the 1938 Chevrolet and I was too young to drive, Christmas did a lot of driving for us. He usually took us everywhere we needed to go except to church. He taught me to drive long before I was old enough to get my license; so then I drove the family to church. Christmas ate dinner with us as that was a part of the work agreement that he had with Dad.

Christmas was the most even-tempered person that I have ever known. In all of my association with him I never saw him get riled-up or say anything out-of-the-way. One day, before he came to work for us, he and I were helping Dutchman Altman put in tobacco. Dutchman hadn't taken the cured tobacco out of the barns ahead of time. He asked me and Christmas to come and help him immediately after we ate dinner.

Now this was while everyone else was taking a two-hour rest and, of course, there would be no extra pay. (It was normal to take a two hour break at midday.) As soon as I finished lunch, I returned to help Dutchman unload the barn of tobacco. Christmas was slow getting there, and he asked Dutchman how much extra money he was going to get. This made Dutchman mad. He "popped-off" and said a lot of things that he regretted afterwards.

Christmas didn't say anything else; he just looked at Dutchman and walked slowly by him on the way to go talk to Susie, his wife, who was at her sister's house. Dutchman realized the seriousness of the things that he had said. He didn't know but what Christmas might be going to get a gun. Dutchman ran in his house and got his gun and loaded it.

Dutchman had two boys, Gordon and Lenair, who were probably four and six years old. They were hanging on to Dutchman, crying and screaming, "Daddy, don't kill him! Daddy, don't kill him!"

This scare was too much for a young fellow like me to have to endure, but I did try to calm down the situation. Christmas had gone to tell Susie that he was going home. He then walked back by Dutchman's house on his way home. He never lost his cool and for that reason prevented what could have been a tragedy. From that day forward my respect for Christmas grew with each moment that I was with him.

I have no knowledge of Christmas ever abusing or hurting anyone either physically or verbally. He would not talk about people to their back; he would not meddle in other people's business; he was totally honest. The only hurt that he did to anyone was to himself.

His problem was that on weekends he took his money and bought something to drink and drank all weekend. When he was drinking, he never got mean or disorderly. I think his drinking really made him more peaceful. When he was drinking, if he went to Johnsonville or Hemingway and walked down the street, the police officers locked him up.

I don't ever remember any disturbances caused by him in either of these little towns, but, if he walked the streets and had been drinking, he was surely put in jail. This was a sure source of revenue for these little towns, because they knew Dad would bail Christmas out by Monday morning in time to go to work. Dad would tell Christmas, "The next time you get in jail, I'm just going to leave you in there." This didn't do any good as Christmas did not change.

Dad would tell him that he was going to run him off, and Christmas would say that he wasn't going anyplace 'cause he was going to stay with Dad forever. Dad told him once, "I'm going to leave you in jail and let you rot." Then he said to Christmas, "Aren't you ashamed of yourself?" Christmas' response was, "No, I ain't 'shame." Once he was in a wreck and his hip was broken; the town police kept him in jail without treatment for several days.

Dad finally realized that he had to do more than change Christmas; he had to try to change the town police in Johnsonville and Hemingway from taking advantage of Christmas and him. Soon afterwards Christmas was in jail again and the town representative came to tell Dad that he had Christmas locked-up. Dad told the police, "Just keep him. I am not going to pay another fine for him." This shocked the officer, but they still kept Christmas for several days. They thought Dad would give in, but they were wrong.

After they were convinced that Dad was not going to pay the fine and no one else would, they let him out. I don't think they wanted to continue feeding Christmas, even though Christmas said that he had some 'poor eating' while in jail. This did the job! As far as I know, Christmas never got locked-up again.

Christmas and I became very close friends after he came to work for us in 1939. Other than his weekend drinking habit, he had a lot of qualities that I tried to emulate. Any job that he did, he did it well and tried to please Dad. This made me want to be more like him because I wanted to please Dad also.

We sawed oak trees that were at least thirty-six inches in diameter. Due to my height, I had to reach up when we started sawing a block off of these big trees. Christmas made me think that I was really doing good; but now I know that all I was doing was steadying the other end of the saw, and he was really doing the sawing.

He taught me how to saw, chop wood, shuck corn real fast, but most of all he taught me how to crop tobacco and keep up with the other croppers. He taught me how to stack hay on a wagon with a flat body so that we could haul twice as much as anyone around. We worked as a team and really depended on each other.

When the day's work was done, we usually had plans that continued on into the evening. During the fall and winter, we did a lot of coon and possum hunting. Several nights a week we took Rover, my dog, and went hunting. Many nights we would build a fire and just sit and talk while waiting on Rover to tree something. The coons and possums that we caught were divided equally. The hides were sold and the money divided. We worked real hard during the week so that we could go hunting or fishing on Saturday.

During the fall and winter months we went squirrel hunting. In the spring and summer we went fishing. Our squirrel hunting was usually done with Rover either on the Woodberry place in "Powell's Corner" or on the Greenwood place at Kingsburg. Hunting and fishing helped Christmas and my family to have something to eat.

The fishing that Christmas and I did was with lead lines. In Marion County we fished in Graves, Crooked, Dog, and Honey Lakes and in Florence County we fished in Hannah's Lake. Christmas could catch fish when nobody else could. He always brought back more fish than anyone who went fishing with him.

He really tried to help me learn to fish because he wanted me to enjoy it so I'd go with him often. I got pretty good, but I never quite attained the proficiency in this art that he had; with him it was truly an art. He would spit on his bait, talk to his bait, and talk to the fish. He would say, "Fishy, fishy, come on and get your dinner; now come on to papa!"

There were some tremendous cypress trees in Hannah's Lake. Some of them must have been fifteen feet in diameter. Most of them were hollow, so Christmas would roll his line up to about three feet and anchor the boat around these trees. He would then fish in the hollow places - sometimes sticking his cane all the way in the hollow of the trees. You could always bet, when Christmas went fishing, he would bring home some meat for his family.

All the years that I worked, hunted, and fished with Christmas, I never heard him use a curse word; either he didn't curse, or he respected me enough not to curse in front of me. He had a lot of inner wisdom and the innate ability to use it wisely. I relied on his counsel a lot.

Many times I asked him questions. One question that I asked him was about sex. He would say things like, "Ask your Dad," or "Wait till you get old enough," or "You'll know when the time comes," or "I ain't telling you cause I might tell you wrong."

Once we were having a hotly contested school trustee election. I asked Christmas who he was going to vote for, and he told me that he couldn't vote. I asked him why and he said, "Negroes can't vote." I couldn't believe this. Who would not want Christmas to vote? How had I been protected from this bigotry in my home and in the schools? The blacks weren't talking about it and the whites surely weren't, so at the age of fourteen I didn't know blacks couldn't vote.

My association with Christmas made a big impact on my life and has greatly influenced what and who I have become. He will always be a pleasant part of my memories of the past. I feel a lot of remorse that he had to endure so much discrimination during his lifetime.

"Thanks, Christmas—for being there and for being my friend. Thanks for your guidance and for the good times we had together. I know I'll see you again."

Chapter 33

ROVER, MY BEST FRIEND

Robert Cornwell, son of Mr. Pete and Mrs. Lucille Cornwell, used to visit us quite often during the summer and holidays. He always stayed several weeks at the time. His parents were our landlords in "Powell's Corner."

Robert loved to hunt, so he bought a hound dog that was supposed to be a real good tree dog. He gave him to me to keep. It turned out that all this hound dog wanted to do was run foxes; he wouldn't tree a thing unless that tree had bread or food for him.

Ted Hemingway from Hemingway was a hunting guide for Mr. W. W. Montgomery, and he also did fox hunting on the side. He found out that we had a fox hound and that we wanted a tree dog, so he traded Rover to us for the hound.

Rover was a mixture of boxer bull with about one-fourth terrier. He was not quite as big as a boxer but big enough to take care of himself. I got him when I was nine years old, and he was probably four or five years old at that time. It didn't take long for us to become close friends. He was red and white spotted with ears that stuck up. He walked like he was proud of himself.

When he was young, he was a tough hombre in a protective way and could handle himself with the best of dogs. He was not mean but would fight when he was forced to...... and when in a fight, he could take care of the situation. If he and I were going someplace and we came up on a dog, he would get in between me and the dog. If the other dog wouldn't back off, then there was a dogfight on hand.

Rover turned out to be a good tree dog, but he was so protective and temperamental about me that it interfered with his effectiveness as a hunting dog. If just he and I were hunting, he would hunt real well. He would tree squirrels in the daytime and coons and possums at night. If someone went with us, he would go out and hunt a little while but would keep coming back to me. I guess he was checking on me to be sure that I was okay.

When my hunting partner was Christmas, Rover hunted real good. I guess he just got used to and approved of Christmas. But, if we went hunting with a group and had other dogs, he absolutely would not hunt. All he would do was just follow right at my heels. I don't know whether he wanted to protect me or was insulted because we had other dogs along.

My pal Rover always knew when I would be getting home from school and would be waiting for me. He would stay with me the rest of the day. When I was going to Trinity School, there were a few times when he came all the way from "Powell's Corner" to school. The teachers didn't think too highly of a dog coming to school.

On one occasion he even came to Trinity Methodist Church. It was in the summertime, and, since there was no air conditioning in those days, the doors were wide open. So, here came Rover walking down the aisle.

Dad didn't appreciate that one bit, and I was so afraid that Dad was going to give him away or something. Dad only liked dogs that would run deer, so Rover wasn't his favorite; it didn't take much for Rover to really get in the "doghouse" with him.

From that day on I tried to shut him up in a pen before we left for church. Many times when I was plowing, Rover followed right behind me up and down each row.

When we moved from "Powell's Corner" to "The Backwoods," Howard Davis became my new next-door neighbor. We were also in the same class in high school.

About every afternoon after school Howard came over to visit. Sometimes our visiting turned into playing and wrestling. As long as I was on top, Rover was completely at ease; but, if Howard got on top of me and Rover thought he was hurting me, he went after Howard with a vengeance.

During high school, I worked at Bernie Poston's Service Station and General Store on the weekends and any day that Dad could spare me from the farm. It was about three miles from our house in "The Backwoods" to Bernie's store. I walked some of the time, but, most of the time, I drove the 1938 Chevrolet.

Everyday, after Rover had finished his breakfast, he came to Bernie's and stayed with me the rest of the day. He would just lie under the car until quitting time and then he rode back with me in the car. Of course, if I had walked to work, he would walk back home with me.

In early September of 1943 I left home to go to Pfeiffer Junior

College at Misenheimer, N. C. At this time Rover was 14 years old. Mom said that he stayed and moped around the house for a few days and then just disappeared. I'll never know what happened to him, but I have a feeling that, wherever he was and whatever happened to him, he was looking for me. The bond between us was very strong, and when I lost him, it really hurt.

My memories of Rover protecting me, hunting for me, wanting to be with me, and actually risking his life at times for me will never be forgotten. "Thanks, Old Pal, you won my heart over and over again, and you wrote this chapter for me."

Chapter 34

MY PARENTS' "DO-GOOD" RULES

Over the years Dad and Mom developed a list of guidelines which we were expected to follow. When I was growing up, these guidelines seemed awfully strict. It seemed to us that other children had more "leeway" to do certain things than we did.

If there were any questions or doubts in our minds as to whether something was acceptable or not, we'd ask our parents. We knew this was the only way to stay out of trouble. Our parents were always together on what was right and what was wrong. If there were ever any split decisions, we didn't know about them.

Dad and Mom encouraged us to think on our own, but they cautioned us to think and try to do what Jesus would do in any situation. If we made a decision that they did not agree with, they didn't disown us, but we were certainly reminded time and time again that what we had done was wrong. There was a concerted effort by all the children to please our parents when it came to morals, ethics, and spiritual values.

We were not that diligent when it came to how well or how quickly we performed certain chores that were assigned for us to do. However, sometimes when we didn't do what they wanted done as quickly or as well as they expected, we were harshly penalized. The punishment was usually a good tongue lashing. But, if it was a second or third offense, there was a leather strap hanging by the door of the room where Dad used to sit and read that was used on us. If the offense happened outside the house, there were a lot of peach tree switches handy.

Dad always encouraged us to play with black children when we were growing up. He felt that the moral and spiritual values being taught in the black families were "first-rate." He wanted us to be exposed to those values. It was made clear that we were not to take advantage of them in any way, and we were expected to share what we had with them.

Two of my best friends for several years were Hiram and Nelson Ellison, who lived on the farm in "Powell's Corner." Boys were encouraged to play together and girls were encouraged to play together as the sexes were somewhat kept separate.

Once when I was about five years old, I walked to the store at Kingsburg with Edna, Ora Lee, and Arthur Junior Poston. I was the youngest of the foursome. On the way we passed by a black lady, Maybelle Woodberry, and her daughter. Arthur Junior, Edna, and Ora Lee called them "Ole Black Niggers."

A few days later when Maybelle saw Dad, she told him about the episode but failed to tell him that I wasn't involved. Dad came home and got all over me and was about to tear me up. I pleaded that I hadn't done anything to get a whipping for. He didn't punish me but promised to talk to Maybelle again to find out whether I was telling the truth or not. When he talked to her again, she verified that I was not involved. He came back, and he seemed relieved, even though he made no apology. I think this helped my credibility for many years to follow.

Even though there were ten children in my family, we were all watched very closely. Our progress at school was monitored by my parents and close contact was kept with the teachers. If anyone of us left home for any reason, our parents knew where we were going, what we were going for, and when we were expected back.

As we grew up, we were not permitted to waste much time. Duties were always laid out for us to do during the school year and also during the summer months. Our lives were somewhat regimented, but you know what! -- it didn't hurt a one of us.

All ten children came through this strict environment as God-fearing, law-abiding, and hard-working people. All of us finished high school and three finished college. All were married and there have been no divorces. All have done well in their professions -- only one remained on the farm. None have ever been arrested or had any scrapes with the law.

The following is a list of "do-good" rules that we were expected to abide by:

1. Children should be seen but not heard.
2. Don't sass an adult.
3. Say yes sir, no sir, yes ma'm, no ma'm to adults.
4. Address adults with Mr., Mrs., or Miss.
5. Answer when you are called.
6. You will go to school when you are not sick, or have to work, and you will graduate from high school.

7. If you get a whipping in school, you'll get another one when you get home.
8. Spare the rod and spoil the child.
9. Be courteous.
10. Don't lie.
11. Don't gossip.
12. Keep your nose clean.
13. Don't start a fight, but don't run away from one if it's forced on you.
14. Don't be two-faced.
15. Don't say anything to a person's back that you can't say to his face.
16. Always say thank you.
17. Always wear clean underwear.
18. When leaving the house, Mom would say, "Be pretty and don't tell anything."
19. Eat everything you put on your plate.
20. Don't take anything that doesn't belong to you.
21. Don't drink "rot-gut" liquor.
22. Observe Sunday and keep it holy.
23. Treat other people as you would like for them to treat you.
24. Pay back more than you borrow.
25. Look a person straight in the eyes when you are talking to him or her.
26. If anything is worth doing at all, it's worth doing good.
27. Let your word be your bond.
28. A stitch in time saves nine.
29. Go to church on Sunday.
30. Don't put off until tomorrow what you can do today.
31. If the ox is in the ditch, take him out.
32. Don't bite off more than you can chew.
33. The chickens will come back home to roost... meaning... what you sow you will also reap.
34. When you belittle someone else, you belittle yourself.
35. "Do not let the sun go down on your anger." (Ephesians 4:26)

36. "Know this, My beloved brethren. Let every man be quick to hear, slow to speak, slow to anger." (James 1:19)
37. "We know that in everything God works for good with those who love Him, who are called according to his purpose." (Romans 8:28)
38. "I will be with you; I will not forsake you." (Joshua 1:5)
39. Fornication and adultery are sinful.
40. No sex until you get married.
41. Idleness leads to mischief.
42. What you do speaks so loud I can't hear what you say.
43. Bring up a child in the way he should go and he will not depart from it.

"Mom and Dad, they worked! Thanks for the love, foresight, and endurance."

Chapter 35

THINGS THAT I REMEMBER ABOUT DAD

Dedication
He was totally dedicated to God, to his family, to his beliefs, to his church, to masonry, to deer hunting, to fishing, to politics, and to less fortunate people.

Strictness
He was uncompromisingly strict on his children. He always saw that there was plenty of work to keep us busy—this would keep us out of trouble. Anytime there were differences between the children, he would solve the differences.

Expectations
He had high expectations for each child. After he or she reached about the age of ten, he thought they were mature enough to know right from wrong and should start thinking and working like adults.

Confidence
He had total confidence that each child would not stray from the high ideals that he had set for them. The amazing thing about this is that none of them disappointed him.

Hatred of alcohol
He had the most intense abhorrence of the use of whiskey and beer of anyone that I have ever known in my life. Relationships with some people were affected by this hatred for alcohol.

Respect
He had total respect from the people in the community -- this included blacks and whites who either knew him or knew of his reputation. His word was his bond. He lived by his principles, and he was a friend to man. The respect that people had for him made life a little easier for all the family, as we could get credit to get anything we wanted. All the family tried very hard not to tarnish the high respect that the community had for him and Mom.

Constant Reading
As I remember my Dad, he was always reading something. He read the daily news from front to back. He read every magazine that we took from cover to cover. He read all the church literature

that he received. Friends kept him supplied with books.

Perfection
As I think back, one thing that stands out was his need to have everything done as nearly perfect as possible. He always worked on his tobacco plant beds several weeks in the winter until he had them just like he wanted them. Before he started tilling the land, he had to have it totally cleaned off. He could plow the straightest row of anyone I ever saw. When he built something, you could be sure it was built right. He would not take short cuts or try to rush through and sacrifice quality.

Dad's Sunday Morning Prayer:
"Almighty and Most Merciful Father, we have erred and strayed from Thy ways like lost sheep. We have left undone those things which we ought to have done, and we have done those things we ought not to have done. We acknowledge and bewail our manifold sins and wickedness, which from time to time we have grievously committed by thought, word, or deed against Thy Divine Majesty.

Forgive those who are cold, careless, and indifferent about their own soul's salvation. We beseech Thee to have mercy on us and to accept this as our bounden duty and service, not weighing our merits but pardoning our sins. We do earnestly repent and are heartily sorry for these our mis-doings—the remembrance of them is grievous unto us. Please grant that we may hereafter serve Thee and please Thee with a newness of life to the honor and glory of Thy name, through Jesus Christ our Lord, who taught us to pray:

Our Father, which art in heaven, hallowed be Thy name, Thy kingdom come, Thy will be done, on earth as it is in heaven. Give us this day our daily bread. Forgive us of our trespasses as we forgive those who trespass against us. Lead us not into temptation, but deliver us from evil; for Thine is the kingdom, and the power, and the glory, for ever and ever. Amen."

I Remember Dad's Curse Words
All the time that I was with Dad, I never heard him take the Lord's name in vane. He did have his own selection of words that he used when he got disturbed, worried, mad, or mashed his finger or something like that. He would come out with one or more of the following: Dog gone it! Plague take it! Dad burn it! Dad gum it! John Brown! Infernal! Hell fire!

Bits and Pieces of Songs Dad Sang to us
"Up jumped Lillie, Lilllie Lang Dum, Billy Dum Coy oh me.
Coy up the Gayro, guilting Caro…coy oh me.
Run fella run, the patterol will catch you
Run fella run, it's almost day.
The fella run, the fella flew
The fella tore his shirt in two.

Old Dan Tucker and Henry Clay
started out to ride in a one horse sleigh;
The sleigh was broke and the horse was blind,
and he had no hair on his tail behind.
Get out the way, Old Dan Tucker
You're too late to get your supper.

Way down in Columbus Georgia,
I want to be back in Tennessee.
It's a rainy night in Georgia. It's raining all the time.
Mr. Jailman, my son didn't steal that chicken,
That chicken just followed him home.

When they cut down the old pine tree,
And they hauled it away to the mill;
To make a coffin of pine for that sweetheart of mine,
When they cut down the old pine tree."

I Remember Dad Taking Me to the Tobacco Market
One of the highlights of my early memories was Dad taking me to Mullins to the tobacco market. I was four years old and small for my age. We went in a red Model T truck that did not have a cab, so we just rode along and let the wind blow on us. When we got to Mullins, we passed several tobacco warehouses. There was someone at each door hollering, "Drive right in." They were trying to get people to sell tobacco at their warehouse.

Dad always sold at Paul Hardy's warehouse, so when we got to Mr. Hardy's warehouse, they hollered, "Drive right in," … so we did. The tobacco was unloaded and put in baskets and lined up in rows. The place was loud with people working and hollering, and trucks were coming in and going out constantly.

We had to wait a few hours before the sale started, but when it did start, that was the most amazing thing that I had ever seen. There were probably twenty-five people in the line going up and down the rows of tobacco. This long line of people included the warehouseman, the auctioneer, recorders, and buyers from each tobacco company.

Some of the companies were American Tobacco, R. J. Reynolds, Brown and Williams, Imperial, and many more. The auctioneer was talking so fast; I really couldn't tell what he was saying. After the sale, if the farmer didn't accept the price they offered, he turned the tag over and those baskets that he wouldn't sell at the price that was offered were left in the warehouse and sold the next day.

The warehouse workers took the baskets that were sold to the various companies, and the tobacco was then put in large wooden hogsheads, which are large wooden barrels. This experience was a lot for a four year old boy to take in.

After the sale, Dad took me to a hot dog stand and bought me a hot dog and a Ne Hi orange drink. This was the first time I had ever had either of these. I ate the hot dog, but there was no way I could drink all that "Big Orange." Then we went to several stores to try to find a suit for me. We could not find one small enough (I must have been little for my age). I finally tried on one (which I almost got lost in) and I told the clerk, "It's too big, but I'm going to have it anyway."

This was a full day for me. I slept about all the way back home. At that time I didn't know why Dad took just me with him on this trip, but after I had children of my own, I know that he took me because he loved me with an unconditional love. "Dad, I may not have told you back then that I loved you and appreciated going with you, but I really did."

Paul's Dad sitting on the front porch of the house in Possum Fork

Doctor bills paid by my Dad for Grandfather and friends

FLORENCE, S. C. 11/15 191_1_

M_r_ E. P. Prol---

IN ACCOUNT WITH

DR. F. H. McLEOD

To Professional Services	$35	00
By Cash	25	70
	$9	30

JOHNSONVILLE, S. C.   **DR. A. G. EADDY**   REG. No. 1564   OFFICE HOURS: 8:30 to 10 a.m. 2 to 3:30 p.m.

For_____ Address_____

℞ Dixie Ellison   2.95
                2.00
                $4.95
Homer Ellison   20.0
Jesse Ellison   1.55
                2.00
                $3.55

_____ M. D.

No._____ Date_____

Tax Receipts

Office of COUNTY TREASURER
Florence County

No. 12__

Florence, S. C., _____ 191__

Received of Mr. _M. R. Paston_

_____ Township

One Dollar Commutation Road Tax for Year 1912.

$1.00

_____
County Treasurer

Office of the County Treasurer
FLORENCE COUNTY

NUMBER 3202

Florence, S. C., _Dec 24_ 1916

Received of _M. R. Paston_

Pee Dee Township

One Dollar. Commutation Road Tax for year 1916.

$1.00

_____
COUNTY TREASURER

$1.25   OFFICE OF   No. 203

County Treasurer, Florence Co., S. C.

DOG TAX RECEIPT

Florence, S. C., _____ 192_7_

Received of _M. R. Paston_

One and 25-100 Dollars for Dog Tax for Year 192_4_

School District _35_

CHAS. T. HAYNIE,
County Treasurer

Bill of Sale for Dad's first Sporty Buggy
purchased in 1907 when he was 19 years old.

handwritten promissory note and bill of sale

P.O. Savage, R.F.D. #1 – Box 33 –

$55.00   Florence S.C. 12/21" 1907.

On the 15" day of August 1908 next, I promise to pay to the order of J. W. Jones at Florence S.C. Int. from date at 8%

Fifty-Five /100 Dollars.

Value received. Witness my hand and seal.

Due .... M. K. Poston   (SEAL)

The State of South Carolina,
County of Florence

WHEREAS, I am indebted to J. W. Jones in the sum of Fifty-Five /100 and have given my note therefore, of even date with these presents [which is hereto annexed], payable on the 15" day of August. A. D. 1908

NOW, in order to secure the payment of said note, and in consideration of the sum of Five Dollars to me in hand paid, I do hereby grant, bargain and sell unto J. W. Jones the following goods and chattels to-wit:

One Top Side Spring Buggy made by Ottinger Buggy Co. with Rubber Running Gear & Bead body also one settle Buggy, Harness & Lap Robe — Same as bought of J. W. Jones this day & date.

tion, for   cash after giving notice by advertisement of 25 days and shall apply the proceeds of said sale to the discharge of said debt, interest and expense, and pay surplus to the said mortgagor or his assigns.

IN WITNESS WHEREOF, I, the said mortgagor, do hereunto set my hand and seal, the 21st day of Dec. 1907

SIGNED, SEALED AND DELIVERED
IN THE PRESENCE OF

W. E. Elliott
M. M. Poston

M. K. Poston   (L. S.)
                (L. S.)

Dad bought 2 mules and put up 2 cows
and all future calves as collateral.

CHATTEL MORTGAGE — Pee Dee Printing Co., Florence, S. C.

$350.00 Hemingway, S. C. Jan - 9, 1930

I promise to pay to HYMAN MOTOR COMPANY, Inc., or order, the sum of Three Hundred Fifty and no/100 DOLLARS, value received, payable at their office at Hemingway, S. C., as follows:

$175.00 on the 1st day of Sept., 1930
$175.00 on the 1st day of October, 1930

I agree that on default of payment of said installments at the time stated, then the full balance of this obligation remaining unpaid shall thereupon mature and become due and collectable without further notice or demand. This obligation to bear interest from date until paid at the rate of eight per cent. per annum. Now, to secure the payment of this obligation, I do hereby convey by way of mortgage to the said HYMAN MOTOR CO., Inc., their executors, administrators and assigns the following personal property, to-wit:

One Black Mare Mule about 6-years old
One Black Mare Mule about 6 years old.
One Cream Colored Milch Cow about 8-years old
& all Increase, with Short horns.
One Cream Colored Milch Cow about 2-years old.
with white spot in Face & all Increase.
The above Mules are very Closely Mated
and are Fresh shipped

TO HAVE and to hold, all and singular, the said goods and chattels unto the said HYMAN MOTOR CO., Inc., and their executors, administrators and assigns, now in my possession and which I represent to be mine and free from encumbrance; and should the mortgagor default in the payment of the sums of money at the time stated, or attempt to move the above named property or any part thereof from where it now is then the said HYMAN MOTOR CO., Inc., or their assigns may enter and seize and sell the same, after three days notice, to satisfy this debt and expense of seizure and sale.

I further agree to pay all cost, including the probating and recording of this instrument, and ten per cent. attorney's fees; also one dollar for each visit to my premises for collection of installments past due, and that this mortgage shall stand as security also for any _____ indebtedness to the said HYMAN MOTOR CO., Inc., in excess of the amount of this obligation and mortgage or otherwise.

Also, that if in the judgment of HYMAN MOTOR CO., Inc., the within described property should at any time become so depreciated in value as to impair the security of the amount for which it is given to secure, then the said HYMAN MOTOR CO., Inc., shall have the right to immediately seize and sell the same as per terms herein stated.

SIGNED, SEALED AND DELIVERED IN THE PRESENCE OF

_____ (L. S.)

M. J. K. Poston (L. S.)

Chapter 36

THINGS THAT I REMEMBER ABOUT MOM

Unselfishness
Mom was totally unselfish. She gave her love, her devotion, and her energy to her family. She never thought about herself; she was always thinking about someone else.

Unwavering Love
Mom truly loved each one of us with a capacity that could not have been earthly inspired; that love had to be inspired by connections from above.

"Christlikeness"
The life that she lived was an example of Christ being alive in her. Christ was visible in her daily life—not necessarily by what she said, but rather in what she did and what her life stood for.

Quiet Prayer Life
Mom never seemed to be too tired or too weary to kneel at her bed to pray. This took place each night after we were all tucked away for the night. Her prayers were silent and quite long, as she had a lot of us to pray for.

Bed Checks
There was never a night when we were small that she didn't come to our bed to check us before she went to bed. If we weren't asleep, she asked each one if something was bothering him or her. If we were asleep, she made sure we were covered up. Then she checked us several more times during the night.

Being There
Of all the things that I remember about Mom, the one that stands out most in my memory is her being there. There were usually three or four of us children going to school all the time. When one graduated, another one started.

After a tough day at school, it was always a warm, loving, and secure feeling to have Mom meet and greet us when we got home. Whatever she was doing was put aside until she had seen and talked to each of us. We had to tell her what had happened at school, and she told us what had happened at home. When she wasn't there when we got home (which was very seldom), it just didn't seem right. There was no sunshine; it was just a house and not a home. Because of this experience, I didn't ever want Leta to work. I wanted her at home when our children, Wayne, Anne, and Stan, got home from school.

Storytelling to the Small Children

Mom was an excellent storyteller. Usually after she had finished all of her chores, she gathered the small children in front of the fire and told stories until bedtime. She could make the characters and events seem so real. Of course, we went through "The Three Little Pigs," "Little Red Riding Hood," "Jack and Jill," "Goldie Locks," "The Troll," "Jack and the Bean Stalk," and many others.

One story that stands out in my mind was so vivid that we actually acted out the characters. It was supposed to be true but had been passed down through several generations. It was about a young woman who taught school several miles from her home.

Her name was Jennifer. She was unmarried and boarded with a family near the school during the weekdays. On weekends she went to her home. The school was at Blossom and Jennifer's home was on the Davis Plantation near Savage. This was a distance of about nine miles. The only way they had to travel was with horse and buggy.

On the day the story unfolds, the weather was cold and it was beginning to snow. Jennifer's father told the family that he would go for Jennifer on this Friday afternoon as the weather looked too bad for either of Jennifer's brothers to go. So they hitched up a young black gelding horse to the buggy as this was the fastest horse on the plantation.

The father left about noon with his shotgun, extra food, and extra lap robes. The weather by this time was getting rough. He had to travel on the River Road or Stage Coach Road, which ran parallel to the Pee Dee River. The trip to Blossom was uneventful—just slow with the horse doing a lot of slipping and sliding on the icy road. He picked up Jennifer about three o'clock. They wrapped up good with the lap robes and started for home. Jennifer was so glad to see her dad and to be going home. She was just gibbering with excitement.

The weather was getting increasingly worse; visibility was zero as snow was coming down so fast. Snow was already six inches deep and traveling was treacherous. Clouds were so heavy—night was coming early. Jennifer and her father were traveling cautiously. The road was narrow and tree limbs spanned the entire width of the road.

At an unsuspected instant, a large wild animal lunged out of a tree and landed on the horse's back. The terrified horse took off running as fast as he could. Jennifer and her father looked out and saw instantly that it was a big, black panther that had come out of the Pee Dee Swamp. The horse was going real fast and the buggy was bouncing all over the rough road. Jennifer's father took two shots at the panther but missed with both shots.

The panther was looking for his supper, so he was bearing down on the buggy. The buggy turned over as they were going around a curve and hit a tree. The horse broke loose and kept going. Jennifer was knocked unconscious and her father was hurt, but he didn't have time to think about his aches and pains. The vicious panther was bearing down on them.

Her father looked up and saw a little two-room house that had been abandoned. He picked Jennifer up and carried her as fast as he could to the house -- kicking the door open when he got there. The panther was just steps behind—not making a sound. Jennifer's father bolted the door and checked the wooden windows to be sure they were securely fastened. The panther did not catch them because he had lingered by the over-turned buggy a short while before sighting his prey running toward the house.

Snow was continuing to fall and daylight was fading fast. The panther apparently hadn't eaten for several days as he seemed terribly hungry and quite determined to have Jennifer and her father for supper. Jennifer's father watched him through the cracks as he went around the house and under it trying to get to his prey. The panther could smell them, and he kept looking for a way to get into the house.

After several unsuccessful attempts, he climbed up on the roof and started looking down the chimney. Jennifer's father knew that if he didn't get a fire going in the fireplace soon, the panther would come down the chimney. He scraped up every piece of wood that he could find and started a fire. He tore boards off the partition between the two rooms and burned them to keep the fire going. He knew that if he kept a big fire going, the panther would not come down the chimney.

Jennifer regained consciousness after about an hour, but she had a very bad bump on her head and was in and out of consciousness for the rest of the night. Her father kept the fire going all night and kept Jennifer near it to keep her warm. The lap robes, food, and shotgun were lost when the buggy turned over and hit the tree.

The noise of the panther's footsteps on the roof and his threatening growl were horrifying. Occasionally he let out with a screeching noise that sounded like a woman screaming in distress. Sometime after daylight the panther jumped off the roof and meandered off toward the dense swamp of the Pee Dee.

Jennifer's father was still afraid to leave the safety of the house. He was afraid that the vicious animal was out there hiding—just waiting for them to come out so he could have them for breakfast. Jennifer was really not well enough to travel on foot, plus she had no boots, and the snow was over a foot deep.

The horse did not stop until he got home and that was sometime after dark. He whinnied and let the family know that he was home. They went out to see what was going on, and to their sorrow and alarm, they found that he had broken out of the harness. No buggy was in sight, and the horse was bleeding with two deep gashes across his back. He was totally exhausted. The family feared the worst may have happened to Jennifer and her father.

Snow was still falling, so they rubbed the horse down, put him in his stall and fed him. Then they summoned some of the neighbors and explained the situation to them. It was agreed that there was nothing they could do until daylight. The knowledge that it might be too late to save Jennifer and her father grieved the family.

The next morning the snow had stopped, but it was cold and cloudy. Jennifer's two brothers arose early and summoned several neighbors to help them. They hitched up two teams of mules and wagons, loaded extra lap robes, food, and supplies and started out to try to find Jennifer and her father. They gathered several of the best hunting dogs around the area and carried them along.

Traveling was slow and there was a lot of slipping and sliding through the snow. After traveling several hours, they spotted the overturned buggy, which by this time was almost totally covered with snow. They surveyed the area and found no bodies; then they spied the little house with smoke rising out of the chimney. They ran to the house and called out to Jennifer and her father. The door to the house burst open and there was a joyous reunion.

After Jennifer's father explained what had happened, it was decided that one wagon would take Jennifer and her father home. The other wagon of people would take the dogs and track the panther down and shoot him. They fed Jennifer and her father the food they had brought along; then they wrapped them up in the lap robes and carried them home.

The men on the other wagon took the dogs and tried to track the panther down. The dogs worked hard trailing him through the thick swamps. The panther was too smart; he just "out-panthered" them and got away. After several hours and no panther in sight, they gave up. They came back by the buggy, turned it on its wheels, tied it behind the wagon, and pulled it home. There was much rejoicing when they got home and everyone was safe.

Extra care and caution was always taken after this experience when Jennifer was carried back and forth to her school teaching job. A panther was spotted several times after this, and it was believed to be the same one; but he was always wise enough to go back into the swamps and not get killed.

Reading to the Small Children

Mom was a good reader and would often gather the small children and read to them after her chores were completed. She read Bible stories and stories she found in magazines. She also read news items from the daily paper that she thought we would be interested in and could understand.

One story that I remember most was an article in the Progressive Farmer in 1932 on the Twentieth Anniversary of the Sinking of the Titanic.

As I remember, the size of the ship was enormous. It was the largest passenger ship ever built at that time or since. It was almost 900 feet long or the length of our tobacco rows. The gash in the hull made by the iceberg was over 300 feet long or the length of our garden. Mom gave us these comparative measurements so we small ones could better understand the size of the ship.

We just relived the whole episode of what happened— especially the part about the men letting the women and children have first priority over the lifeboats. Since the Titanic was supposed to be unsinkable, there were only enough lifeboats for half of the passengers.

    We listened as Mom told us how the brave men helped the women and children board the lifeboats. Then they kneeled on the deck of the Titanic, prayed and went down with the ship. The ship's band assembled on the deck and played music until the ship sank. The music continued until the last man went under. I can remember how proud I was of these men, who gave their lives to save the women and children. I just thought that when I got to heaven I would tell them what a great and unselfish thing they did.

Songs that Mom Sang
The Old Rugged Cross
On a hill far away stood an old rugged cross,
The emblem of suffering and shame;
And I love that old cross where the dearest and best
for a world of lost sinners was slain.
So I'll cherish the old rugged cross
Till my trophies at last I lay down;
I will cling to the old rugged cross,
And exchange it someday for a crown.

Amazing Grace
Amazing grace! how sweet the sound
That saved a wretch like me!
I once was lost, but now am found,
Was blind, but now I see.
'Twas grace that taught my heart to fear,
And grace my fears relieved;
How precious did that grace appear,
The hour I first believed.

Let the Lower Lights Be Burning
Brightly beams our Father's mercy
from the lighthouse evermore;
But to us he gives the keeping
of the lights along the shore.
Let the lower lights be burning!
Send the gleam across the wave.
Some poor fainting, struggling seaman

You may rescue, you may save.

My Bonnie Lies Over the Ocean
My Bonnie lies over the ocean,
My Bonnie lies over the sea.
My Bonnie lies over the ocean,
Oh bring back my Bonnie to me.
Bring back, bring back
Oh bring back my Bonnie to me—to me
Bring back, bring back
Oh bring back my Bonnie to me.

The song that Mom loved most and sang more than any other was an Indian love song. She dearly loved the chorus of this song:

Red Wing
There once lived an Indian maid,
A shy little prairie maid,
Who sang a-lay, a love song-gay,
As on the plain she'd while away the day.
She loved a warrior bold,
This shy little maid of old,
But brave and—gay,
He rode one day to battle far away.

She watched for him day and night,
She kept all the campfires bright,
And under the sky, each night she would lie,
And dream about his coming by and by;
But when all the braves returned,
The heart of Red Wing yearned.
For far, far away, her warrior gay,
Fell bravely in the fray.
Chorus:
Now, the moon shines tonight on pretty Red Wing.
The breeze is sighing—the night bird's crying,
For afar 'neath his star her brave is sleeping,
While Red Wing's weeping—her heart away.

Reciting Poetry to the Small Children
Mom had a very keen memory. She often recited poems that she had learned in school. Her best loved poem was "Annabel Lee" by Edgar Allan Poe. She could recite all six verses, but I will give only the first two verses below:

> It was many and many a year ago,
> In a kingdom by the sea,
> That a maiden there lived whom you may know
> By the name of Annabel Lee;
> And this maiden she lived with no other thought
> Than to love and be loved by me.
>
> I was a child and she was a child,
> In this kingdom by the sea;
> But we loved with a love that was more than love,
> I and my Annabel Lee;
> With a love that the winged seraphs of heaven
> Coveted her and me.

Mom's Quilting Parties
A family of twelve needs at least eight beds to sleep in. And since heating the house comfortably was always a real problem, a lot of quilts were needed to keep us warm. Consequently, there was a lot of quilt-making done so that each bed had several quilts. Therefore, during the winter months there were a lot of quilting parties by the women.

I remember Mom used greige homespun for the bottom of the quilt. She always saved enough cotton to make several quilts from the cotton that was ginned. Then, she took scraps of different fabrics that had been used in making dresses and shirts for the family. She sewed these scraps together to make the quilt top. She took these little pieces of cloth and made attractive designs out of them. I still think that she was most artistic with some of the designs that she came up with. Of course there were no patterns—she made her own, which made her even more special.

With all the materials ready, Mom took four long wooden quilting rods and shaped them the size of the quilt. She then clamped the rods at each corner. The rods were then hung from the ceiling with wire so that the quilt would be about thirty inches from the floor or a comfortable height to sit in a chair and quilt. The bottom of the quilt was then laced to the quilting rods very tightly, so there was no sag. The cotton batting was then rolled out evenly on the quilt bottom. The fancy quilt top was then placed on the frame and tacked so it would not move. Before the quilting began, Mom took chalk and a string and drew lines where she wanted the rows of stitches to be made.

After all the preliminary work was finished, it was now time to have some fun. When Mom had everything ready, she invited the neighbors to come to her quilting party. She usually had eight women—two for each side and each end, and she cooked a feast for their dinner.

I always looked forward to these quilting parties because of all the good food that was served. These women had a big time as was evident by the chatter heard all over the house. They usually had a devotion, which was followed by prayer and singing. They actually sang off and on all day. Mom had to keep the coffee pot going to keep everyone happy. By the end of the day, there was usually another quilt ready—except for the hemming which she did herself.

It was usually my job to keep the fire going in the fireplace. It is my firm belief that many women came to know Christ at these quilting parties. I believe that these types of gatherings are a missing link in our society today.

Mom always made a quilt for each of her children when they got married. I still have the last quilt that she made as she died a few months after I got married.

Chapter 3

GRANDMA GREENWOOD

Grandma Greenwood was stricken with the deadly flu of 1929, which killed her husband, my grandpa. She lived until 1936, but she never really got over losing Grandpa. Everyone who knew her before he died said that she was never the same after his death.

Grandma and I always had a very special relationship. I stayed with her a lot, particularly before Uncle Mack's son, Norman, was born. She would send somebody to get me, and she would keep me several days at a time. I was just a little boy, being only ten years old when she died in 1936. We were more buddies than anything else; wherever she was, I was right there with her.

I can remember so well how she used to have several acres of peanuts planted on the farm. She would have them pulled up and put in stacks to dry. When they were dry, she would go from stack to stack picking them off the bushes. I was right at her heels, and you know how much I was helping her! Peanuts are good to eat, and, as I remember, she did quite well selling them and bartering with the folks on the farm to work for her.

Grandma lived on the Mollie Davis place, which she rented from Isolene Davis. Isolene was a midget woman, who lived in Asheville, N.C. This house that Grandma lived in had three stories and twelve rooms. It had an upstairs porch that had a big bell on it. It was said that the bell was used to let the slaves know when to stop working. Of course, this was when the Davis family lived in the house, as it was built in 1841.

All of the hardware, such as door locks, were imported from England. The house was built on the Old River Road that ran along the Pee Dee River from Georgetown to Cheraw. The house was in a grove of big oak trees and had a white picket fence around it. Across the road from the house, there were open fields of about four hundred acres. Down to the right and across the road, there was a big fancy barn and stable that housed about twenty mules.

To the left and across the road, there was a commissary. It was not in use, but I understand that, in the heyday of the River Port at Davis Landing with all the traffic on the River Road, this commissary was a very busy place. There was a little one room school house to the left of the house that couldn't have been more than twenty-four feet wide and thirty-six feet long.

The house that Grandma lived in was the first house that I had ever seen with plastered walls. The rooms were big, and every room on the first and second floors had a big fireplace. The Davis family apparently had a lot of money as this house was an edifice typical of the antebellum times in which it was built.

It always made me feel good to know that I was related to someone who lived in such an impressive home, even though they didn't own it at that time. The place was purchased by the Greenwood brothers after Grandma died in 1936. Apparently Grandpa was a pretty good provider, and Grandma must have been a good homemaker. They seemed to have gotten along a little better financially than most people at this time.

Grandma was a small woman probably weighing no more than a hundred pounds. She wore her hair in a little ball pulled to the back of her head. Her hair had just started turning gray when she was in her late sixties or early seventies. She had the normal wrinkles for a woman her age, but, of course, I could see only her inside, and she was real pretty to me.

Grandma always wore a bonnet and an apron. She didn't wear the high-top, button-up shoes that a lot of elderly women wore during this era and she didn't smoke a pipe. She loved music and kept an organ or piano for years and years. Her daughter, Alma, learned to play but never very well; so they got a self-player piano, which they thoroughly enjoyed.

Grandma was a wise lady and had a lot of counsel for all of us. She had some serious concerns about her sons and their drinking problems, and the fact that Furman and "Bubba" never did get along very well. This created a lot of grief for her. She did keep most of them going to church, and she was thankful for this.

Apparently she had some premonition about her on-coming death for about two or three years prior to her death. Every time I went to see her, before I left to return home, she would take me off to another room. She had me sit down in a little, low homemade chair, and she sat right in front of me and talked.

She talked to me about doing the things that would be pleasing to Jesus and to my parents. She told me not to drink or curse, to be kind to others, to mind my parents, etc. These little sessions were not domineering, as they were just simply born out of love. Grandma's love, care, compassion, and counsel had a big impact on the person I am today.

Adelia Virginia Marsh Greenwood
August 2, 1860-June 28, 1936

John Travis Greenwood (1848 - 1929)
Adelia Marsh Greenwood (1860 - 1936)
Grandma and Grandpa were a devoted couple.
Picture taken about 1928.

Grandma Greenwood's house on the Old River or Stagecouch Road. The house was built on a 1400 acre farm in 1841. The house had eleven rooms with a fireplace in each room.

Chapter 38

GRANDPA GREENWOOD

John Travis Greenwood was born in 1848 somewhere in Marlboro County. There is very little known about his family. I do not know if he had brothers or sisters, or where he lived in Marlboro County. He died in 1929, so I can't remember a great deal about him.

He was twelve years older than Grandma, and he was forty-two years old when his first son, Furman, was born. This gives me reason to believe that (either due to his family situation or the Civil War) he did not get married until late in life. As far as I know, he was always a farmer.

During the flu epidemic in 1929, the whole Greenwood family came down with flu. There was nobody, except our mother, to take care of them. Even though Mom had seven children, with the youngest one, David, only a year old at the time, she stayed up there several weeks nursing them.

The only child at home who could do any cooking at all was Lance, who was only thirteen. He could cook some of the worst-looking biscuits that any of us had ever seen. Mom decided one day that she had better check on us, so she came home for a few hours to see how we were getting along without her.

I was three years old at the time. She picked me up and was hugging me, and I was enjoying it so much! She asked me if I wanted her to come home, and I told her, "Go back and make Grandpa and Grandma well and we will eat Lance's "wobbly" biscuits until you get them well."

She made us some real "un-wobbly" biscuits and then went back to nurse our grandparents. She said that she told them what I had said and that it meant a lot to them. Grandpa died, but my wanting them to get well so badly seemed to have created a special bond between Grandma and me. This bond lasted until her death.

Grandpa was our only link to anyone on the Greenwood side of the family who had been in the Civil War. The older children asked him a lot of questions about what went on during the war and how it affected him. The main thing that I remember that the older children told me was that Grandpa said he was only a boy and his father was either in the fighting or was killed during the fighting.

He said that he and his mother had very little to eat. They had one milk cow, and, when the Yankees came marching through on their way from Georgia to North Carolina, they killed their only cow. This just made a bad situation even worse because then they didn't even have milk to drink.

I've never heard of any bad habits that Grandpa had. He and Grandma had a good marriage. He worked hard and was a good provider. He lived to be eighty-one years old and kept the family under his control as long as he lived. Grandma lived seven years after he died. She never forgot him or stopped loving him. Up until her death, she talked about him as if he was still around. He made a big impact on his family, and they never forgot him.

The loving way that the family talked about Grandpa helped me to get to know him better and love him more. He made a difference in my life even though I barely remember him. Just hearing things said about him made me want to grow up to be like him.

I feel that he's been with me throughout my life which has helped me to know that there is life after death. Having this realization, it is quite clear that for me to have eternal life I simply have to "do good, love mercy, and walk humbly with God." (Micah 6:8).

John Travis Greenwood
September 20, 1848-January 14, 1929

Chapter 39

UNCLE "BUBBA"

John Lamar Greenwood, my Uncle "Bubba," was born in 1892. He was two years younger than his older brother Furman. Furman gave him the nickname of "Bubba" because he could not say Lamar. This nickname stayed with him all of his life.

When "Bubba" was growing up, he got into more than the usual amount of trouble. He was rowdy, combative, and developed a drinking problem early in life. The direction of his life took a drastic turn during his mid-twenties, as he was drafted into the service of his country during the First World War. He was drafted in the Infantry and served throughout Europe. He never talked much about his experiences -- unless you caught him when he was drinking.

It has always been my belief that Uncle "Bubba" was a real good and a tough soldier. Over the years I picked up bits and pieces of some tough situations that he had been in. His very nature created some problems between his superiors and himself.

During the lull in one of the battles that he was in, he and one of his officers had a real donniebrook and the officer really chewed him out. In a few minutes the officer was killed by a shot from an unknown origin. A lot of his buddies accused him of doing it. Apparently none of the command thought that he had anything to do with it, so no charges were ever brought against him. His superiors actually gave him a R and R pass for several days away from the front lines.

He always said (when we boys questioned him about it) that he had none of that man's blood on his hands. I really believe that he had nothing to do with this officer's death; he always felt real badly over this incident and the problems that he had with this officer. It was an incident in his life that he never forgot. The trials that he endured during this war left hidden scars that only the grave erased for him.

"Bubba" never got married and had very few serious relationships that I knew about. For some reason either real or imaginary, he developed the belief that he could not trust a woman. For as long as I could remember him, he was a confirmed bachelor.

He never really liked the idea of working. He just didn't want to have anything to do with what was called work. He always found some way of getting by without doing any. He stayed with Grandma, Uncle Furman, and Aunt Alma until after Grandma's death in 1936. He contributed very little to his upkeep... Uncle Furman was the bread winner.

In the late twenties or early thirties, he got hold of some poison whiskey and he almost died. For a while we didn't know whether he was going to make it or not. He finally pulled out of it, but he did lose some use of his arms and legs. He used crutches for a while, and then for years he used a cane. During this episode, he requested and received disability benefits from the Veteran's Administration, which continued for the next approximately sixty years. This helped in his quest to get by without having to work.

Uncle "Bubba" bought a 1931 Chevrolet Coupe with a rumble seat. A year or two later he was off on a drinking spree with Leroy Poston, and they had a wreck; he was almost killed. Leroy was driving, so naturally we children blamed him and called him, "That mean Leroy."

Mama also blamed Leroy and had a go at him the next time he passed the house. When the truth really came out, it was determined that "Bubba" jerked the wheel away from Leroy and caused the car to go out of control. When the car went out of control, it partially threw "Bubba" out and drug him along a barbed wire fence for a long distance.

"Bubba" was cut all to pieces. One ear was practically cut off, deep gashes were on his face, and multiple cuts were on his body. It was thought that he wouldn't make it, but he was tough and pulled through. His problems caused Grandma a lot of grief. He promised her that if he lived he was going to "straighten-up and do-right." After a slow recovery, he did taper down some on his lifestyle, but "straightening-up" was not to be for sometime to come.

After Grandma died, only "Bubba," Furman, and Alma were left at home. "Bubba" and Furman had never gotten along well even though they lived in the same house. They never spoke to one another and just didn't communicate. Now that Grandma wasn't there to keep them straight, things got really bad.

One Saturday night "Bubba" had been to Florence. When he came back, he decided that Aunt Alma and Aunt Minnie, Uncle

Mack's wife, were going with him on a trip to Florida. Uncle Furman came in about that time and said that Alma was not going anywhere. This "threw fat on the fire," and they had a "free-for-all" that was hard to break up. Uncle Furman finally got his gun and that put "Bubba" on the move.

"Bubba" came to our house sometime that night and spent the rest of the night and the next several nights with us. Furman sat on the front porch with his gun waiting for "Bubba" to come back as he had promised to kill him. Dad had to go to their house and do a lot of talking to get Furman to put the gun down. He did put the gun away; Furman had a great deal of respect for Dad. Probably no one else could have gotten him to put it away.

Later "Bubba" had a little mobile house built, which was probably eight by twelve feet, that he placed across the road perhaps nine hundred feet from the big house. He lived there for the next ten to twelve years. He and Furman might see each other, but they wouldn't speak to one another.

As I have said before, it was more "Bubba's" problem than Furman's. This status continued until Furman became ill in the late forties with diabetes and his sickness became progressively worse until his death in 1950. Before his death, the two of them finally got to the point where they could tolerate each other. "Bubba" moved back in the house and actually started helping Furman look after his farming interest.

"Bubba" was never a flashy dresser; he went clean but was never a real stylish dresser. He always walked jake-legged after his bout with poison whiskey—his feet flapped every time he made a step. He did like to drive a late model stylish-car.

I remember when he bought a new 1934 black Ford, which was trimmed in yellow with yellow spokes in the wheels. The doors opened to the front, and I thought that was the prettiest car that I had ever seen. It was one sharp-looking vehicle!

"Bubba" was always real close to us Poston children. Often he came by to see us during the week. We were all attached to him; he could do no wrong in our sight. When Mack and Jessie got married and each of them had two boys who lived right near him, this more or less just cut us off from him.

This hurt us all very deeply, and the closeness of the bond that had developed more or less just faded. It was kind of like we children were used to satisfy a personal need that he had, which could now be satisfied by other children, who were more convenient. This attitude had a great deal to do in his influencing Alma to cut the Poston children out of inheriting their rightful share of Furman's estate.

Late in life "Bubba" did change his lifestyle. As far as I know, he did stop drinking and smoking. He still liked to chew tobacco. He started going to church pretty often and really tried to learn more about the Christian faith. He sought a closer walk with Jesus.

His favorite biblical passage was the Twenty-Third Psalm. He struggled with his faith. I had a number of long conversations and several prayer sessions with him. He always seemed to have a little problem with surrendering everything to God and letting God have his way in his life.

"Bubba" taught me that I could admire him without admiring his lifestyle. He showed me that I could love him without loving what he was. All ten of us children cared a great deal for him, but none of us wanted to emulate him.

John Lamar "Bubba" Greenwood
June 4, 1892-June 13, 1985

John Lamar Greenwood   1892 - 1985
Uncle "Bubba"
A tough rifle infantryman who fought
in France and Germany in WWI

Chapter 40

UNCLE FURMAN "PUM"

Uncle "Pum" got his nickname from his brother, who was two years younger and couldn't say Furman. He was the oldest of a family of six children. He was born in 1890 and lived a fairly normal life for a boy growing up in the Savage Landing area of the Pee Dee River.

His life took a turn in another direction during World War I. He was drafted to serve his country at a time when he was about twenty-six years old and single. Some married men were drafted at this time; but it was mostly the single men in their twenties who were greeted by their President to serve their country and defend the Constitution of this great land of ours.

Uncle "Pum" served in the Field Artillery throughout Europe. He had taken part in some rough and tough battles during his service that left invisible but everlasting emotional scars. We never learned much of what he went through. We would get him to talking and try to pen him down on something, but he would just change the subject. I remember him as having always been an old man.

As we children became older, we quit calling him Uncle "Pum" and called him Uncle Furman—probably more out of respect than anything else. Uncle Furman never got married, and I've never heard of too many serious relationships that he had. I heard that, when he was young, he drank a good bit and could be right rowdy at times.

I must hasten to say that he never displayed any of this to us. He was a good-looking man, who dressed the part. He had a very smooth mannerism in his communications and presented the image of my conception of what a Kentucky Colonel was.

Uncle Furman and I always had a close relationship. When I was growing up, he would get me to come up to his house to go hunting with him. A lot of times we would just sit on the big front porch and talk. He would just take all the time as if nothing else in the world mattered, and he made me feel important. I won't ever forget those conversations; they made me think more of him, but they also encouraged me to think more of myself.

He was always loyal to his church, which he attended every Sunday, but he wasn't really "turned on" for the Lord. However, he did become more committed later in his life. It has always been my belief that, if he had found a good woman and gotten married, he would have made a very positive impact in the political, social, and spiritual life of the community.

The one big problem that Uncle Furman had was that of getting along with his brother "Bubba," who was two years younger. They were a lot alike—both veterans, both bachelors, and both drank pretty much. They just didn't get along, and at times it became serious. I covered this in my story about "Bubba," as he really was the bigger part of the problem.

I think this problem of the two not getting along caused Uncle Furman more shame and grief than it did to "Bubba." Neither one of them really made a great deal of effort to mend fences or to set things right between them.

Uncle Furman was a successful farmer. During the years 1937 and 1938, he, Uncle Mack, and Uncle Jessie were given the opportunity to buy the Mollie Davis place from Isolene Davis, a descendant of the original Davis family. They were talking about the amount needed for down payment, which would have to be divided between the three of them.

Uncle Jessie and Uncle Mack, both married and doing well financially, felt that Uncle Furman may have a little trouble coming up with his third. Furman had always driven a good late model car, kept up with the latest thing in radios for the home, and had splurged money on his drinking; so, he did cause them a little anxiety. However, when it was time to put up shares, Furman had money actually buried in several places; so he was better set for the down payment than they were.

In the mid-forties Uncle Furman became ill with diabetes. This curtailed his activities and shortened his life. In the years before his death in 1950, he became a devout Christian, a Master Mason, and actually fell in love with a young lady from Hemingway. The affair never developed as his health became progressively worse at a fast pace.

Uncle Furman and my Dad were always pretty close, and in his later years he tried to model his life after that of my Dad. When he became sick, he deeded his third of the place to his sister, our

Aunt Alma, so that he could draw a veteran's disability benefit check each month. This was a paper transfer needed because he could not have any assets in his name and draw this check.

My Dad and I were told by Uncle Furman that our family would inherit a third of his estate. This actually did not happen, as in later years when Alma was somewhat senile due to age and health, she was persuaded to exclude the heirs of our mother. The estate was divided between the heirs of the two brothers, Mack and Jessie.

This deeply hurt all of the heirs of my Mother, but there was nothing legally that any of us could do to reverse this dishonorable, disgraceful and greedy decision. It was like saying to each of us, "You've been down in the cellar all of your life, so now stay there."

We each have the consolation of knowing this wasn't the way Uncle Furman wanted it, so it only increased our love and respect for him. Each of us has become reconciled to the knowledge that we and our heirs don't have to worry about fighting over the estate, and that's a consolation the other heirs don't have.

Furman's contribution to my life was to increase the value of my self-worth. He helped me to think more of my abilities and potential and less of my financial status. His counsel helped me to strive to reach for goals that seemed unattainable. Right after Leta and I got married, he helped us with the down payment on our first home.

"Thanks, Uncle Furman for loving me and wanting my lot in life to be better."

Joseph Furman Greenwood
September 7, 1890-February 26, 1950

Joseph Furman Greenwood 1890 - 1950
Uncle Furman
A good strong soldier who fought with the artillery in
France and Germany in World War I

Chapter 41

AUNT ALMA

Mattie Alma Greenwood was born June 6, 1900. She was the fourth child of John Travis and Adelia Ann Marsh Greenwood. Alma grew up to be a very pretty woman; she was quiet and somewhat shy. She had a seventh or eighth grade education, which was more than most people obtained in those days.

She had to walk several miles to school, and usually Jessie and Mack went with her. The school that she went to was a two-story building located on a sight by the current St. Mark Church. Alma was six years younger than my Mother, Yulee, and was only thirteen years old when Mom got married.

I know very little about Alma's growing-up years, as she never talked much about her past. If she had any serious love affairs, I don't know about them. She was twenty-six years old when I was born, and I remember her from the time I was about three years old. I don't know of any serious relationships that she had after that time.

Alma broke away from the tradition of her family when she joined the Baptist Church at Kingsburg; all of her family were members of Trinity Methodist Church. This denomination change upset several members of the family.

She tried to learn to drive, in an effort to become more self-sufficient, but she didn't get any cooperation from her brothers. They offered her very little help in instruction, nor would they let her use their cars for practice. This presented a real problem for her in trying to go to the Baptist Church. Consequently, Alma never was a regular attendant at the Kingsburg Baptist Church. Late in life she again joined the Trinity Methodist Church and this eased the pain that had existed for a long time.

Alma apparently thought she had to stay at home and take care of her parents. Her mother was forty years old when Alma was born and her father was fifty-two; so, they were getting up in age as she grew up. After Grandpa and Grandma died, she stayed on and kept house for the two brothers, Furman and "Bubba."

Alma never had any source of income; she had to rely on what Furman and "Bubba" gave her. Before Furman died, he deeded his interest in the farm over to her, so he could get a veteran's disability retirement check. This transaction was only a paper transfer. After Furman's death, she did get Furman's third of the farm.

"Bubba" managed the farm and eventually controlled what happened to it. Alma was a good Christian woman who would not knowingly do anything wrong. She was surrounded by a few strong-willed people to whom she probably felt indebted, and they controlled her entirely. The eventual "cutting out" of the Poston family from their rightful share of Furman's estate was not her will, but I believe that it was the will of those around her.

Alma had a lot of health problems throughout her life. Even though she lived to be eighty-seven years old, she was sickly a lot. Nellie, my sister, at different times went to Alma's and stayed for weeks at the time taking care of her. Alma was always close to the Poston children and we thought she was interested in our well-being. She always wrote to the Poston boys who were in service during World War Two and kept us up-to-date on what was going on.

She was not outgoing and was somewhat self-centered. She was not talented, so she did very few craft projects—probably due to some of her personality traits. She did not make a big impact on my life. This was probably due to my not realizing that she had needs also. Alma was the last of that generation of Greenwoods to pass away, and this has left a void in my life.

Mattie Alma Greenwood
June 6, 1900-March 8, 1987

Chapter 42

GRANDMA POSTON

Emily Ann Creel Poston was born in 1852 somewhere in the Marion District of what is now Florence County. The only things we know about Grandma's life while she was growing up were learned by asking her specific questions. She was a very private person; she just didn't talk much about herself.

Her husband, Edward Pinkney Poston, was five years older. They had their first child, Uncle Zack, in 1869 when she was only seventeen years old. She must have gotten married at the age of fifteen or sixteen. They had nine children over a period from 1869 to 1897 and two of these children died in infancy.

Grandpa died in 1911 leaving her with several teenage children. Grandpa had lost everything he owned prior to his death, so Grandma was left with a real-life struggle. I am sure that the tough struggles she had in life caused her to turn her feelings inward; she was not an outgoing person. Even though my Dad had a big family of his own, he still tried to help her whenever he could.

Uncle Zack remained single for a long, long time, so he and his sister, Aunt "Culia" who never got married, stayed with Grandma. Uncle Zack later married Bertha Harris, who lived only a short while after their marriage. However, they continued to live with Grandma until Aunt Bertha's death.

In those days there was no Welfare or Social Security, so elderly folks had to depend on their children for support. So, Uncle Zack was Grandma's only real support. Bless his heart! He tried, but he didn't own anything. Farming was the only thing he knew and he had to rent or sharecrop. Survival was a real struggle for them.

I remember Grandma only as an elderly lady. She was seventy-four years old when I was born and eighty-four when she died. I remember her as a small lady who wore long dresses, an apron, a bonnet, and high-top, button-up or string-up boots—I think they called them shoes. She wore glasses all the time that I knew her. She smoked a corncob pipe, which was a common thing for older women to do at that time.

Grandma was a very independent lady and kept herself busy

doing things for herself and for others. When she came to visit us, she was so quiet we might not know she was on the place, but wherever she was, she was always busy doing something. While I knew her, she kept in good health, and you only heard the normal grunts and aches that came from elderly people.

Grandma was our last link to anyone in the family who lived through the Civil War. We kept asking her about how life really was during the Civil War. We didn't get much information from her. She would say that she was young and couldn't relate much of the politics of the war. She remembered food and everything else being very scarce. She remembered going hungry at times. The Yankees didn't march through the area where she lived, so she was spared that ugly sight.

Grandma always expressed some bitterness concerning the reconstruction after the war. She made it very clear that none of her family ever owned slaves. She felt that poor white people suffered more than the colored during the years right after the Civil War. Federal programs helped the colored people but continued to strip away what the white people had.

She mentioned the fact that there were bands of colored people who attacked white people and took whatever they wanted from them. She said that, if the white people took their complaints to the Yankees, they would be told that the Southern white's lost the war and if the colored people robbed them, it was just their tough luck.

Grandma felt that the white's were forced to do something to protect their lives and property as the Yankees were upholding the colored people in their misdeeds. She thought this situation created the birth of the Ku Klux Klan. Some southern white people felt that if they didn't do something, they would be annihilated. History over the 100 years that followed tells us where that fear led to.

Black people today should realize that a very small percentage of white people owned slaves. Let me hasten to say that if only one had owned slaves, that would have been one too many. However, the whole white race should not be held accountable for what a few greedy white people did over a hundred years ago.

Blacks have to understand and accept some responsibility for the animosities that grew out of their misdeeds during the reconstruction era. Blacks also have to recognize that some of their forefathers back in Africa were the ones that captured and sold the slaves to the white traders. There is guilt on both sides and the answer to the problem is to accept each other as brothers and sisters in Christ, to seek forgiveness for past sins, and to let the Holy Spirit lead us to new heights in race relations.

Emily Ann Creel Poston
August 26, 1852-March 30, 1936

Please note a copy of a Ku Klux Klan application which was found in my Dad's effects after his death. It was never filled out.

Application for the Ku Klux Klan found among Dad's possessions. It was well-worn but never filled out.

Chapter 43

UNCLE ZACK

Zack Poston was born in 1869 in the Marion District, which later became Florence County. He was the first child born to Edward and Emily Ann Creel Poston. I can remember Uncle Zack only as an old man, as he was fifty-seven years old when I was born.

He was nineteen years older than my Dad. He was a little taller and heavier than Dad, but they looked a lot alike except he always wore heavy, dark-rimmed glasses.

Uncle Zack was a good-looking man, who was always neat, and he dressed well, considering his situation. I used to like to watch him walk. He had a nice, easy stride that made him look very distinguished.

We weren't very close, so I don't know a lot about any bad or good habits that he had. He did smoke and chew tobacco, but I don't know of any real bad drinking habits that he had. The main thing that I do remember about him was that he really loved Coca Colas, and he would drink several everyday.

Uncle Zack was a bachelor until late in life. He was 61 years old when he married Bertha Harris in 1931. When they got married, they just moved into the house with Grandma and Aunt "Culia." Aunt Bertha did not live very long after they got married. She died in 1933. As far as I know, they had a good marriage. Uncle Zack always seemed happy when he was around her. I'm sure their life would have been better, if they could have lived away from his family.

Uncle Zack, Aunt Bertha, Grandma, and Aunt "Culia" visited us several times a year....usually on Sunday.... and they ate Sunday dinner with us. They always came in Uncle Zack's Model T, which was a two-seater with a convertible top. It had curtains, and it had robes to be used in rainy and cold weather.

The only difference between Uncle Zack's Model T and Dad's was that Dad's had two little square rear windows and Uncle Zack's had one long wide rear window. I think his car was a 1926 model, which was two years newer than Dad's, and the window change was an improvement in the later models.

I don't remember that Uncle Zack did a lot of hunting and fishing. He usually spent all of his leisure time just "hanging-out" at the Daniels Brothers' Store at Salem. To my knowledge, he was never active or took any interest in the political life of the community.

Uncle Zack died in 1936 of Bright's disease, which is a disease of the kidneys. Most of the time Bright's disease can be helped medically, but he had the incurable kind, which caused a slow, painful, and agonizing death. Dad was made executor of his estate, thus having an accounting of all his indebtedness and an appraisal of the value of his estate. I am including these records, as it was a typical estate of a family during that era, who owned no land and usually sharecropped. Please note that he owed $18.15 to Daniel's Brothers' Store at Salem. The price of some of the items were:

gas	20 cents a gallon
cigarettes	18 cents a pack
cokes (called dope)	6 cents a bottle
salmon	15 cents a can
aspirin	5 cents a pack
Black Draught	20 cents a pack
oil	20 cents a quart
Groves Chill tonic	20 cents a bottle.

Please note that the value of the estate was $312.05, and bear in mind that this was an accumulation of two generations, as it was Uncle Zack's parents' estate plus his. Note that mules were the most valuable possessions that he had; the mules were appraised at $160, which is over half of the total appraised value of the estate. Note the Model T was valued at only $25. I think it would be difficult for a reader who didn't live during this era to visualize the desperation and how tough it was just to persevere from one day to the next.

Life Estate of Uncle Zack Poston
Page 1

Estate of J. T. Poston June 29-36
List And Value of Personal Propty

2 universal Sweep Stocks 1 @ 2.00 1 " 2.40	4.00
1 Boy Ditrie	1.00
1 S.B. White Dixie	2.50
1 Side Harrow	.50
1 lot Sweeps	1.00
2 pitch forks	1.00
3 Hoes	1.00
1 Rake	.35
2 Shovels	.75
1 Wash Pot	.25
1 Axe	.50
2 Plow Gears	5.00
1 Two Horse Wagon	12.50
2 Bridles	1.00
1 Fert Distributor	.50
1 Forge	2.00
1 Basket	.25
1/4 Bu Measure	.40

Life Estate of Uncle Zack Poston
Page 2

Item	Value
1 Model T Ford	25.00
1 Bay Mare Mule	60.00
1 Horse "	100.00
1 Monkey Wrench	50
2 End "	25
2 Socket "	50
1 Brace 3 Bits	50
1 pr Plyers 1 Screw Driver	10
1 Cold Chisel 1 Wood Chisel	10
1 Stilson Wrench	50
1 Hand Saw	50
1 Cross Cut Saw	1.50
1 Iron Square	50
1 pr Beams	25
1 Bop Juice Iron	.25
1 Basket	.25
1 Cook Range (Sold)	3.00

Life Estate of Uncle Zack Poston
Page 3

14 Quilts	L	$10.00
1 Table	L	2.00
1 Organ	L	10.00
1 Small Mirror & Brush	L	25-
2 Pictures & Frames	L	1.00
1 Chain Horse	L	5.00
1 Double Gun	L	7.50
1 Car Robe	L	1.00
1 Set 20 ft Lot Flues	L	5.00
4 Pillows	L	75-
		$312.05

Appraisal Made June 29-1936
By   E. F. Evans
     H Delion Poston
     J J Daniels

Copy of debts owed by Uncle Zack
at the time of his death in 1936

Chapter 44

AUNT "CULIA"

Tula Calene "Culia" Poston was born in 1879 in the Marion District near Salem, which later became Florence County. She was the second daughter born to Edward and Emily Ann Creel Poston. No book written about any heir of Edward and Emily would be complete without the inclusion of Aunt "Culia."

Aunt "Culia" never got married; she lived her entire life for other people. She was always a giver. Her education was very limited, but she could read and write without any problems. She was one of the most honest, hard-working, unselfish women that I have ever known. If she ever said a bad word or did anything out of character, none of us knew about it. She set the perfect example for each of us and, believe me, her example was a tough act to follow.

As long as Aunt "Culia's" mother, my grandma, and Uncle Zack, her brother, lived, she felt that she had to take care of them. Yet, every time a child was born at our house, she was always there. She always stayed several weeks with us until Mom was strong enough to do everything that needed to be done on her own.

So, all ten of us children were initiated into the world with the help of Aunt "Culia." She never asked for, nor did she receive anything in compensation for all this hard work. She felt like a second mama to each of us. She was always interested in how we were doing, particularly after World War II began and we children were scattered all around the world.

Aunt "Culia" was not a flashy person, but she was always clean and neat. She always wore an apron and a bonnet. She wore long dresses and high-top, laced-up shoes, until later in the forties when the high-top shoes became unavailable. Then she started wearing low-cut shoes.

She dipped Railroad Mills snuff constantly—this being her only vice, if this was a vice. Her height was probably five feet six inches and she was always real thin, probably never weighing more than one hundred pounds. Even though she was small in stature, nobody could outwork her. She always had a good outlook on life and a real good sense of humor.

As far as I know, she never had a serious boy-girl relationship or ever considered marriage. It just seemed to me that she was a confirmed and happy old maid. When Grandma and Uncle Zack died in 1936, we all hoped that she would come to live with us; but, she said that she felt better satisfied staying with her youngest sister, our Aunt Rozela. When she passed away in 1951, we all grieved the loss of this cherished loved-one who had played such a vital roll in our growing up years.

The fruit of her labor of love will have its influence for generations to come. She gave to each of the ten of us children something that no one could take away: The desire to love someone else more than we love ourselves and to look at the goodness in others rather than the badness. I think no one could give greater gifts than these.

Tula Calene "Culia" Poston
September 28, 1879--October 1, 1951

Chapter 45

"THE WELL DIGGER"

There can't be anything more frustrating to a farmer than to have a lot of animals and not have sufficient water for them to drink. Farmers who lived on the eastern side of Lynches River in what was called "The Backwoods" had a difficult time keeping a constant supply of water.

The normal depth of wells was twenty to thirty feet. The earth at these depths was a sand clay, which caved very easily as the underground water drained to Lynches River in the spring of the year. The well on the farm that we lived on in "The Backwoods" had a history of being the worst well in the area for caving-in and going dry.

The very first spring that we lived on this farm in "The Backwoods," the well caved-in and we were out of water. Christmas, my friend, and I put a hand pitcher pump down about twenty feet deep that gave some water, but this was not enough for all of our needs. So we had to haul water in a sixty gallon barrel each day either from the Roger's well or from the Eaddy's. This hauling water was not only time consuming but cumbersome.

Dad was always coming up with ideas to make our existence easier. One day he came up with the idea that we could find a hollow cypress log big enough to use as a casing to slide down in the well to keep it from caving-in.

The search was on to find a hollow cypress tree at least four feet in diameter. We needed about thirty-six feet in length, as this casing for the well curbing had to extend four feet above ground level.

Dad found the right tree in Lynches River swamp behind Doug Collin's house. This was a distance of about four miles from our house. Dad decided that we could go over there and saw it into sections, and, if we did it on Saturday while David and I were out of school, we could do some fishing at the same time.

On the designated Saturday morning Dad, David, Christmas, and I got up early, ate breakfast, and took off walking with fishing canes, cross-cut saw and ax. The reason we were walking was because there wasn't enough gas in the car to make this trip and then get us to church and back home on Sunday. Gas was rationed at this time, and we received only a three gallons per week allotment to start with after the Japanese bombed Pearl Harbor and World War II began.

When we arrived at the river, the decision was made to fish for a while and then cut the logs. We did some serious fishing until about two o'clock. Since we didn't carry a lunch, we were already hungry, but we went to the tree and started sawing anyway.

We cut the tree into four-foot sections. If they had been any longer, we couldn't have handled the weight. We encountered all kinds of problems trying to saw the tree. It was so big that we couldn't pry it open enough to keep the saw from hanging up. It took the rest of the day to saw nine sections of the tree.

When we finally got home, we were starving and completely worn out. Mom had cooked a big pot of Hopping John (dried field peas and rice). As hungry as I was, I didn't think I'd ever fill up on what I thought was the best food I'd ever tasted.

The next week we had to haul the logs out of the swamp. We used the wagon and hauled two sections at a time. After four days, we finally got all the sections to the house.

The next chore was to set up a hoist to lower the sections down in the well. We tried to match them up as we had sawed them so each section would align straight in the well. One by one we let each section down.

When the casing reached the bottom and extended several feet above the ground level, it was time to start digging the well deeper to let the casing slide down. This part of the project had not been discussed. We all just kind of looked at each other without speaking for a while. Then after Christmas and I collected our thoughts enough to talk about it, we started asking, "Who's going down there to dig the well?"

We knew that Dad was the boss, and he would tell us what to do and when to do it. That pretty well took him out of it thus leaving only two of us to choose from ....Christmas or me. I thought drawing straws might be a good idea, but Christmas didn't think too highly of this plan.

Christmas came up with every excuse in the book as to why he couldn't do it. He was too tall and wouldn't be able to stoop over and dig when he got down to the bottom. Then he thought he was too heavy and might break the chain. He was afraid that Dad and I wouldn't be able to pull him back out. He finally said, "I ain't 'gwing' down in that hole no matter what!"

After Christmas made his declaration about not going down in the well, I started giving my own reasons for not going. The main reason that I harped on was that I was fourteen and too young to die. Really, I was just plain scared but wouldn't admit it.

I was afraid all along that I might be the one called on to go down to dig the well, but there didn't seem to be an escape for me. I wanted so desperately to run but I didn't think I had anywhere to go.

The preparations were made to lower Mom's fourteen year old son (going on forty) down into that thirty foot well. I got in the bucket very cautiously with a short-handled shovel and a dip pan. I had taken off my shoes and rolled up my overalls. As I was slowly lowered down, the darkness became blacker and blacker. When I reached the bottom and looked up, I knew then what the light at the end of the tunnel looked like. And that's the truth!

With the short shovel and pan, I started scooping dirt and water and putting it in the bucket. Christmas then pulled it up. Little by little I went deeper, and as I did the cypress casing kept easing down.

Everything sounded so different down in that hollow log. Each time I filled the bucket and sent it up, I drew back as close to the side of the casing as possible so if the chain broke or slipped in Christmas' hand, the bucket wouldn't come down on my head. This digging, scooping, and sliding went on for several hours, but to me it seemed like days. Finally Dad said that he thought we had gone deep enough, so I smoothed out the bottom of the well and they pulled me out.

When I reached the top of the well and got out of the bucket, I was just a muddy glob. Believe me, daylight had never looked so good and I just wanted to hug everybody. In a few days water had run back into the well and had cleared up. The water tasted a little like cypress to start with, but after a few weeks, it either cleared up, or we just got used to it. Dad's idea had pretty-well solved the water shortage problem, as the cypress casing did keep the well from caving in.

I never did go around bragging about my well-digging experience because I was afraid someone would want me to dig out his well. I always figured that I had dug out two wells -- my first one and my last one. This was an experience that a growing boy would never forget. It made a deep impression on me and gave me an appreciation of the rough and difficult times that our forefathers had.

Chapter 46

"THE WILD MAN"

A clear stream of water flowing gently downstream is an attraction that no child can resist. The temptation to wade, to make water wheels, and to sail imaginary boats to foreign shores is irresistible to children. Parental punishment is a small price to pay in exchange for a few minutes of these incredible pleasures. When we lived to "The Backwoods" on the farm that we rented from Mr. Henry Holliday, there was just such a stream of water right behind the barn. The water was clear and flowed nearly all year. There was a lot of thick undergrowth on each side of the road.

This cool, clear stream, which we called a branch, was just too much temptation for "Sis," Jerry, Prince, Lou Dottie, and Louis Rogers. "Sis" and Jerry were my sister and brother, Prince and Lou Dottie were Christmas' children, and Louis Rogers was a neighbor. The ages of these children ranged from about five to about seven.

It was just impossible for Mom to keep "Sis" and Jerry out of this branch. They would slip off every time Mom's back was turned and go down to the branch to play in the water. Their little feet stayed wet, they ruined their shoes, and they kept getting sick, but nothing deterred their enthusiasm for playing in the water. The thrashings that Mom gave them didn't change a thing.

Much to the dismay of the children, a rumor surfaced that a "wild man" had been spotted in the area in and around this popular branch of water. This created lively conversation and speculation, but there was a lot of skepticism among the older children. Still, the children were cautioned to be on the lookout for any mysterious noise or any strange person they might see in this area.

The older children downplayed the rumor and said that someone was making up all this stuff—that there was really nothing to it. The younger children actually became concerned and cautious, but the older children just tempted them right back to the water. Talk about this savage creature continued for several days, but the children continued playing in the water.

Then one fateful day it happened, and it came with a big splash. The "wild man" decided to make an appearance. He was an awful looking creature who looked like he was from a foreign world or the wilderness. He wore a huge coat and an old beat-up hat. There was fur all over his face—only his eyes were visible. He walked through the branch in oversized rubber boots and eased downstream for about 100 yards. Then he began working his way back upstream.

At this same time these children were preoccupied. The "wild man" could see that they were just playing in the water and having such a good time. He started splashing the water, growling, breaking sticks and bushes, and coming menacingly toward the children.

One by one the children stopped what they were doing to stare at the beast. Immediately they ran screaming and crying toward their homes as fast as they could go. They were calling for their mothers, but most of all they were running. If they had been in an Olympic race, they would have won.

Louis Rogers didn't even stop at our house; he cut across the field and went straight to his house. Prince and Lou Dottie were able to make the turn at the first gate and find their mother.

"Sis" and Jerry couldn't make the turn at the first gate, but they made it at the second gate. They didn't stop until they got inside the house. It took some calming down and some cleaning up to get these children back to normal.

This episode pretty well ended the playing around in the old branch behind the barn. For some reason, there was never any inclination for this "fivesome" to go back down there again. The "wild man" was a much talked about topic for a long time. There have always been questions in the minds of these children as to whether the "wild man" was real or not. The deep, dark secret remains—just who would have been so devious as to have scared those little, innocent children?

Chapter 47

LOST IN THE PEE DEE RIVER SWAMP

The dense growth of trees, bushes, briers, and vines in the swamps of the Pee Dee north of Ellison Landing created a very safe haven for animals but was a very treacherous environment for hunters. Darkness of night just added dread to what was already a spooky situation.

On one particularly ominous night, my destiny turned into hours of foreboding anxiety. Two of my friends, Christmas and Fellow Woodberry (Christmas' father-in-law), and I went hunting in the swamps as described above. We hunted for several hours; we more or less followed the dogs as they treed either possums or coons.

This following of the dogs led us into an area that we really weren't very familiar with. We had a very successful catch, so about eleven o'clock we decided to go home. We started walking toward where we thought we had left the car. We walked and walked but didn't seem to be finding our way out of the swamp.

Fellow said, "I can get us out; I know how to follow the lower tail of the moon," which was in its first quarter. We started following the moon's tail, and we kept this up for several hours, but somehow we always came back to the same place.

Then Christmas said, "I can get us out by following the stars." So, we followed the handle of the Big Dipper for a long time having the same results as following the moon. Then we realized and admitted that we were "bad lost." By this time all three of us were tired, weary, and, frankly, a bit apprehensive. We decided to stop walking, build a fire, and stay put until daylight. We were hopeful that after daylight we could find our way out.

So, we built a big fire and raked up mounds of leaves to sleep in. Two of us slept while the other person kept the fire going and kept watch for any wild animals that might wander by. The usual screeches and hoots of owls kept the brisk night eerie. This went on for the duration of the night—each person taking a turn at tending the fire and keeping watch for the unexpected.

When it became daylight and we looked around, we couldn't believe what we saw. We could see the car but couldn't get to it.

During the night the river had risen and backed up all around us. We were virtually on an island. This had confused us all night. Each time when we came out to the water we turned around because we knew we hadn't crossed any water when we first went hunting.

After finding out where we were, our next problem was to find a place where the water was shallow enough to walk across. We finally found a place where we could jump from log to log and worked our way off the island.

It was mid-morning when we got home, and it was too late for me to go to school. (Of course I didn't mind missing school!) My parents were quite concerned but relieved when they learned that we were safe.

I was only fifteen when this happened, and this was a frightening experience. I thought that if Dad had been along, we would not have gotten lost. All night long I had wished I could have reached out and taken his hand and let him lead me out. I needed his strength and self-assurance more than I thought I'd ever needed it before.

During this night of anxiety, I quietly turned to my other Father and asked Him to calm me down and help us get out of this mess. It is impossible to describe the feeling that was in my being when I woke up and saw the sun shining on the car, which was no more than two hundred yards from where we slept.

Chapter 48

THE INFAMOUS SQUIRREL HUNT

In 1942 Nellie, my sister, was dating Edward Whaley, who was home on furlough from the Navy. Edward was visiting his relatives, Uncle "Hass" and Aunt Sue Jones. Mr. "Hass" was a retired Baptist preacher and owned a nice farm and home at Gresham.

There was a swamp behind his house with some of the tallest cypress trees that I had ever seen. Mr. "Hass" invited Edward, Howard Davis, my friend, and me to hunt squirrels on his place. We took Rover, my dog, to tree the squirrels.

Edward had a double-barreled shotgun, and I had a twenty-two caliber, single-shot rifle. Howard didn't have a gun, so we let him shake the bushes to scare the squirrels. If we couldn't find them, his shaking the bushes would make them move, and then we could see them in the tall cypress trees.

Squirrels were plentiful and Rover had more fun than he had ever had chasing those squirrels. As soon as he treed one and we killed it, he had another one treed. He was just besides himself; he was back and forth all over the place.

Rover didn't know where the land boundaries were, and frankly I don't believe he cared 'cause he was having too much fun. We were all enjoying ourselves too much to notice that we had wandered over on to Mr. Bill Thompson's land. We had not seen any "no trespassing" signs posted.

It was a good thing that we carried the rifle because a number of the squirrels went to the top of the cypress trees. They were so high that the seven and a half load in the twelve gauge gun would only sting the squirrels and not kill them.

At times when the gun failed to reach the squirrels, we'd knock them out with the rifle. We killed twenty-two squirrels on this hunt in about three hours, which was the most prolific short hunt I'd ever been on.

When we got out of the woods, we decided that we wanted to have a feast of squirrel and rice and invite all the neighbors. We went to the home of Mr. Walt and Mrs. Maggie Richardson to see if they would help us.

Mrs. Maggie agreed to cook for us, if we would clean the squirrels. We proceeded with the cleaning and she cooked the squirrels and rice in a big pot. She was known all around the area for her good cooking.

This was a feast like I had not seen; all the neighbors were invited. With all the fun going on (plus Gresham was loaded with pretty girls), we forgot the time and stayed real late. By the time we did get home, our parents were concerned about us.

If the story could stop here, I believe I would live five years longer than I'm going to because of the turn of events. Two days later Edward came to our house to tell me that we had been sued for trespassing. Mr. Bill Thompson was saying that we had trespassed on his land, so he took out a warrant and sued us. He didn't know Howard's name, so he just sued Edward and me.

He said that he was going to lock us up and throw away the key. Howard just rubbed this in since Mr. Thompson didn't name him, and this made the situation even worse. I was scared like I had never been scared before. I was only sixteen and had never had a scrape with the law.

I anticipated the worst thing that could happen—this being serving time on the chain gang. I could visualize the striped suit on me and feel the chains around my ankles.

I couldn't eat; I couldn't sleep; I couldn't concentrate in school. I was in a daze. Every car that I saw coming, I thought it might be the sheriff coming to take me to jail. Each day at school I kept looking for the sheriff to come pick me up.

Edward's furlough was soon up, so he had to go back to his ship. There was no way the civilian law could get to him. This just left me alone and that made it even worse. I thought if I had to be locked up, at least I wanted some company because I didn't want to be cast away and lonesome. I could not forget Mr. Bill's threat about throwing away the key.

Just before Edward left to go back to the Navy, his father, Mr. Edward Whaley, Sr., came to Gresham. He was a little upset over the things that had transpired. Well, he paid Mr. Thompson a visit and I don't know what he did or what he said, but he got his attention.

Whatever he said must have been mighty persuasive because Mr. Thompson immediately dropped all charges against us. I have been told that what he said wouldn't be found in a Sunday school book. When Edward came and told me the news, I believe that was the best news that I had ever gotten up to that point in my life. I ate a big supper that night, went to bed, and slept soundly all night. What a relief! I was so happy that I wasn't going to be a jailbird.

After this episode, my esteem for Mr. Whaley "skyrocketed to the top." I thought he could fix anything. He was one of my favorite people as long as he lived.

Max, "Sis" and Jerry really thought this scare was justified as they believed I was the "wild man" who had frightened them so shamelessly a few years earlier.

Chapter 49

B. L. POSTON, AN INSTITUTION

Bernie Lafar Poston was born October 5, 1901 and died April 8, 1961. Charlie and Emily Owens Poston were his parents. He was born and lived his entire life in the Poston area.

Bernie's grandfather was Andrew Poston, who was instrumental in establishing Poston as a thriving community during his lifetime. Andrew was born in 1829 and died in 1916. He served as an officer during the Civil War.

Having survived the tragic war, Andrew returned to a land that was devastated by the ravages of the conflict. The future looked very bleak. His efforts to rebuild were hampered by the economy and the federal restrictions that were placed on the southern white people. However, Andrew was not easily defeated and during the remaining years of his life he amassed great wealth.

Andrew was a community leader. He was someone who many people looked to for guidance in all their difficult situations. He served on a commission that recommended to the State Legislature that Florence County be formed from parts of Marion, Williamsburg, Darlington, and Clarendon Counties.

At the peak of his accomplishments, he owned a plantation of about 3000 acres. He also owned a steamboat, a general merchandise store, a cotton gin, a gristmill, and a sawmill. It has been said that he was the first person in the area to cultivate tobacco commercially. Andrew was a tough act for his heirs to follow and none of them have come close to his accomplishments.

Bernie's father, Charlie, became a prominent merchant and farmer in the Poston area; he died in 1920 at the early age of 54. His death came before Bernie or any of his brothers were old enough to take over the vast empire that their grandfather had established. The family fortune was pretty well depleted by the time all of the children were grown.

Bernie entered high school but did not finish. His primary work experience while growing up was clerking in his father's store in Poston. This huge store was located on Main Street right by the railroad track. The store was a general merchandise store that carried everything that was needed by the people who lived in this area. After Mr. Charlie died, Owens (Bernie's oldest brother) took over the running of the store. There was not enough business to support two families, so Bernie pulled out of the business and opened a store in Kingsburg. I'm sure that the experience that he gained while working in the Poston store helped him when he started his own store.

In 1932 or 1933 Bernie borrowed a few hundred dollars, rented an old store from Doug Collins, and opened a general merchandise store at Kingsburg. The store was in a good location for traffic going from Florence to Georgetown on Highway 51 and also for traffic going to Mullins, Marion, or Myrtle Beach on Highway 378 and Highway 41.

More cars were on the roads now, so Bernie decided to put in a gas tank and sell gas. About the same time that he opened his store, the railroad opened a line running from Poston to Florence, which went through Kingsburg. A Post Office was opened in Kingsburg across the road from the train depot. A few years later a bus line, The Pee Dee Coach, began running between Florence and Georgetown. Bernie's store was one of the main bus stops and this became a very thriving segment of his business.

A very large logging firm out of Lake City and Sumter did large-scale logging on the Marion County side of the Pee Dee River, and they used Bernie's station as their refueling center. Bernie sold to most of the farmers in the area—extending credit for as long as a year or until their crops were sold. Thus, he built a tremendous business with both black and white clientele.

Bernie's success pretty well dried-up the other mercantile businesses in Poston including the one run by his brother, Owens. This increased the importance of Kingsburg as the economic center for this community for a long time to come. Only in the years to come would the importance of this change be known as Bernie's emerged as the economic center for the community.

The store and station actually became a landmark for that area of the state and remained so throughout the thirties, forties, and fifties. The prices he charged were relatively high, but he sold everything that a person needed. The location of his store was convenient for everyone in the area and credit was available for all who needed it.

Bernie married Daisy Bryte Sherer from Sharon, South Carolina. She was teaching school at Trinity at the time. This union produced six children: Aggie Jean, Bernice, Isabell, and triplet boys, who died right after they were born.

Bernie was a Methodist and a strong supporter of the Trinity Methodist Church. He was a trustee of the Trinity School District 35 for a number of years. Being a somewhat shy person, he did not like to get up and talk in public.

Bernie was a caring person and would readily help people who were in trouble. People knew they could depend on him and a multitude of them did. He was intelligent, witty, and always had something interesting to talk about. A good number of farmers in the area would catch up with their work and come to the store just to talk to him.

During the winter months Bernie kept a big heater in the middle of the store with several rocking chairs around it. His store became a very popular place. When the children in my family were small and went in the store, he usually gave each of us a piece of candy. Sometimes when Dad went to the store alone, Bernie would fix up a little bag of candy and send it to us. These charitable deeds were never forgotten by us children.

Bernie was an avid hunter and fisherman, and he was successful at both of these sports. I don't think any man who ever lived enjoyed stalking and killing a wild turkey more than Bernie.

Chevrolets were the only cars Bernie would drive. His cars were always good, and always clean. He was a fast driver, so when you saw him coming or going, there was usually a cloud of dust following him.

I started working part-time for Bernie in 1940 immediately after I got my Social Security card at the age of fourteen. I started working on Saturdays from seven a.m. until eleven p.m. for a dollar and a half a day. This was very good, I thought, because this was twice what I got for a days work on the farm.

This job developed into working on Saturday, Sunday afternoon, and any evening after school that Dad could spare me away from the farm. This job helped me save a little money to buy clothes, books, etc. for school. After I finished high school, I worked for fifteen dollars a week until I was drafted into the army. This money helped me and my family during those difficult economic times.

When I was discharged from the Army, I came back and worked for a couple of years until I married Leta Mae Tanner. She was working in Kingstree as secretary for the Rural Electrification

Administration, so I got a job at Stanley's Grocery in Kingstree. I was making forty dollars a week. I didn't know what I was going to do with all that money—but I soon found out.

Bernie and his business played a vital roll in the welfare of my family and the welfare of many other families during the most difficult economic crisis that we Americans have ever experienced. All of our lives were touched by him, and I am proud to say that most of our lives were made just a little better by Bernie's compassion, care, and concern.

The store was used as a Voting Precinct for elections. A lot of politics and concerns of the community took place around the heater in Bernie's store. He worked long hours day-in and day-out, usually opening up about six a.m. and closing about eleven p.m. He probably burned himself out as his health began to fail when he was about 55. He died at the age of 59. The entire area was affected by his death.

Chapter 50

JOHNSONVILLE HIGH SCHOOL

We hear a lot about school consolidation today, but consolidation actually began to happen in the early thirties. My own school, Trinity High School, consolidated with Johnsonville High School in Johnsonville.

There was a distance of about five miles from Trinity to Johnsonville, and this presented a real problem to the children of the rural community. This particular problem was solved, at least for the older children, when Mr. Luther Richardson located and bought a Model T bus. The county paid Mr. Luther a few cents per mile to haul the high school children to Johnsonville.

The poor little grammar school children were teed-off all the time because the bus came by and picked up the big high school children and left the little ones to walk to school. This happened in rain, sleet, or snow—the little ones walked and the big ones rode the bus.

The Model T was not the most dependable transportation known to man at this particular period. There were a lot of tire blowouts, break downs, and engine-heating problems.

In 1934 the situation began to look a little brighter when Mr. Luther bought a new Chevrolet truck and built a homemade body. The seats were long boards that ran from front to back on each side of the bus.

There were double-wide boards in the middle that ran from front to back. Children seated on the outside rows faced the middle rows. Children on the inside rows sat back-to-back and faced the children sitting on the outside rows.

This bus was more dependable, so Mr. Luther started running several routes carrying all the children to Trinity School. Then he transported the high school children on to Johnsonville. This took care of the white children, but the black children still had to walk to their little school at Kingsburg.

As the buses became more dependable and the roads were improved by better drainage and scraping, traveling to Johnsonville

High School became almost routine. The only thing that kept it from being routine was the spring rains that flooded the Lynches River causing the water to rise and run over the road. When this happened, traffic going to Johnsonville was cut off for days at a time.

I always looked forward to these spring rains because I knew that I could set gill nets in some of the low places where the water had backed up and catch a lot of fish. This meant food for the table and some extra cash. I could always sell fish.

Johnsonville School was big compared to Trinity. It included all the grammar and high school children of the Johnsonville area, plus the high school children from the Vox, Prospect, and Trinity areas. The total enrollment was probably three hundred and fifty students. The number of students going from Trinity was usually about thirty.

Johnsonville had two buses, plus the bus from Trinity and the one from Vox making a total of four buses. At the time I was going to high school, very few students had cars. Gas was rationed and most people couldn't afford to own a car. Mr. H. M. Floyd, the Principal, and Mr. L. J. Carter, the Agriculture teacher had cars. Only a few of the teachers had cars, so parking was not a problem.

There was a no-smoking policy at the school. If you got caught or if a teacher even smelled smoke on your breath, the consequence was a good whipping by the principal. After the new gymnasium was built, this provided a good place for the boys to hide and do their smoking.

The area around the back steps of the gym was a place where all the bigger boys gathered at recess whether they smoked or not. There were occasions when the non-smokers were punished for associating with the smokers. This happened when the smokers were actually caught in the act. Girls just did not smoke, and to my knowledge none of them were ever chastised for smoking.

During the years that I was in high school, we never had a football team. All the country boys had to go home to work on the farm and there weren't enough town students to field a team. I did not participate in any sports or any extra curricular activities as any extra time that I had was spent doing farm work.

The first two years that I was in high school, we didn't have a gymnasium, but the town boys and girls had basketball teams. The games were played in an old tobacco warehouse. The floors were not finished, the boards were loose, and there was an awful noise when the ball was advanced from one end of the court to the other. Needless to say, we weren't very competitive.

We had a new gymnasium the last two years that I was in school. However, the situation remained about the same as only the town students (who didn't have to do farm work) were the only ones who participated in the basketball program. We probably won a few more games but still weren't very competitive.

The new gym had the prettiest floor that I had ever seen, but it was absolutely a "No-No" to walk on it unless you had tennis shoes on so the floor would not be damaged. I never had tennis shoes, so I never got to walk on that beautiful floor. It was a big temptation just to get out there and walk all over that floor; but I respected the authorities and stayed off of it.

Students in high school were divided into three social groups due mainly by the consolidation of the different school districts: the Johnsonville group, the Vox group, and the Trinity group. There was very little fraternizing between the groups.

The Johnsonville group being the larger and more cohesive pretty well got their way about everything they wanted to do. A large number of the Trinity group were children of sharecroppers, so they had very little influence on the school programs. They were kind of like spare tires —they went along and were used only when one of the main tires went flat.

In any election of class officers or selection of things like class rings, the Johnsonville group always got who they wanted or what they wanted. The teachers usually lived in Johnsonville and were more aligned with the Johnsonville students, so they did very little to help the situation. Actually, there was very little that anyone could do. The Vox and Trinity groups were somewhat complacent about the whole situation.

The worst day that I can remember at Johnsonville High School was my very first day. It was a custom at the school to have all new boy students run through a belt-line, which was formed by upperclassmen.

I'm sure the big boys just didn't realize how hard they could hit. I came out of this belt-line with whelps, bruises, and scars that lasted for weeks. The boys who wouldn't go through the belt-line had a rougher time than the ones that did because they were then ostracized by the other students.

Johnsonville was very fortunate to have had Mr. H. M. Floyd's guidance and expertise as principal in leadership for so many years. His being there left its mark on the entire community that will last for many years to come.

Most of the teachers who were at Johnsonville while I was going to school there were dedicated, well-prepared, compassionate and interesting. They were also interested in the welfare of the students.

Occasionally we had a teacher who had a short fuse like the one supervising the lunchroom on one particular occasion. Students always lined up in front of the lunchroom at recess and waited for the door to open. The teacher in charge took up the tickets and kept order.

On this particular day I had asked a friend to save me a place near the head of the line, which was a normal occurrence. The supervising teacher saw me come to the front with my friend and assumed that I was breaking in the line. He told me to go to the back of the line. I tried to explain that my friend had saved me a place. He screamed at me, "Go to the back of the line!"

When I turned and started down the stairs, he gave me a shove and I went flying down the steps. I missed the bottom step, tripped, fell, and busted my knee. The students who had witnessed this incident had a lot of compassion for me and tried to help.

The young teacher just ignored me. I learned later that he had a young child who had just developed a serious illness, so I forgave him for this unexpected push down the stairs.

Punishment was normally rendered fairly to the guilty parties. One day in English class I had the privilege of experiencing this impartial punishment. The teacher had to leave the room. Ernest Junior Huggins had been bothering me something awful, and after the teacher stepped out of the classroom for a moment, I just lost my cool and we "locked horns" in front of the class.

Just about the time Ernest Junior and I got in high gear, Mr. Floyd walked in and wanted to know what we were doing. Of course, after looking up at him, we said, "We're only playing." He said, "Good, let's go to the office because I want to do some playing too."

He took us to the office and gave us a real good strapping.

He had us bend over his desk and then whacked us with two yardsticks. This hurt a little, but my pride was 'cracked' real bad.

The thing that concerned me more than anything else was the fact that Dad and Mr. Floyd were good friends. I knew that when Mr. Floyd told Dad about this episode I would really get a tanning from Dad.

For a long time after this episode, every time they got together, I would 'draw up' because I knew what was in store for me. Well, Mr. Floyd never got around to telling Dad on me, and I never did get that second beating.

Mr. Floyd probably knew that I'd get another whipping at home if he told Dad. He showed a lot of compassion by keeping this secret. After that I considered him one of my best friends, and I gave him no more problems. I helped him in every way possible. His counseling was wise and I am thankful that I was fortunate enough to receive some of it.

My graduating class was the Class of `43. We had only eleven grades back then, so I was only sixteen when I graduated. All boys were drafted in service as soon as they reached eighteen. It was urgent that all boys not fail any grades, or they would be drafted and not get to graduate.

There were 41 students in our class (22 girls and 19 boys). Everyone of the boys was drafted and served his country in various branches of service. It was a fortunate group of young men as none of them lost their lives in the conflict.

In 1943 the war effort was at the height of mobilization so every unnecessary activity was eliminated. Sports were curtailed, May Day activities were stopped, the Junior-Senior Prom was canceled, and there was no Yearbook.

Our commencement exercise was held at nine o'clock at night so the farmers would have time to get out of the fields, eat, get dressed, and get to the schoolhouse in time for the program. This late hour also allowed the building to cool down as there was no air conditioning in those days.

Our Class Motto was: <u>Today We Follow, Tomorrow We Lead.</u> As I write this chapter fifty years later, I note that we did follow and we did lead. We succeeded and we failed. We moved on and we stayed behind, but we always tried to better ourselves and make life better for those who followed us.

As leaders we had some successes and some failures. We have gone from the mule and wagon to rockets on the moon since my graduation. The economy is much better now, but the world is much more complex. Crime and violence are our worst enemies. Let's pray that the next generation can accomplish more than we did.

Chapter 51

SEX AND SEXUALITY

I grew up in an environment in which there was a great deal of secrecy about sex. You did not ask any questions, and you were told very little.

Boys were told that "boys were made of snails, rails, and puppy dog tails," whereas " girls were made of sugar, spice, and everything nice." Boys were told that they should not hit girls (even if girls hit them) -- they were instructed to just walk away. It was a cardinal rule that boys didn't fight girls.

Boys could play with girls as long as there was no physical contact; touching girls was a no-no. Boys were so instructed, that if girls were working and boys weren't, then the boys should step right in and help them. If girls were carrying something heavy, boys should stop what they were doing and carry the objects for them.

Girls were watched over by the adults very closely; they were protected and kept out of "harm's way." Girls were never sent to work in fields that were far from the house, nor would they be sent to the woods to gather and carry wood to the house.

Boys were taught to tip their hat and speak politely to girls and ladies. Boys were instructed to always open the door for a girl or a lady, and they should never walk in front of her but always beside or behind her.

When walking beside a girl or lady, a boy had to be sure he was walking on the side of the girl that was considered most dangerous. We were always taught that boys were to protect girls no matter what peril they might have to put themselves in.

Girls were considered to be more fragile, petite, graceful, even tempered, delicate, weaker in strength, more tender, and less athletic than boys. Girls could not participate with boys in football, basketball, baseball, or even in shooting marbles.

You never saw a girl pulling up or acting on a gymnastic bar, doing push-ups, doing high jumps, or broad jumps. The games girls normally played were hopscotch, jump rope, ring-around-the-roses, and pretty-girl station, but most often they played with dolls and tea sets.

At Trinity Grammar School boys and girls were normally kept separated during recess breaks. The girls' toilet was in one back corner of the school ground and the boys' toilet was in the other back corner, so girls played on one side of the schoolhouse and boys played on the other side. Teachers were always on the yard during recess to supervise the activities.

The nearest thing to a sexual crisis happened in our home when the three oldest boys, Merrill, Lance, and "Bunkus," were very small. Merrill and Lance had been assigned the task of feeding the mules and cows and were working in the barn. "Bunkus" just tagged along.

Merrill and Lance were going to school and "Bunkus" hadn't started as he was only five years old. Merrill and Lance had picked up some new terms at school and had figured out how to spell them. They wanted to communicate their new knowledge between themselves and didn't think that "Bunkus" (at the tender age of five) should be told the new things they had just learned. They thought that if they just spelled out the things they wanted to tell each other that "Bunkus" wouldn't be able to understand.

They underestimated their younger brother. Things were pretty normal until all of the family were seated at the supper table. "Bunkus" spoke up and asked Mom what was the meaning of some spelling he had just learned. He spelled out a five-letter word that started with a "P" which had sexual connotations.

Everything and everyone became totally silent and still. Mom broke the silence when she inquired of "Bunkus," "Where in the world did you hear that?" He looked over toward Merrill and Lance. They just choked up and couldn't swallow, and curiously, they completely lost their memory.

Panic did set in for a short while, but Mom, with all of her innate wisdom, took control of the situation. She explained that children sometimes hear and learn things from other children that may or may not be correct. She told them that when they heard things they didn't understand they should come to her, and she would try to give them the correct explanations.

Mom didn't have psychology in school, nor did she have any preparation for a situation such as this one, but she had a God-given talent to think wisely and come up with the right answers at the right time.

This was really the only open family discussion about sex that I know of. There were plenty of single, individual questions that came up and Mom usually handled them on a one-on-one basis. For reasons of fear or respect, none of the children ever went to Dad with any questions concerning sex, love, or marriage; it was always Mom who we depended and relied on.

I don't want to make it appear like we didn't have a lot of unresolved problems and unanswered questions, because we really did. It was as sure as death and taxes that you would get no answers or advice from the schoolteachers. You may get a few answers from the ministers, but their answers were few and far between.

In church and at home, the one thing that was stressed whenever the opportunity arose, was that boys and girls should be chaste and save their virginity until they got married. We boys were told not to try to do "mannish" things until we became a man and were capable of assuming the duties and responsibilities of a man.

The scriptural bases used as guides for the teaching and leading of young people in the community by the churches and parents were as follows:

Exodus 20:14--"You shall not commit adultery."

Exodus 20:17--"You shall not covet your neighbor's wife."

Matt. 5:28----"But I say to you that everyone who looks at a woman lustfully has already committed adultery with her in his heart."

Matt. 19:18----"And Jesus said, You shall not kill, You shall not commit adultery, You shall not steal, You shall not bear false witness."

Heb. 13:4----"Let marriage be held in honor among all, and let the marriage bed be undefiled, for God will judge the immoral and adulterous."

Lev. 20:10---- "If a man commits adultery with the wife of his neighbor, both the adulterer and the adulteress shall be put to death."

1 Cor. 6:9--- "Do you not know that the unrighteous will not inherit the Kingdom of God? Do not be deceived; neither the immoral, nor idolaters, nor adulterers....."

Mark 10:11---"And he said to them, "Whoever divorces his wife and marries another commits adultery against her..."

Mark 10:12----"....and if she divorces her husband and marries another, she commits adultery."

These scriptures were used over and over at home, at church, and at Sunday school as a guide or road map to live by. They were also used as a warning of what would happen if one strayed from the "narrow path" as it was laid out.

In our family, it was stressed that we not start dating too young. Maybe we could start when we were about eighteen. We were not to get too close or think about marriage until we were at least twenty-one and until boys were able to support a wife.

The religious ethics and sexual morals as depicted by Erskin Caldwell in his book Tobacco Road were light years away from the ones that we grew up with on a tobacco farm. There may have been some illicit sex going on, but it was discrete; you didn't hear a lot about it.

The Ku Klux Klan was active in the community during the twenties and thirties, and this organization didn't sanction too much "hanky-panky." It is quite possible that the fear of this organization kept some people from doing things that they might have done otherwise.

If a person got caught doing something wrong like stealing, wife-beating, being drunk in public, or not taking care of his family, it was not unusual for him to be taken for a "ride" and "worked-over" pretty well. This was a friendly reminder and was about all it took to keep wayward people in tow.

Times were hard and people were very poor, but families, churches, and Masonic Lodges were strong. People somehow kept their dignity, self-respect, and faith in God.

I can remember several husband and wife separations, but I really can't recall a divorce. I can only remember talk about five illegitimate white children and only a few black children.

The morals and religious values were no different between the blacks and whites. To my knowledge, I knew of no homosexual men, and I had never heard of a lesbian woman until I was in service.

I can't say that there was no venereal disease in the community, but I had never heard about this disease until I was drafted into the Army. I can recall only one reported case of rape and two cases of adult incest. It must be remembered that the community was close-knit, and life was very simple during this period.

There was work that was considered to be "man's work" and work that was considered to be "woman's work." You were more apt to see men cross over to do something that a woman normally did than you were to see a woman cross over to do a "man's work."

Work that was considered as "man's work" was work that required more brute strength than brains. It required a lot of lifting, pulling, pushing, chopping, digging, shoveling, sawing, and handling of mules and heavy equipment.

"Man's work" normally carried with it more danger such as the felling of trees, blowing-up stumps with dynamite, handling and breaking mules, digging wells, and managing untamed livestock. This was the type work that had to be done in all kinds of inclement weather.

"Woman's work" included cooking and feeding the family, keeping the house clean, washing clothes, gardening, watching out for the children, milking the cows, sewing clothes for the family, and canning. Women also helped on the farm doing such things as chopping and picking cotton, hoeing and gathering tobacco in their "free" time.

Doctors were usually men because they had to get out in all kinds of weather (day or night) and travel from house to house. Their traveling was done on horseback, horse and buggy, or Model T Ford cars.

Mail carriers were men as they had to travel on very poor roads, in all kinds of weather, on horseback, horse and buggy or Model T Ford. When mail carriers started delivering mail in cars, they carried an extra can of gas, a can of water, extra spare tires, a shovel to dig out of bogs, and a chain.

The chain was used by farmers who pulled them out of a bog with a team of mules. If his car broke down, the carrier might have to spend the night at someone's house until he could get help.

Door-to-door salesmen quite often got stranded. Salesmen spent the night with us on several occasions. My Dad always tried to help people who were in trouble. The stranded guest that I remember best was the tax collector. Dad owed some back taxes, which made him feel a little sensitive.

All railroad work was heavy, laborious, and physically strenuous, so only men were hired for this work. When women were hired off the farm, it was usually as store clerks, cafe waitresses, nurses, or clerical workers or bookkeepers in other businesses. There was no competition between men and women for each other's jobs since "man's work" required physical strength and "woman's work" didn't.

The pay was much less for women. It is great to see women attain equal pay for equal work in the job market today, but they should never forget the physical bodily abuse that men endured while creating the gap in equality to start with.

In the 1940's men were taught to respect and protect women. For example, remember the Titanic, the world's largest passenger ship!

Since it was supposed to be unsinkable, there were only enough lifeboats for about half of the passengers. The men on the Titanic helped the women and children board the lifeboats. Then they kneeled on the deck of the ship and prayed as they went under with the ship.

Women should never forget the men who have been forced to go to war to defend our Constitution. Many made the ultimate sacrifice so that we can enjoy our freedom today. No woman has ever been drafted to serve on the front lines in the Armed Forces of the Unites States yet.

Growing up during this era was much less complicated than it is today. There was always something to do on the farm which kept children too busy to get into a lot of trouble.

Even as a young child, I had a curious mind. Once I asked Mama where babies came from and she said that a stork brought them. My next question was, "Where did the stork get the babies?" She then told me that the stork found them in hollow logs. I then asked, "How did the babies get into the hollow logs?"

By the time I got to this question, Mom tried to change the subject. But I surprised her with yet another question which was, "Why does the stork stop at our house more than he does at our neighbor's house? Some of them don't have but one child?"

Mama said, "The stork just must like us better." By this time I was shooed away.

I was about six or seven before I found out that boys and girls weren't equipped the same. We were continuously instructed from potty training on that we were not to expose our private parts.

One day a little neighbor girl, who was two or three years older than I, was at our house playing with my sister Nellie; she was sitting a little carelessly. Her panties didn't cover everything that they were supposed to, so the first thing I did was ask, "What's that?" I really thought she had broken "it" off.

The answer that I got was a knock on the head and they ran me out of the room. This was what I really deserved, but that wasn't the way I felt about it back then.

What I learned for the rest of my young, growing-up years was from boys talking about sex behind the toilets at school, and they didn't know much more than I did. When I was attending high school, the war was going on and gas was rationed, so getting the car to go on a date was next to impossible.

Serious dating was discouraged by my parents until we became about eighteen years old. There were no telephones so about the only opportunity we had to talk to girls was on the bus going to school or at Methodist Youth Fellowship at church on Sunday nights.

Sometimes someone would have a hayride, birthday party, chicken bog, or maybe a marshmallow roast. I really didn't have a lot of interest in girls. I enjoyed hunting, fishing, reading, building things like model cars, hiking, and exploring. And, of course there was <u>always</u> a lot of work to do.

I never had a serious girl friend until I met my future bride, and this was after I was in the army. There was a girl who was two grades ahead of me in high school, whom I absolutely adored. She didn't know about my crush on her as girls were usually attracted to older boys and certainly not to one two years younger. The age difference didn't discourage me too much. She remained my secret infatuation for a long time.

As we grew up, our parents continued to stress total abstinence; in fact, they pretty well demanded it.

The sexual mores of the community did change some during World War II (and not for the better). All able-bodied men between eighteen and forty-eight were away from home fighting the war. This left a lot of young brides at home alone. Some of them had small children, and they had a very difficult time. The war caused long separations for a lot of families. I guess we could say that the war years were the point in time when our sexual values began to change.

There are some analysts today who say that poverty has caused the breakdown in family values and the deterioration of sexual morals. When we were poor, we had very high standards for family values and attitudes toward sex. Many poor people have high morals and deep religious convictions.

What has happened is that many have strayed from what Christ taught about our moral obligations, love, marriage, rearing children, and the golden rule. Also, some of our government programs, which do nothing to discourage out-of-wedlock births, have played a major roll in the breakdown of families.

Not all the changes are bad though, as we can now talk openly about sex without feeling that it's a dirty subject. When my children were growing up, I just could not bring myself to talk about and answer questions on sex; and I have always regretted this. I hope and pray that I don't make this same mistake with my grandchildren.

Chapter 52

WE RAISED OUR BOYS TO BE MEN

The following was related to me by Wallace Taylor, who was a neighbor, a close friend, and sometimes a driver for Dad. Wallace told this to me after Dad's death; unfortunately I was unaware of it during Dad's lifetime.

The incident I am referring to happened at a highly political agriculture meeting. Dad was always very active in the political affairs of the community, county, and state, and his presence was usually felt.

This incident happened shortly after I had been drafted into the Army. I was the fourth son in the family to march off to war as Lance, "Bunkus," and Nellie's husband, Edward, were all in the Navy. "Bunkus" was in Europe and Lance and Edward were in the Pacific.

I am sure that the strain of having four members of the family to worry about was having its toll on Mom and Dad. This must have been an awesome experience for them.

The day of the meeting came in early 1945. Dad didn't drive, so he got Wallace Taylor to drive him to Florence to the meeting. Wallace said that the meeting was well-attended as the room was full.

Wallace told me that after the meeting began one of the designated speakers was making his presentation, and in this presentation he included a family matter. Apparently the speaker's oldest son had reached eighteen and was subject to being drafted into the service. The speaker worked a statement into his talk, "that he didn't raise his boy to fight war and he didn't want him to go to Europe or the Pacific to fight somebody else's war."

Wallace said that he didn't believe Dad heard another word that the speaker said after that statement. He said he really couldn't contain Dad. Remember, Dad had four family members who were fighting the war at this time.

Wallace told me that Dad asked for and got permission to speak as a rebuttal to the man's speech. He said that Dad got up and approached the podium with a very calm and professional demeanor.

He looked at the gentleman who had just talked, and he said, "Mr. Doe (not his real name) I have seven sons and a son-in-law. Four of them are already fighting the war that you didn't raise your son to fight. And if this war goes on much longer, I'll have two more sons who will also have to go.

He continued, "No, Mr. Doe, I didn't raise my boys to be warriors, but with God's help my wife and I have tried to raise our boys to be God-fearing, Christian men. As Christian men they will be able to fight all of life's battles, and, yes, if some of those battles are waged to try to stop Hitler and his Nazi army and Tojo and his fanatical Japs, they will do it."

Wallace said Dad continued to say, "Our country is in deep trouble; our freedom and our Christian way of life are threatened. When my sons had to leave, they didn't want to go; they love their family and home, but they left with their heads high. Their country beckoned them so they rose-up and answered the call."

Dad continued, "This country is not perfect, but it's worth fighting for, and, yes, if it means my going and helping our boys with this war, I'll go, even if I am fifty-seven years old."

"We pray for the safety of our boys, but we pray for the safety of all our American boys. We know that some will make the supreme sacrifice. Our prayer is that those who do get killed will be ready to meet their Master."

"We pray that this war will soon be over and most of all that we will win. When we win the war, we pray that we'll use the victory for the advancement of Christianity here on earth."

According to Wallace, the crowd went wild after Dad closed his remarks. They stood up and yelled and applauded. Several men went down front, picked Dad up, lifted him on their shoulders, and carried him around the room. He said that it took quite a while for things to get back to normal so they could continue the meeting.

I am so glad that Wallace told me about this, but I wish he had told it to me before Dad's death. I knew all my life that he was devoted to his country, but I would have loved telling him how proud I was of him for standing up in that meeting and saying what he believed in.

Chapter 53

BITS OF HUMOR

Hold Him! Hold Him!

In the fall of 1936 after the leaves had turned brown and fallen off the trees, we were rounding up some hogs to put in a floored pen. Usually hogs were put in an enclosed floored pen for about two to three months so they could be fed lots of grain to fatten them up before butchering them.

"Bunkus" was seventeen years old this year, strong as a bull, and was right in the middle of catching the hogs. He caught one by the tail and continued to hang on. Dad yelled, "Hold him! Hold him! Don't let him loose."

In a moment the hog squealed and ran off. Dad said, "I declare to goodness! I told you to hold him and not let him loose."

"Bunkus" walked over to Dad and handed him the hog's tail and said, "I didn't let him loose; his tail just pulled off."

That Chicken Just Died

The first snow that I had ever seen fell in the winter of 1936 when we were living in "Powell's Corner." I was ten years old and I thought this was the most beautiful thing that I'd ever seen.

What was even more wonderful was the fact that we didn't have to go to school. With this beautiful snow and no school, we children were so excited. We were all so hyperactive and really got "under Mom's feet."

"Bunkus" showed me how to make a deadfall to catch birds. It was decided that we would catch enough birds to make a bird pie.

We took a short board about two feet long and twelve inches wide and propped it up on one end with a stick about eight inches long. This board was put about forty feet from the porch so the birds couldn't see us.

The snow was then cleared from the area around the deadfall, and feed for the birds was spread under the board. "Bunkus" tied a string to the stick and we stood on the porch holding the other end of the string - waiting for a bird to get under the board.

When a bird reached the danger zone, we pulled the string,

and Bing! We had another bird for a pie.

That day there was an old hen that was bothering my deadfall and keeping the birds away. I got so mad at her that I picked up a stick and threw it at her. My aim was a little too good. I had a direct hit, which flipped the chicken over. She was flopping around "just like a chicken with its head cut off."

I cried for a moment because I knew Mom wasn't going to take this killing of one of her prize hens too lightly. Laying hens were valuable because they laid eggs and eggs always sold for money.

I went running in the house crying and told Mom, "I chunked a stick at a chicken and she died." I think I wanted her to believe that the stick scared the chicken to death.

Mom was upset, but she told me to go back and bring the hen to her so she could clean it for cooking. I went back out to get the chicken, but to my surprise, that old hen got up, unfurled her feathers, and took off running to the hen house. So, back into the house I went with the good news that the hen "came back alive."

Cock-A-Doodle-Do

During the depression, one thing that had to be guarded and protected carefully was your chickens. You had to protect them from possums, foxes, owls, hawks, wild dogs, and hungry people. Chickens were a valuable asset; you could sell eggs anytime for fifty to sixty cents per dozen. So great care was taken to be sure you didn't lose any chickens needlessly.

When we lived on the King Farm, we lived right beside a country road that people traveled constantly on the way to and from Poston. This constant traffic created opportunities for the chickens to be picked up, put in bags, and taken away.

We were losing a lot of chickens, so Dad decided to do something about it. He built a new chicken house that could be locked up. All chicken houses had roosts for the chickens to get up on and roost during the night. Dad's new venture was a big chicken house with some tall roosts in it.

Of course, at five years of age, I was helping Dad build the chicken house. What young boy in his right mind would miss an adventure like this?

Just before the house was finished, I decided to try out the roosts. I got up on the top one which was high as I could go and perched on the roost like the chickens did. Then I decided it was time to crow like a rooster. I let out with a big, "cock-a-doodle..." but I never finished with the last "do" as I lost my balance and bang! I fell off the roost right on my head, and that was "all she wrote" for several hours. I came around about three hours later surrounded by some concerned parents and brothers and sisters.

When I came to and realized where I was, I told Dad, "I don't want to be a rooster anymore!"

Over My Head One Time Too Many

When I was growing up on the farm, I was called on to do many things that normally would have been done by a person more mature in years and larger in stature. There were many tasks that had to be done, and there was no one else to do them; so, I did them even though I was "over my head" most of the time.

Almost invariably during the summer months, feed for the mules and cows ran low, so we had to cut green corn tops to supplement the regular feed. In 1938 we had four mules and two milk cows, so it took a lot of corn tops to feed these animals.

One Saturday afternoon I was assigned the task of feeding all of these animals with corn tops. We normally cut enough on Saturday for two days, so it took a big wagon load on Saturday. This was done so we wouldn't have to cut tops on Sunday, our day of rest.

Even though I was only twelve years old, I caught and hooked up a pair of mules. David, who was only ten years old, was helping me. Together we set out to cut and haul a load of green corn tops.

This fearsome twosome with all of our size, maturity, and strength cut the corn tops. Then when it came time to load the wagon, we stacked the corn tops every which way on the wagon.

When the wagon was loaded, we traveled to the barn and began unloading it. The difficult task was to figure out where to start because the corn tops were all jumbled on the wagon. In all this confusion, as I was trying to sort out and throw the corn off, I slipped from the wagon body and fell right on my head.

The lights went out for me and stayed out for several minutes. When I came to, I found that I had knocked another hole in my head and both arms were sprained at the elbows.

Needless to say, I was almost helpless for several days and received a lot of attention from most of the family. Some members of my family didn't think too highly of my going around with both arms in a sling because I was constantly telling them that I was a wooden people.

I didn't have to cut any more corn tops for the rest of the summer, so that eased my pain just a little.

Doctor I Can't Breathe Through My Nose
After I became an adult and began to have trouble breathing through my nose, I went to the doctor and explained my problem to him. He took a light and looked to see what was going on.

After a while he asked, "You can't breathe through 'um...eh?" He then left and went to get another doctor to look at me. They looked and began to ask more questions.

One doctor asked me, "Do you remember breaking your nose?" I said, "I don't remember breaking it, but as a boy I fell out of trees, off wagons, out of chicken houses, was hit in the nose by a baseball, and things like that."

Well," one doctor explained, "You have broken your nose three times and it looks up there like an S curve on a mountain road."

The doctors decided they could straighten out some of the curves. They tried to chisel out some of the humps, which helped a little, but it didn't clear up all my breathing problems. I guess I just had one too many bumps when I was growing up!

Oh! Oh! Down It Goes With A Gag
Probably no one enjoyed chewing tobacco any better than my Dad -- I might add he chewed most of the time. On just one occasion he might have taken issue with that statement.

There were some wild hogs that were eating up the corn in the "crappy field" in "Powell's Corner." A black man, "Uncle" Henry Eaddy, had some dogs trained to catch wild hogs, so Dad got him to help catch the ones that were eating up the corn.

Arrangements were made for the wild hog catch on a particular warm morning. As the dogs began to catch the hogs, the people who were involved had to move fast to get the hogs tied so they could be transported to a pen that was built especially for wild hogs.

In all the hustle and excitement of trying to tie the hogs and keep from getting cut up by the hogs, Dad made a quick swallow and "oh, oh".... in a gulp his big chew of tobacco was gone.

He got on his knees and gagged and heaved desperately trying to bring it back. He was nauseated something awful, but he just couldn't bring it back. Needless to say, he didn't help with the hog catching any more that day.

That big chew "down the hatch" squelched his hog catching, but it didn't squelch his desire to chew Beechnut tobacco.

What In The World Was That?

When Nellie's children were young, her husband Edward was in the Navy; so they traveled and moved a lot. Usually during transfers and moves, she and the children would come home on extended visits. The family always looked forward to their visits, and it was always sad when they left.

On one of these visits, Dad was in for a real surprise. He had the most comfortable rocking chair that was ever made. He had taken the rim of a wagon wheel to make rockers for the chair, which made that chair rock and sit like no other.

One cold day in 1948 Dad had built a big fire in the fireplace and was sitting back in that envied rocking chair. The comfort of the rocker and the warmth of the fire soon lulled him into a peaceful slumber.

Also sleeping soundly in a crib right behind Dad's chair was Jean, Nellie's daughter who was about a year old. She quietly woke up, finished her bottle, and stood up in the crib right behind Dad's bald head.

We don't know why, but she picked up her bottle, which was a heavy glass bottle, and whammed it right on Dad's bald head. Jolted out of a deep sleep, he jumped straight up out of his chair and yelled, "What in the world was that?"

Everyone in the house heard him and ran to see what was wrong. When they got to the room, what they saw was Dad standing holding his head which had a big knot on it. Jean was just standing in her crib with a great big smile on her face.

It Ain't Funny!

In the fall of 1947 Edward and I got out of service at about the same time and started a house-painting business. Our first assignment was the Brogdon house in Gresham.

On our first day of painting, we were really making progress -- just painting away, but someone began to run some interference. Nellie and her daughter Carol, who was three years old, happened to be visiting Mrs. Brogdon while we painted.

Carol must have escaped notice of Nellie for a few minutes, but she was really noticed when she reappeared. She was covered with white paint. Her face was white, her hair was white, and her clothes were completely covered. A clown has never looked so funny.

Edward and I just bent over double laughing -- she was unrecognizable. Carol looked at us and said, "What you laughing about? It ain't funny."

This was not only our first but also the only house we painted. Edward decided that painting was not for him so he re-enlisted in the Navy and I went to work for Bernie Poston.

Do You Have Any Loose Oysters?

When Lance was growing up and maturing, he was the prankster of the family. He got more enjoyment out of pulling something on someone than any person I have ever known. After Dad bought the 1938 Chevrolet, a whole new world opened up for him, as his territory (for pranks) expanded.

A short while later he started dating Hanna Mae Evans from Salem. On one of their dates, he put Hanna Mae up to go into Bernie Poston's store and ask him if he had any "loose oysters." Bernie's reply to her was, "Yes, ma'am." She then told him, "You better try to catch them before they mess up everything in the store."

Bernie turned several different colors and was absolutely speechless. After that incident, he was always leery of his "loose oysters." In fact, he quit carrying them in his store.

Fishing, Chewing, and Spitting

When I was sixteen years old, I went fishing with Uncle "Bubba" in Round Lake on the Greenwood Farm. Round Lake covers about five acres and is surrounded by the Pee Dee River Swamp. It was completely encircled by big trees full of Spanish moss that draped out over the water.

In order to get down to Round Lake, we descended a steep hill about fifty feet. Uncle "Bubba" had steps cut out in the hill and kept a rope there to assist in getting down and back up the hill. Because it was so secluded and hard to get to, very few people fished in the lake. When we went there, we usually caught a nice bunch of fish.

On this particular day after a nice lunch and visit with the Greenwoods, Uncle "Bubba" and I went to the lake. Each of us had two canes, a can of worms and some crickets. We paddled out to the middle of the lake and just drifted and fished. The bluegill bream were eating up the bait and we were really catching fish and having fun.

Uncle "Bubba" was chewing Red Coon tobacco. He was just fishing and spitting and having the time of his life. I decided that I wanted to get in on some of that fun, so I asked him for a chew of that Red Coon.

I cut off a big whack of his tobacco, put it in my mouth, and started chewing and spitting. It wasn't long before I became nauseated and started throwing up.

That nausea put a stop to my fishing, chewing, and spitting, as all I did was hang over the side of the boat -- I was so sick.

It was good that we had already caught a bunch of fish because I didn't catch another fish; in fact, I didn't put my hook back in the water. This didn't break me from fishing, but it did break me from chewing as I've never taken a chew since that momentous day.

My Lord! What Was That?

At the mature age of five, I thought I was old enough and big enough to shoot firecrackers at Christmas just like my big brothers and sisters. Neither my parents nor my brothers and sisters thought I was ready for this, so they forbade me from doing this.

Since I didn't totally agree with them, I started looking for the opportunity to light one of those big noise makers. My big brothers seemed to get such a thrill out of seeing how long they could hold the firecrackers and how high they could throw them. I felt that I just had to experience this thrill.

The time finally presented itself when I found a two inch firecracker which had gone out before it blew up. The fuse was burned down about halfway, so you might say it had a short fuse.

I slipped a box of matches into my pocket and tried to figure out where to hide from my brothers and sisters so I could experience this thrill all by myself. The best place I could think of was under the house.

Well, I crawled up under the house far enough so no one could see me. I took out my firecracker and matches and carefully struck a match. Then I eased the short-fused firecracker to the match and...Boom! It blasted off before I could even think of throwing it.

The place that I had selected to accomplish this feat just happened to be directly under Dad's rocking chair, and he was sitting in it. All that was separating us was one thin layer of boards. The blast must have shook the floor and rattled the windows. Dad yelled out, "My Lord! what was that?"

Everyone rushed out of the house to see if we'd had an earthquake or been hit by a bolt of lightning. The sudden blast had really stunned me. At first I was blinded, my ears were ringing, and my right index finger was split open.

Needless to say, I had gotten everyone's attention, and believe me, I didn't touch firecrackers for several years after this incident. My parents didn't whip me. I'm sure they thought I had been punished enough.

Sunday Morning Ritual

Dad went to Sunday School every Sunday morning. He always studied his lesson religiously every week whether he was going to teach or not. He spent a lot of time on the preparation of the lesson.

There was one problem and that was that he didn't have a specific place to put his book after he finished studying. Often on Sunday morning he couldn't find his Sunday school book and this caused a crisis at our house. Everyone had to stop whatever he or she was doing to help him find that book.

He always thought someone else had moved it, misplaced it, or hid it. It always started out with, "Who's had my Sunday school book? Why would somebody move it from where I left it?" And then he would say, "Somebody just had to hide it and I can't understand why they would do that."

Meeting Grace

"Bunkus" was stationed in Houston, Texas in 1944 where he met and married Grace Nunn. After they were married, they came home and all the family got to meet Grace.

I was away at Pfeiffer College so I was not home to meet her. However, later that year "Bunkus" went to sea, so Grace came to visit us. By this time it was summer and I was home from school.

I was busy everyday -- plowing the fields and going barefooted. My feet had already gotten tough so it was uncomfortable to have to wear shoes.

Grace wrote that she would be coming by bus, and she told us when she would be arriving in Florence. There were only two people at home who could drive the car, Christmas and me. Dad decided that he could do without me easier than he could Christmas. Therefore, I was delegated to go meet my new sister-in-law (whom I'd never met) and bring her home.

So, I had to "scrub up," put on my best pair of overalls, and my only pair of shoes, which hurt my feet. The family all tried to tell me what Grace looked like, and, of course, I'm not going to repeat that part of their instructions.

When I finally made it to the bus station, Grace's bus had already arrived. I went through the station trying to pick out someone who looked like the description that I had been given.

I made no progress at all until I started asking the younger women, "Is that you, Grace?" One young lady said, "No, but for you I'll be Grace." Well, Grace spotted me before I spotted her and said, "You gotta be Paul."

She was nice, especially when she didn't say my big nose gave me away! Grace later told me she was sorry that my feet were hurting from the shoes. She said that she felt real pity for me as she really thought I had hemorrhoids.

Chapter 54
LOCAL TOBACCO CUSTOMS

Tobacco was the main money crop in the area during the 1920's, 1930's, and 1940's. Smoking was advertised and promoted as the "in-thing." There was no knowledge about it being injurious to your health. It created money for the grower and jobs for a lot of workers in the fields and in the factories.

People in our area promoted tobacco by using it in every form that was available. Most of the men involved in growing or processing it used it personally either by smoking, chewing, or dipping.

Women smoked very little back then, but a lot of them dipped snuff on the sly. Some of the older women smoked pipes, but you very seldom saw this unless the woman was up in her seventies or eighties.

Boys usually started smoking between the ages of twelve and fourteen. They mostly started with five-cent bags of Bull Durham or Golden Grain roll-your-own. Parents usually didn't sanction their son's smoking until he was sixteen to eighteen; so boys had to slip around to smoke until they became old enough for it to be accepted by their parents.

Smoking was absolutely a no-no for girls. Those girls who did smoke were talked about and looked on with disfavor. It was thought that if a girl would smoke that she would do other things that certainly weren't acceptable. The double standard was obvious, and there were no efforts to try to hide it or change it.

The practice of chewing was unsightly and unsanitary. Cuspidors were provided in stores, courtrooms, railroad stations, railcars, and most all public places. The big problem was that a lot of people did not use the cuspidors -- they just spit on the floor in the various buildings and on railcars.

Also, you would find big wads of chewed tobacco on the roads, streets, sidewalks, and most anyplace you walked. You really had to be on the lookout where you stepped, especially when you were barefooted.

When you talked to someone who was chewing, you had to

be very careful not to get too close or you might get sprayed with tobacco juice. People did not look at themselves in mirrors very often as there were not many mirrors at this time; so, it wasn't unusual to see a man with tobacco juice streaming down both sides of his mouth.

As long as I can remember, my Dad chewed. I always thought that he was a little more careful than most people we knew who chewed. I never saw the streams of juice running down the sides of his mouth.

The practice of smoking cigarettes, cigars, and pipes also presented some problems. Buildings were poorly ventilated, and when several people "lit-up," the air became filled with smoke -- causing much difficulty in breathing.

Smoke odor was always left in buildings, homes, or cars after someone had been smoking. This was a terrible odor and was hard to endure.

A lot of smokers accidentally burned down their homes, and some of these mishaps were caused by young boys hiding out to smoke. Some of them even set their barns on fire! Once a barn caught on fire, there was no way to put it out. Sadly many times the livestock also burned along with the barn.

The dipping of snuff was not as obnoxious as chewing. I guess the primary reason was due to the gender of the people who were doing it. Dipping was done mostly by women, and they were discrete and more careful. A lot of women actually tried to hide the fact that they were dipping.

My mother tried dipping for a while late in life, but she was never open about it or a regular user. I don't believe she ever really enjoyed it.

Some Common Brands of Tobacco:
Smoking

Cigarettes:	Pipe and Roll Your Own:
Lucky Strike	Prince Albert
Camel	Lord Calvert
Chesterfield	Half and Half
Old Gold	Sir Walter Raleigh
Cools	Bull Durham
Philip Morris	Golden Grain

Chewing Tobacco:

Brown Mule	Apple Sun Cure	Black Maria
Red Coon	Blood Hound	Days Work
Brown & Williamson	Work Horse	Beech Nut
Gentleman's Choice		

Cigars:
King Edward
Tampa Nugget
Hav-a-Tampa

Dipping:
Navy
Tube Rose
Society Sweet
Railroad Mills
Dental Scotch

Chapter 55

COMMON ILLNESSES AND THEIR CURES

Doctors were called in only if someone had a life-threatening illness or a woman was having a baby. By the early 1920's doctors had put away their horses and buggies and were driving cars.

Roads were awful, which made the driving of cars a very bumpy and hazardous way to travel. It was not unusual for a doctor to spend the night on the road with his car mired-up to the axle in mud, while his patient was suffering.

People had no money, so doctors had to wait until the end of the harvest season to receive their pay. Sometimes they were paid with chickens, eggs, milk, butter, or even pigs. Many times they just didn't get paid at all. These hardships caused doctors to have a pretty rough life.

The three doctors who were in our area were: Dr. W. H. Poston of Pamplico, Dr. A. G. Eaddy of Johnsonville, and Dr. J. W. Johnson of Kingsburg. These men were all perceived to be pretty good doctors, and I think they did well considering their limited knowledge and the medicines that were at their disposal.

Doctors were usually assisted by midwives in delivering babies. It was the responsibility of the doctor to get all new births recorded at the Court House. Births usually didn't get recorded if just the midwife delivered the baby.

If a doctor decided that a patient had an illness that required an operation, he sent the patient to McLeods Hospital in Florence, S.C. The hospital had to wait for its money just like the doctors. Medical insurance was unheard of back then.

Common Illnesses

malaria	mumps
influenza	measles
pneumonia (double & single)	whooping cough
grip	dropped pallet
fits	gout
dropsy	"can't help its"
high blood	"mulligrubs"
low blood	croup
rheumatism	seven-year itch
sugar blood	cholera marbus
pleurisy	scarlet fever

The three illnesses that people feared the most were influenza, pneumonia, and malaria. When one of these struck a family member, it was not unusual for the entire family to come down with it. It was not uncommon for two or three members of a family to die when an epidemic occurred.

Medicines Used as Common Cures

Quinine	Cod Liver Oil
Bitters	Groves Chill Tonic
Castor Oil	Black Draught
Epsom Salts	Calomel
Crazy Water Crystals	Sloan's Back-Ache Pills
Aspirin	Dr. Smith's Cough Drops
Mustard Plasters	Lard and sulphur (for the itch)
Asafetida Plasters	

Note! Every spring all children had to be "cleaned-out" by taking a round of Black Draught at night followed by Castor Oil the next morning. This was an unhappy experience for all participants and made becoming a grown-up something to look forward to.

If a child became irritable, the first thing a mother did was get the bottle of Castor Oil. Nothing helped a child straighten-up his contentiousness quicker than the sight of that bottle. Castor Oil was a parent's leverage for good behavior -- and it got results!

Commonly used medical remedies during the 1920's and 1930's

Settle The Stomach

Neutralize the excess acidity. Stop Dysentery. Avoid Indigestion. Use the old, faithful remedy. Ask your dealer for a 75c bottle of

Ante-Fermen

STOP HEADACHES RIGHT NOW

Take CAPUDINE is the answer. CAPUDINE contains several ingredients so proportioned and balanced to act together producing team work which provides such quick, easy relief.

CAPUDINE is liquid—already dissolved. It naturally takes hold quicker without upsetting the stomach. Can you afford not to take the best? Try it for periodic pains and cold aches also. 10c-30c-60c bottle.   Ad.7

Help Kidneys

If poorly functioning Kidneys and Bladder make you suffer from Getting Up Nights, Nervousness, Rheumatic Pains, Stiffness, Burning, Smarting, Itching, or Acidity try the guaranteed Doctor's Prescription Cystex (Siss-tex)—Must fix you up or money back. Only 75¢ at druggists.

Cystex

WHEN EYES ARE RED and inflamed from sun, wind and dust, you can allay the irritation with Dickey's Old Reliable Eye Wash At All Druggists
Price 25c   Dickey Drug Co., Bristol, Va.

Don't Read This

Unless you are interested in a medicine which has helped over 700,000 women and girls. Take it before and after childbirth, at the Change of Life, whenever you are nervous and run down. 98 out of 100 say, "It helps me!"

LYDIA E. PINKHAM'S VEGETABLE COMPOUND

SORES BOILS CUTS BURNS

Are Relieved Promptly By

GRAY'S OINTMENT

Used Since 1820   25c at Drug Stores

Chapter 56

DIFFERENT FOODS WE ATE

Florence County is in the lower part of South Carolina near the old rice fields of Charleston and Georgetown. Rice became a basic food in the diet of the residents of this area. We ate rice in one form or another everyday. It was cooked plain to be used with gravy, or it was cooked with chicken, pork, fish, or vegetables.

Cornmeal and grits were even more widely eaten than rice by the poorer people. Cornmeal was used for fritters, hoecakes, muffins, mush, and dumplings. We ate grits every morning and many times at night.

Flour was used for biscuits, pancakes, cakes. pies, and dumplings. Flour and cornmeal dumplings were cooked in the pot with chicken, other meats and vegetables.

We either raised, hunted, or fished for all of the meat we ate. We usually had some type of meat at every meal. We ate sausage, home-cured bacon, ham or fatback, chicken, and guineas.

Hogs, chickens and guineas were raised on the farm. Dad did a lot of hunting and fishing. This added a lot of meat for our table.

Hardly a week passed that we didn't have squirrel, possum, coon, venison, wild duck, wild turkey, or fish to help fill the hungry stomachs of the twelve people in our family. It really was not as much a sporting thing with my Dad as it was providing food for the family.

Sweet Potatoes

One of our main food crops was sweet potato. We planted big fields of them every year and always tried to grow enough to last through the whole year. At one time we tried curing them in the tobacco barn to keep from putting them in the earthen banks, but this was not successful.

Potatoes were always dug in the fall before the first frost. We let them dry for several days and then they were put in a dirt bank. This bank was made by piling up a big pile of potatoes, covering them with pine needles about eight inches deep, and then putting dirt on top to keep them from freezing.

A vent was made in the bank to keep the potatoes from sweating and rotting. When the weather warmed up in the spring, the potatoes had to be taken out of the bank or they would start sprouting.

Milk

Milk was another main staple in our diet. We usually kept two cows at all times so that we were assured of having one of them milking at all times. A cow would normally milk for about two years and then dry-up before she had another calf. So, for several months she would not be giving milk -- making two cows a necessity.

Wheat

After we moved to "Powell's Corner," we began to grow wheat. We planted enough wheat so that we would have flour to last all year. Dad shipped the wheat to Darlington to be made into flour about twice a year. The flour was then shipped back from Darlington to Poston by rail.

Corn

Corn was one of our main crops, and we always planted enough to last a year. This corn was used for feed for the livestock and for grits and meal for the table.

We had to shell corn every week and then take it to Poston to Mr. Douglas Furchess' gristmill for grinding into grits and meal. He didn't charge money for this grinding; he just took out a given number of quarts of corn per bushel for toll.

Vegetable Garden

A large garden was an absolute necessity for our family. We usually planted at least two acres with such vegetables as Irish potatoes, green beans, butter beans, squash, tomatoes, okra, peas, and others.

Spring and summer were very busy times for everyone but especially so for Mom. She tried to can enough vegetables to last through the winter, which was about three to four hundred quarts.

Field peas were planted in between the corn rows and were harvested in the fall. This provided us with green peas when all other vegetables were about gone. This also provided us with dried peas for the winter months.

The farm at "Powell's Corner" had large grape vines, a big pear tree, and several nice peach trees, so canning fruits and jellies was added to all the other canning that was already being done.

Hog Killing

Hog-killing and meat-curing were big ordeals at our house. We usually killed and cured-out about sixteen hogs a year. Most of the time we killed eight at the time.

Hogs that were to be killed were put in floored pens to keep them from eating acorns and other undesirable food. Then they were fed corn to get them real fat before butchering time.

We chose hogs that weighed about three hundred pounds each for butchering. When they were thought to be fat enough to kill, we waited for a very cold day so the meat would not spoil. Several neighbors would be asked to help because there was a lot of work to be done in a short time.

The hogs were shot with a rifle and then the throats were cut so they would bleed properly. Next, water was boiled in a big black pot over a fire in the yard and then put in a fifty-five gallon drum.

The drum was placed in the dirt at an angle so the hog could be slid in. His back end was always put in first until it was scalded; then that end would be taken out and his head was put in. When he was thoroughly scalded, he would be taken out and all the hair would be scraped off.

Next he would be hung up by his back legs -- up high enough so the head would not touch the dirt. He was then split open from the belly side and all the intestines, heart, liver, and "lites" were taken out.

The intestines were cleaned to use for sausage casings and for chitterlings. All the fat portions were cut, stripped off, and put in a big wash pot with fire under it. This process dried all the lard out of the fat. The lard was then put in cans and used for shortening throughout the year.

Cracklings, which were skins that had been cooked until they were crisp, were eaten and cooked in meal to make "cracklin" corn bread. The loose, lean meat was ground, seasoned, and made into sausage. Hams, shoulders, sides, and loins were salted down in a big wooden box, where they remained for several weeks.

After the meat had been in the salt long enough to be

considered preserved, it was taken out, washed off, and hung up in the smokehouse. Then the process of smoking began.

A fire was kept burning under the meat for several days. Only hickory wood was used, which gave the meat a hickory flavor. The smoking also made a coating on the meat. This coating helped keep insects off the meat and also helped keep the meat from spoiling.

After the smoking process was completed, the meat was coated with a paste made of flour, salt, black pepper, and other seasonings to keep out insects and hold the flavor in. Then the meat was wrapped in heavy paper, and, if everything was properly done and the seasons were normal, the meat would keep for at least a year.

All parts of the hog were used in one form or another. The feet were pickled. The head, ears, tongue, and other parts were made into sauce meat. Sausage was smoked along with the other meat that required smoking.

Poultry

We usually kept about a hundred chickens. This number of chickens allowed us to eat chicken often and provided all the eggs that were needed with some surplus ones to sell. People would always buy eggs, and they sold at a good price. All stores would take eggs in exchange for things in the store.

Chickens had to be watched very carefully day and night. Hawks and owls would get them in the daytime and coons, possums, and wildcats would kill them at night. Also, the biggest crime problem in our area that we had after prohibition was chicken stealing. Chicken houses had to be padlocked every night.

We kept a small flock of turkeys for a number of years, but, with all the moving we were doing, it became too much of a hassle -- turkeys just don't adjust to environmental changes very well.

Also, foxes became a problem as they killed the old and the young turkeys. During the thirties when there was a severe food shortage, turkeys were prime targets for hungry people to steal for food.

When turkeys were kept by a family, they were used for meat and for eggs. Turkey eggs are larger than hen eggs. They are not as tasty as hen eggs, but they are nutritious. There was very little demand for turkey eggs.

A small flock of guineas was always kept for food and for eggs. Guinea meat was dark, but it was excellent meat to eat. Guinea eggs were small and tasty; you could sell them for a little less than chicken eggs.

Guineas were hardy and smart. They usually outsmarted the foxes, coons, and possums. They slept in trees at night and they could fly real well. Therefore, they were not easily caught by varmints or by people. They were a profitable addition to our food supply.

Making Syrup

We grew some sugarcane for making syrup. The land in Florence County wasn't particularly suited for cane, but that didn't keep us from planting it.

Stalks used for seed the next spring were cut in the fall of the year. None of the leaves were stripped off, as the foliage was used to protect the joints through the winter. The "seed" canes were piled in a large pile and covered with pine needles and dirt to keep the stalks from freezing.

In the spring the sugarcane stalks were removed from the dirt bank, all foliage was stripped off, and the stalks were split from end to end. These split stalks were then put in a shallow furrow and covered lightly with dirt.

The shoots from the joints would come up and grow to about eight to ten feet tall. The diameter of the stalks was about two inches. When fully grown, the stalks were cut off at the ground with a large knife or machete. The leaves were stripped off and the cane was loaded on the wagon.

There were only a few cane mills in the area, so the cane had to be hauled several miles. "Uncle" Dan Davis and Mr. Luther Richardson were two of the more prominent mill operators.

When we went to "Uncle" Dan's mill, we were in for a treat. He gave us a sample of the cane juice to drink and a sample of the syrup he was cooking. Sometimes he might even have a biscuit, and he'd let us sop some of his specialty.

The machine that squeezed the juice out of the stalks was two large metal rollers pressing against each other in a vertical position. The rollers had gears on the top to make the rolls turn toward each other. There was a long wooden shaft about ten feet long that extended from the rollers.

A mule was hooked to the shaft and was driven round and round in a circle to power the rollers. The cane stalks were fed in the rollers, which squeezed the juice out. The juice ran into a tub at the bottom of the rollers.

The cane juice was taken to the cooking vat, which was a large pan about three feet wide, eight feet long, and eight inches deep. This vat had several segments that were divided by metal strips and were at different levels.

The vat was mounted on a brick furnace, which was fired by wood. The cane juice was poured in the first segment as soon as the furnace was hot. The juice would boil and foam and had to be dipped off. The thicker juice moved to the next segment.

This process would be repeated through several segments until the finished syrup came out in the last segment. "Uncle" Dan didn't charge for this operation -- he just took out a given number of quarts as toll based on the number of quarts cooked out. He was a master at this process.

He wouldn't take up the syrup until it tasted just right to him. When you got home with your syrup, you really had something good to eat.

Honey

For a number of years Dad kept honeybees, which provided an extra treat for us. However, all the moving we were doing created adverse conditions for beekeeping because bees just don't relocate well. So Dad gave his hives away. This slowed down his bringing in honey -- but it didn't stop it altogether.

I have mentioned before that Dad spent a lot of time in the swamps of the Pee Dee and Lynches Rivers hunting for game and searching for liquor stills. It wasn't unusual for him to find a colony of wild honeybees on one of these outings.

The one that I remember most vividly was in the early thirties while we were living on Mr. King's farm. Dad found this colony in the Pee Dee swamps on the Florence County side. He said that it was one of the biggest that he had ever seen. The hive was in the top of a huge hollow elm tree.

Most people would not have known what to do with a situation like this, but Dad did. He worked on his plans for about a week before he made his attack. He decided to wait until Saturday so that the three older boys would be out of school to help him.

The momentous day finally came and all the plans that were made ahead were ready to be put into action. Dad, Merrill, Lance, and "Bunkus" loaded the wagon with saws, axes, shovels, hoes, large ladles, several 50 pound lard cans, and several big pieces of tobacco canvas.

They hitched the mules to the wagon and departed on their journey. They had to stop the mules several hundred yards away from the hive so the bees would not sting them. The mules were tied to trees by ropes to keep them from leaving.

Now Dad and his sons wrapped up in tobacco canvas for protection from the bees. As "Bunkus" related, everyone had to be quiet and cautious as they approached the hive.

The first thing they did was saw the tree down. "Bunkus" said that when this happened thousands of bees just covered them. But, he said that the bees were unable to get in the canvas to sting them.

The next thing they did was saw off the top section of the tree that had the hive in it. The situation was becoming more critical by the minute as the bees were getting more and more angry.

Then they had to split the log so the honeycombs could be reached. By the time the log was split, the whole area was a mass of flying bees. The canvas, which was protecting them from the bees, was so fully covered with bees that their vision was drastically impaired.

The intruders (meaning my Dad and sons) did not give up as they struggled until they accomplished what they went there to do -- and that was to get the honey.

When Dad and his sons got home, they were weary and tired. They had some stings, but they weren't hungry. There were several 50 pound lard cans full of honeycombs with honey dripping everywhere.

Now the job was to boil and squeeze the honey from the honeycombs. When the separating process was completed, we had several gallons of honey and a lot of beeswax. The entire day's work meant that we had enough honey to last for about two years and this greatly enhanced our meager diet.

I could just look at the expression on both Dad's and Mom's

faces and feel the satisfaction that they felt in knowing that they had achieved a feat which their children would enjoy for a long time.

There was so little that I knew about bees and honey-making at that time. It was impossible for me to really appreciate the entire process. For example, I didn't know that there were three types of bees in each colony, the queen, drones, and workers, and that each of them have different functions.

A large colony of bees will have up to 100,000 workers and according to Dad this particular colony had more. A worker will collect less than a quarter of a pound of honey during its lifetime.

A worker flies about twelve miles an hour going to get nectar from flowers and taking it to the hive. To make a pound of honey, a worker probably has to fly over 12,000 miles.

The only purpose of the queen is to lay eggs. The purpose of the drones is to fertilize the eggs and the workers make all the honey.

Berries

During the late spring we went out in the woods and looked for and picked huckleberries, wild blueberries, and blackberries. This was done every year.

This was a time of the year when red bugs (chiggers) were very bad, as they would get on you and just about eat you up. The itching these little varmints caused was unbearable.

To prevent this problem or at least to help the situation, we took strips of cloth and soaked them in kerosene. Then we tied the strips around our legs and arms to try to keep the red bugs from getting to the rest of our bodies.

Huckleberries and blueberries were canned to be used for future cobblers. Blackberries were used to make jelly and jam.

Things We Had To Buy

The things that we had to buy were rice, salt, sugar, seasonings, kerosene, fatback, butt meat, canned salmon, and clothing.

Normal Dishes
1. grits and gravy
2. cracklings (dried pork skins)
3. pot liquor and corn bread

4. chitterlings (hog intestines)
5. pork backbone and rice
6. pork neckbone and rice
7. chicken and rice
8. fried chicken
9. Hopping John (field peas and rice cooked together)
10. Jumping Jack (butter beans and rice cooked together)
11. lima beans
12. black-eyed peas
13. pine bark stew (catfish, pork, tomatoes, rice, onions, and seasonings all cooked together)
14. possum baked with sweet potatoes
15. turnips and turnip greens
16. fried sow belly or hog jowls
17. wild turkey, venison, wild duck, and squirrels
18. fish
19. sweet potato pudding
20. corn dodgers (balls of corn meal dropped in hot grease -- this was eaten with fried fish)
21. tea cakes and milk
22. Pepsi Cola's and cinnamon buns (a delicacy enjoyed on special occasions)

There were no thoughts about calories and cholesterol -- the only considerations were tastiness and the filling of the stomach.

Chapter 57

COLLOQUIAL DIALECT

People who lived in lower Florence County had their own colloquial dialect, and this seemed to be more prevalent in my Dad's family than in my Mom's. This was probably due to the fact that Grandpa Greenwood migrated from Marlboro County, where the dialect was different. Postons had lived in the lower Florence County area for about 160 years.

The educational level of the Greenwoods appeared to be a little higher than the Postons. They were able to obtain more schooling.

Usually when R was followed by A, the R was strong (as in car or Carolina). Likewise, R that was followed by an O was always weak (as in poe for pore or boe for bore). The letter T was never pronounced if it came before an H (as in de for the, day for they, or dem for them).

A lot of words were shortened by leaving a syllable off (for example, bacco for tobacco, mater for tomato, and tater for potato). An unnecessary U worked its way into a lot of words (such as quar for car, guarden for garden, puert for pert, and buer for beer).

Some of the conversations went like this:

Yisdiddy I ailed all day — meaning yesterday I was sick all day.

He fetched a bucket of warter from de well—meaning he brought a bucket of water from the well.

He got drunk and walked rat true de glass doe — meaning he became inebriated and walked right through the glass door.

He was the fust one to ketch de flu —meaning he was the first one to catch the flu.

Colloquial Words

Colloquial	Correct	Colloquial	Correct
fetch	bring	fetched	brought
brung	brought	yisdiddy	yesterday
ain't	are not	yawl	you all
tater	potato	mater	tomato

208

lasses	syrup	dough	though
true	threw, through	nuff	enough
lef	left	Mis	Mrs.
possum	opossum	coon	racoon
bacco	tobacco	ketch	catch
chimley	chimney	wang	wing
fust	first	Satday	Saturday
guin	going	salit	salad
hongry	hungry	thusty	thirsty
PO-lease	police	poke	bag
done	did	run	ran
et	ate	poe	poor
quar	car	purty	pretty
cooter	turtle	stob	short peg
swinge	singe	tuck	took
wid	with	de	the
fur	for	bub	bulb
close	clothes	fard	forehead
chawed	chewed	puert	like
neck	next	dinky	unusual
bile	boil	ball	boil
buer	beer	year	ear
nigh	near	atter	after
ast	ask	tote	carry
furrner	foreigner	guarden	garden
kilt	killed	least	smallest
puney	not feeling well	least	youngest
lightard	firestarter wood	naw	no
near'bout	close	okry	okra
shine	home brew	toreckly	soon
breckfus	breakfast	bum	bomb
toleble	feeling alright	dip	use snuff
pint	point	infernal	a curse word
ranch	wrench	sot	a drunk
plak	play like	git	get
doe	door	flow	floor
scrawny	small	triflin	a deadbeat person

slack	unkept person	heifer	a young girl with shady character
ail	to be sick	warter	water
chunk	throw	chunked	threw

Colloquial Phrases:

I ain't got none	I don't have any
stick in the mud	a contrary person
catty wampus	eschewed
chop cotton	to hoe & thin cotton
lug tobacco	first cropping of tobacco
cuss fight	a war of words
I gotta	I have to
clod desolver	a very big rain
frog strangler	a very, very big rain
cloud bust	a sudden downpour
high flutin	a stuck-up person
bad mouth	to talk about a person
lay-by bacco	last time tobacco is plowed
cain't hardly do	very difficult to do
stir about	to be up and going
hard-up	having a difficult time
hunker down	to bend over
pussle-gut	a person with a big stomach
too big for his britches	a young person doing something he shouldn't do
show nuff	sure enough
raise sand	doing a lot of fussing
pay no mind	doesn't pay attention
wrench-off	to wash off
It's time enough to go!	there's plenty of time left before you have to go.
down in the mouth	not feeling well
no count	not well
Pleg Take It!	cursing phrase
Dad Burn!	cursing phrase
Infernal!	cursing phrase
Dog-gone!	cursing phrase

Hell fire!	cursing phrase
Dad gum it!	cursing phrase
John Brown!	cursing phrase
beat'inest thing	a most unusual thing
stove-up	when you have sore muscles
rat chair	right here
you don't have sense enough to bell a buzzard	you are not too bright
It's tight as Dick's hatband!	it's real tight.
a fly sally	a fast woman
you dish it out with a shovel while I rake it in with a spoon	the out-go is higher than the income.
I ain't know	I don't know

Chapter 58

LOCAL SUPERSTITIONS

Through the years people in the lower part of Florence County built up their own list of superstitions. These superstitions developed into a religion to some of them.

If you didn't believe in these notions, something bad would probably happen to you, such as being struck by lightning or going straight to hell. During the time we were growing up, we were told about these false beliefs over and over — not by our parents but by friends and neighbors.

It took a long time to get all of these superstitions out of our minds. Even today I do not like for a black cat to cross the road in front of me -- particularly if he's going to the left. Some of the superstitions were:

1. A black cat crossing the road in front of you meant bad luck. If the cat went to the left, this meant worse luck than if he went to the right.
2. If you turned a chair around on one leg in the house, you would have bad luck.
3. Thirteen was an unlucky number.
4. If you walked under a ladder, you would have bad luck.
5. Friday, the thirteenth, was a very unlucky day.
6. If your nose itched, someone was talking about you.
7. A whistling woman was not a lady.
8. If you carried a rabbit foot in your pocket, you would have good luck.
9. If you carried a buckeye in your pocket, this would bring you good luck.
10. If you didn't get off the bed on the same side that you got on, you would have bad luck.
11. The first time you went into a house, if you didn't leave from the same door that you entered, you would have bad luck.
12. If you spit on your bait when fishing, the fish would bite.
13. Drinking coffee would turn growing white children dark.

14. If you could kiss your elbow, you would turn into the opposite sex.
15. A cat had nine lives.
16. If you ate fish and drank milk, you would get sick.
17. If you kept goats, your hogs would not get the cholera.
18. If you had a wart, you should pick it and make it bleed; then put the blood on a grain of corn and feed the corn to the chickens; then your wart would go away.
19. If you went to bed mad, the bogeyman would get you.

Chapter 59

GHOSTS?.... OR HAUNTS?.... OR WHAT?

During the thirties and forties, a lot of people believed in ghosts and haunts. This was much more prevalent in black communities than it was in white communities. The children in my family worked side by side with black people on the farm, so we heard these scary tales over and over again.

Black people were deadly afraid of dead people. They were even more afraid of white dead people than black dead people. You never talked to a black person long before the subject of ghosts or haunts came up.

They had just seen Uncle Dan's ghost, or Aunt Lou had spoken to them the night before. I heard this so much until I began to believe in these strange things.

Let me be first to say that several unexplained phenomenon's did happen. Some people might say that these appearances were figments of our imagination. That is all right for those who have had none of these weird experiences to see, hear and believe.

As I have said before, my Grandmother Greenwood lived in a big three story house that was built in 1841. It was on the Old River Road about eight miles south of the Bigham Place.

The Bigham Place was always referred to as a landmark. It was here that the entire family of Bigham's were slain in 1921 -- with the exception of one son, Edmund.

Edmund was tried for all these murders and was convicted. He spent about forty years in prison; he never admitted his guilt. This was a much talked about crime.

People in the area had a real fear that Edmund would escape from prison and come back to murder again. There were tales about a number of lynchings that had occurred up and down the Old River Road.

There was a barn across the road from Grandma's house that housed about 24 mules and horses. There was a tale about a horse thief trying to steal a horse. He was caught and killed on the spot.

There was a tale about a chicken thief getting caught with live chickens that belonged to his master. He was lynched.

All these tales about events of bygone years did create a lot of suspense. During my early years two black men who lived on Grandma's farm and who I knew well were killed by other black persons.

Always when I spent nights at Grandma's house, if I didn't go right off to sleep or covered my head, I always heard unexplained noises.

The real experience came when Grandma died. The house was full of expensive furniture, and I'm sure there was some money hidden around. The family was afraid to leave the house unattended while they went to the funeral. So, they left David, my eight year old brother, Rowena, my thirteen year old sister, and ten year old me to look after the house.

After everyone left, we sat in the living room and played the self-playing piano that Grandma loved so dearly. After sitting quietly for a while, we began to hear strange noises. All three of us heard sounds like footsteps, doors opening and closing, water pouring, and a slight moan.

Well, we did not stay in that house one moment longer. We did our "house caretaking" in the yard as this seemed more prudent at the time. Even in the yard, we still heard some noises, which gave us an incentive to move further out toward the road. That is where we did our "house caretaking" until the family returned from the funeral.

When they came up, we rushed to tell them what we had heard. They checked the entire house and found nothing out of place. **So I ask, "What was it?"**

Once when we lived on Mr. King's farm, an unexplained event occurred. One evening after eating supper, Mom prepared all the small children for bed.

We had only one kerosene lamp, and the older children were using it to do their studying. So, Mom took us pre-school children to the dark bedroom and tucked us in bed. Before she left us, she looked out the window and called us to come as she wanted to show us something.

There was a big oak tree that stood about twenty-five feet

from the window. When we got to the window, there appeared to be a white envelope attached to the tree about four feet from the ground. This envelope was waving. We could see this in the dark as the moon was shining.

Mom sent Merrill and Lance, our oldest brothers, out to see what it was. When they got out to the tree, the apparent envelope was gone; they could not find a thing.

That night Mom's Aunt Jane died. Mom was very close to her aunt. Again I ask, **"What could that apparent object on the tree have been?"**

In the spring of 1933 we were living in "The Backwoods" on Mrs. Mollie Johnson's farm. Mom was cooking dinner on a wood-burning cook stove. There was a big fire going in the stove so the stove was very hot.

All of a sudden, she started hearing something that sounded like bells ringing and the sound was coming from the stove. We were in another room, so she called us to come and listen.

We did listen to this sound for a few moments, and then it faded away. That same day Aunt Bertha Poston died. Aunt Bertha was Uncle Zack Poston's wife. They didn't have any children and we were all very close to them. Now tell me, **"Where did the sound of those bells come from?"**

We lived in "Powell's Corner" for about five years. A number of unexplained incidents happened during these years. There was a large field across a swamp in front of the house that we lived in. This field was called "The Crappy Field." In the middle of the field there was an old tenant house which was probably seventy-five years old.

We built a tobacco barn near the old tenant house. Several tenants moved in the house, but they never stayed very long. Each of them said the house was haunted.

When I was fourteen years old and old enough to cure tobacco at night, I had to stay by myself at the barn. This was for my four hour shift until someone relieved me. Very few nights went by that I didn't hear all kinds of strange noises in that house. My hair would feel like it was standing straight up, and the top of my head would tingle. My little feet wanted to take me home, but I was too scared to run.

First, I didn't want my family to know that I was scared because I was a "big boy now." Also, I didn't want the ghosts (if there were any out there) to know that I was scared because I felt they could run faster than I. Now understand this, I was not the only person who heard these noises; however, if Dad ever heard any, he would not admit it.

Christmas, one of our longtime loyal sharecroppers, absolutely would not stay at that barn to cure tobacco. We had two other barns near the house that we lived in, so Dad assigned those barns to him.

The house in "The Crappy Field" was not the only place that was feared. A lot of people believed the swamp between our house and "The Crappy Field" was spooked.

There was a nice sandy road going through the swamp to "The Crappy Field." The sand was whiter than what you found on the beach. There were a lot of huge rattlesnakes and water moccasins in the swamp that crawled out into the warm sandy road to sun. We always had to be on the alert for those venomous reptiles.

With those creatures in mind, one was already edgy before going through that dreaded swamp. We children had heard of Big Swamp, Little Swamp, Boggy Swamp, and many others, but we named this one "Booger Swamp."

There were tales of people who had lost their lives in quick sand reportedly in this swamp. None of us ever explored far enough into the dense bushes, weeds, and briers to see if there really was quick sand there.

At night there was always a lot of hoots, screeches, and howls from night birds, owls, and wild animals. These sounds were frightening.

The thing that I could never understand was the fact that as you walked through the swamp, you walked into currents of hot air. If you stopped, currents of warm air passed on by.

When I went through the swamp at night by myself and felt one of these warm currents, there just wasn't anyway I could take it standing still. I'd take off running as fast as my feet would take me. I couldn't tell anyone because they would have called me a "scaredy-cat."

During the five years that we were in "Powell's Corner," we

lived in a big two-story house that was built in the 1880's by Mr. John Gregg Woodberry. Mr. Woodberry was a prominent citizen of the area during the late nineteenth and early twentieth centuries.

He was active during the forming of Florence County and was a County Commissioner for several years. He loved his farm and home more than life itself, but he had lost both due to indebtedness in the early depression years of the thirties.

Mr. Pete Cornwell, his son-in-law, paid the note off and assumed control of the plantation. Mr. and Mrs. Woodberry were forced by Mr. Cornwell to move to Savannah, Georgia with the Cornwells so they could be cared for.

After he moved out, very much against his wishes, he could not talk about his land and house without crying. After 70 years he had a difficult time breaking away from what he had loved and labored for.

As I've said before, Mr. Cornwell contracted with my Dad in 1934 to be a caretaker and sharecropper for him on this plantation. Mr. Woodberry became very fond of us as he could see that we were taking good care of his land and home. He visited us every chance that he got, which was as often as he could get someone to bring him. We became very devoted to him.

One night in the fall of 1936 I was sleeping upstairs. I woke up and had to relieve my bladder, which was most unusual for a child. Back then you disciplined yourself to go all night without relief because there was no indoor plumbing.

Well, I decided to go downstairs and out to the path to take care of the situation. As I went down the stairs, I met what looked like a man. It was about the right size and shape of a male person. I stopped and reached out to touch what I was seeing, but I could feel nothing. I had already asked who it was but got no response. I hurriedly went by whatever it was and it disappeared.

I have to admit that I did wake up a few people in my house, and they tried to assure me that everything was alright.

The next day we learned that Mr. Woodberry had died. I don't know what it was that I saw. At the time I was only ten years old, but I do know that I was awake and not dreaming. **"What do you think?"**

Later in life when I was an adult, an unexplained

phenomenon occurred. The Greenwoods were still living in the big three-story house. On December 28, 1954 Aunt Alma and Uncle "Bubba" went to bed at their regular time.

Uncle "Bubba" said that before he went to sleep a white dove flew in the house and lit on the foot of his bed. He said that it just sat there for a few moments and then flew away.

That same night my Dad died in the hospital at Florence. **So,...... "Where did that dove come from? How did it get in the house? Where did it go?"**

Chapter 60

THEY SAY IT REALLY HAPPENED

Picking Chickens

One day Johnny Peterson was absent from school. This created some concern because Johnny hardly ever missed a day. The next day the teacher inquired as to why Johnny was out of school the day before. Johnny said, "We had an accident and I had to pick and clean chickens all day."

The teacher asked, "Johnny, what in the world happened?" Johnny said, "We woke up and the chickens were raising cane like something was about to get them. My Pa got his double-barreled shotgun off the wall, loaded it, and took off to the chicken house."

Johnny continued, "Now Pa didn't take time to put on his pants, and he was wearing long-handled underwear with a split in the back. He eased up to the chicken house and slowly opened the door. After turning on the flashlight, he started looking around to see what was disturbing the chickens. At that very moment Old Blue, our coon hound, came up from behind and "cold-nosed" my Pa. Pa yelled, pulled both triggers, and killed twenty-five chickens!"

Going to Shave

Mr. Jackston did a lot of coon and possum hunting; he would be gone several nights during a week. He was married, but he and his wife did not have any children.

One cold night when he was hunting, the dogs just weren't finding any coons or possums, so he decided to cut the hunt short at about nine o'clock. A normal hunt would go on until midnight or later. When he arrived at his house, it sort of caught Mrs. Jackston by surprise.

A few minutes after he came in and got settled, he went to the mantle and got his straight razor and started sharpening it. This went on for several minutes, and Mrs. Jackston was really getting nervous. She asked him, "What are you going to do?" He said, "I'm going to shave if there ain't nobody in them shoes under your bed."

Broke Arm Eating Breakfast

Billy's brother Joey showed up at school one day without little Billy. The teacher asked Joey where Billy was. Joey said, "Billy was eating breakfast and had a bad accident and broke his arm."

This really raised the curiosity of the teacher — she was wondering how anyone could break his arm eating breakfast. Joey said, "Billy was climbing a persimmon tree to get persimmons for breakfast when he slipped, fell, and broke his arm."

No But I Ain't Lost!

One day little Jack Arnold was walking on Highway 51 on his way to the store in Kingsburg. A man came by in a long black chauffeur driven La Salle with a New York license.

The car stopped and the man asked little Jack if he could get to Georgetown on Highway 51. Jack looked up and down the road and meditated for a few minutes and then replied, "I don't know."

The man then asked, "Well, can I get back to Florence on this road?" Jack looked both ways, scratched his head and said, "I just don't know."

The man being completely exasperated by now said, "Little fellow, you don't know much, do you?" Jack had a quick comeback and said, "No sir, but I ain't lost."

Don't Come Home on Furlough

During World War I John Hartsell, a soldier, was in training at Fort Jackson. It was customary for a soldier to get a delay in route when his basic training was completed and before he was shipped overseas to go into battle.

John wrote his mother and told her that he was coming home on furlough. His mother quickly wrote him back and said, "Son, please don't come on furlough; take the train because furloughs are just too dangerous."

Town Drunk

Charles Brownly was considered to be the town drunk of Poston. Nobody could ever remember him having worked a day in his life, but somehow he was always able to get something to drink.

One Friday night there was an event at Trinity School.

Charles was there even though he was "high as a Georgia pine" from drinking moonshine liquor.

To get to Poston from Trinity School, you had to pass Trinity Methodist Church. On this particular night it was pouring down rain, and when Charles got ready to go home, he had to walk.

When he got to the church, he decided to take a short cut through the cemetery. He was taking a familiar path, as he went this way quite often. But something happened the day before that Charles was not aware of.

A new grave had been dug and left open. It already had several inches of rain water in it. The night was dark and Charles was unaware of this big hole and stepped right in -- and down he went.

It scared the living daylights out of him, plus it jarred him real good. After getting over the jolt, he started scrambling, scratching, climbing, and jumping .... trying to get out.

While all this was going on, a voice came from the corner of the grave saying, "You might as well give up." This was probably from an apparent earlier trapped drunk.

With this sudden incentive, Charles cleared the top of the grave with one leap and didn't stop running for a half mile. When he finally stopped, he was completely sober. And it was said that his alcoholism was completely cured.

Damn A Church With One Door and Two Windows

"Uncle" Joe Whippet was getting on in years and his arthritic back got worse and worse. It got so bad that he was absolutely doubled over, and there was no way he could straighten up. His health continued to fail and he passed away when he was seventy-seven.

Some of the poor folks in and around Poston couldn't afford an undertaker during those days. So, the neighbors would build a pine box, clean and dress the corpse, and have a wake (sometimes for a week). Then they hauled the corpse to the graveyard for burial.

"Uncle" Joe gave them some real problems because he was drawn double and they couldn't get his body to lay straight in the casket. They took ropes and tied them to nails in the casket to hold him straight. So it looked like the problem was solved. Only a very few people knew they had to do this.

When the wake was over, they hauled the corpse by mule and wagon over the rough roads to the little church. This little church had huge oak trees laden with Spanish moss in the churchyard.

This happened in the month of July and the weather was really hot. Everyone was sweating including the preacher as he shouted out his message. The brothers and sisters were shouting, "Amen."

The preacher shouted, "When Gabriel blows his horn, "Uncle" Joe's 'gonna' rise again." The people were very enchanted with what the preacher was saying. They didn't realize that a bad cloud was coming up.

All of a sudden, there was a loud clap of thunder. The ropes broke and "Uncle" Joe slowly raised up in a sitting position. Panic set in; people were scrambling to get out of the door or out of the two windows. They were falling over one another and blocking the one door and windows.

The preacher was having more trouble than anyone else getting out, and in the process he yelled out, "Damn a church with just one door and two windows!"

Pick A Place.... We'll Make A Door

There was a small group of church people who branched off from the regular Methodist Church at Trinity and started a new church. To begin with there very few differences between the services of the two churches, but this changed as new people with different ideas came into the church. Some of the new members began to do some right strange things.

Once a visiting preacher came to preach a revival service. The first night he got carried away with his preaching. He was preaching about the evils of sin and the fact that every person at church that night was going to hell -- if they didn't repent.

The people started shouting and dancing all over the church. There was standing room only as the church was packed. About the time all this commotion was at the height of a frenzy, one of the good brothers took out a box of rattlesnakes. A few of the members had begun snake-handling and worshipping.

This box of snakes started a sudden overpowering fright (the likes that had never been witnessed in Florence County). This place was a madhouse; the doors and windows were people jammed.

The visiting preacher asked the person who had been assigned as his helper, "Where is the back door?" His helper told him that they didn't have a back door. He yelled back at his helper and told him, "Pick a place where you want a backdoor 'cause I'm fixing to make one."

The K.K.K's Little Reminder

It was said that William Laster was a no-good, lazy, trifling, wife-cheating drunk. He had a nice wife and six children, but he made no real effort to support his family. He would not work in a pie factory. His wife had a real struggle trying to keep food on the table for the children.

There was also the problem of clothes for the family and a house to live in. His wife was going through all this while William was staying out at night drinking and "catting" around with women.

The K.K.K. warned him a time or two, but it didn't do any good. Then one night the hooded vigilantes went to his house, picked him up, and carried him for a little ride.

When they got far enough in the woods to where he wouldn't be heard, they stopped the car. They jacked up one of the back wheels of the Model A Ford and tied a leather strap to the jacked-up wheel.

They took the back fender off so the strap would have plenty of room to move. With this done, they took blindfolded William and tied him face down on the dirt behind the Model A. His buttocks was placed so the strap would hit it every time the wheel turned over.

They put the Model A in reverse and revved-up on the engine. It was literally hell for Old William; they absolutely wore him out. It took the hide and some meat off his behind.

But, this 'work over' made a believer out of him! When he got over his punishment, he was a changed man. It was said that he quit drinking, stopped his womanizing, started sharecropping to support his family, and went to church every time the church doors were open.

Chapter 61

A TAP ON THE SHOULDER

When I was about sixteen years old, I thought I was being called into the ministry. I had the receptivity and the desire to become a minister. Nothing would have made my parents happier than for me to enter this calling as my chosen profession. They were so pleased when I made my wishes known.

I still had some reservations because all of the preachers that I had talked to said that I would know when God called me into his service. These different preachers indicated that God would tap me on the shoulder or send a messenger to tell me of these things.

Mom, Dad, and Rev. Sherwood Davis made arrangements for me to go to Pfeiffer Junior College at Misenheimer, N.C. to begin my study for the ministry. I finished high school when I was sixteen, so I entered college when I had just turned seventeen.

Financially, my parents weren't able to send me to college and I knew that, but they wouldn't listen to me. Pfeiffer had a program whereby you could work as many as twenty-one hours a week to cover your $90 tuition for one semester. All books and lab fees were extra.

The college credited you twenty-five cents an hour for each hour you worked. Mom and Dad felt that, if I worked the twenty-one hours a week, they could make the rest of the requirements — with the help of money I had saved working at Bernie Poston's store.

Preparations were started for me to go to Pfeiffer in September of 1943. We shopped around and bought some clothes. I even got two pairs of shoes. This was the first time I had ever had two pairs of shoes at the same time.

I borrowed a suitcase from Uncle "Bubba" because I couldn't afford both new clothes and a new suitcase. Mom got my clothes washed, ironed and packed ready for me to go.

The time for my departure was rapidly approaching, and the closer it came, the colder my feet got. Remember, I had never been out of South Carolina, and the only times I had ever been away from home at night were when I went to Grandma's or camped while hunting or fishing.

The day of apprehension (when I was to depart for Pfeiffer) arrived in early September. I was scared, and, if there had been a graceful way for me to back out, I surely would have done it. At seventeen I felt that I had to grow up and act like a man, so I tried very hard not to show my true feelings.

Reverend Sherwood Davis and Dad took me in Preacher Davis' pretty green 1941 Chevrolet car. Dad and Preacher Davis were busy talking and I was somewhat in a daze. I just answered any questions they asked with short answers.

The distance to the college was about 150 miles and the speed limit was 35 miles per hour, so it took about five hours to get there. Even at that speed, we got there too quickly. I was hoping it would take all day or maybe longer.

When we got to the State Line, I was disappointed; I expected flashing lights and blowing horns and for things to look and feel differently in North Carolina. Nothing happened -- this was a big letdown.

When we got to Pfeiffer, we rode through the little campus and stopped in front of Washington Hall, which was the dormitory for men. We unloaded my things on the front steps and Dad and Rev. Davis just left me standing there.

As they left, they wished me well and told me goodbye. At that moment Dad was the quietest I had ever seen him. It was not until I carried my son, Wayne, off to college and left him that I really knew what he felt that day at Pfeiffer.

I had a feeling of desolation and desperation, but these feelings quickly evaporated. I met and was befriended by other students who were also very despondent. Getting settled in at Pfeiffer was a pleasant transition. Students and faculty were most friendly, helpful, and supportive.

During the school years 1943 and 1944, the total student body consisted of 160 students (136 girls and 24 boys). Most of the boys were ministerial students who had either not reached eighteen or had a ministerial deferment from the service.

The school was very Christian-oriented and the setting could not have been better for someone wrestling with and longing to be called by God into His service. I listened constantly for God to call me, to touch me, to tell me what He wanted me to do.

The fact that preachers had told me over and over that I

would know if God wanted me in His service weighed so heavily in my mind. I just kept trying to follow the teachings of Jesus and the will of God as I knew it.

College life was a new and broadening experience for an impressionable seventeen year old boy, who (as the old saying goes) "wasn't dry behind the ears yet." Being associated with that many pretty girls was a pleasant part of the college life.

I had several close friends but just would not let my relationships get past that stage. In no way was I ready for any commitment other than my chosen future profession.

Pfeiffer maintained some very strict policies with regard to character-building, dating, etc. There was no smoking permitted on campus. Absolutely no use of alcohol was allowed. Attendance was required at both Sunday school and worship services.

Boys and girls could not hold hands, hug, or show any emotions on campus. They were allowed to walk across campus together but could not stop; they had to keep moving. Boys could not enter the girls' dormitory at any time; they could only call for the girls at the front door.

No telephone calls between dormitories were permitted. Dating was allowed on Sunday nights only and that was in the parlor of the men's dormitory with a minimum of two chaperons.

Needless to say, there were neither outbreaks of regularly transmitted diseases nor any shotgun weddings. Some of the boys did accuse the college of putting saltpeter in the water to suppress their sexual drive, but there surely wasn't any truth to this.

The work schedule for students went very well. The school had a large farm, which consisted of about 250 acres of farmland. The farm also had a flock of chickens, a herd of dairy cattle, and a herd of swine. The farm produced all the eggs, milk, and pork that were needed and a lot of vegetables.

At the beginning of the year, the farm manager allowed the working students to work in the various areas for a few days. Then the different supervisors selected the ones they wanted to work for them.

I was selected by the dairyman to help in the dairy. In fact I learned later that he told the manager that if he would give me to him, he wouldn't want anyone else. I'm sure my farming background was the contributing factor in that decision.

We kept an average of eighteen cows milking at a time. The herd was all Holsteins and those cows gave a lot of milk. We had electric milk machines, but there were times when the power went off and we'd have to milk the cows by hand.

One time the dairyman took a few days vacation and left me in charge to do the milking. Of course, the power went off during an electrical storm, but the cows didn't know it ... they still had to be milked.

I had to milk eighteen cows by hand, which took several hours. My hands were completely exhausted from pulling cow teats. By the way, I did miss some classes!

The school year was really a pleasant experience for me. For one thing, I learned how to hitchhike. I just carried my suitcase with the college name on it and wore a little freshman rat cap with Pfeiffer on it. Back then travelers would not pass up college students or servicemen. Consequently, I never rode the bus; my traveling was done by using my thumb.

Academically I got along well, so Johnsonville High must have done a pretty good job preparing me for college. If your grades were satisfactory, the college would let you work more than the twenty-one hours -- if they needed you. During the last semester I worked so many hours that after a total accounting they owed me money instead of me owing them.

As the year ended, I had gained many new friends. It was real tough leaving them and heading back home to the farm.

The one thought that kept bothering me was that I still was not definitely certain about my call into the ministry. I kept praying as it was something that I wanted to do; I kept trying to do what I thought was God's will; I tried to follow the teachings of Jesus Christ. In my own way, I kept listening for a call -- for a signal -- for a sign -- that would signify God's intent for me.

The summer of 1944 was spent on the farm plowing Betty (my mule), gathering tobacco, curing tobacco, picking hot pepper, and all the other chores that came along. When August 20 rolled around, I had to register for the draft because I had reached my eighteenth birthday.

The time had come to make a decision. If I was going back to Pfeiffer the next year, I had to get a ministerial deferment. Dad and I talked about it; he wanted me to get the deferment, but I just didn't feel right about it.

I thought about my brothers and my friends who were fighting in the war, and I thought about the ones who had already lost their lives. I pondered on a poem I had learned in the sixth grade entitled "The Country's Call" by Thompson:

> "Give me men to match my mountains;
> Men to match my inland plains;
> Men with empires in their purpose;
> Men with eras in their brains.
>
> Give me men to match my prairies;
> Men to match my inland seas;
> Men whose thoughts shall pave a pathway;
> Up to ampler destinies."

Then I thought about my parents and family who were making so many sacrifices for me, and there was no question about what I should do. I opted not to return to school but to make myself available for the draft into the Service of My Country.

The chance to join the fighting forces of the United States came within a few months, and my tour of duty lasted two years. My life went in a different direction after my years of serving in the army.

Now I had the GI Bill, which paid for my college tuition, so I went to Wofford College in Spartanburg, South Carolina. I received an AB degree in Business Administration. The profession I chose as my life's pursuit was in textiles. I had a successful and very fulfilling career in textiles, but there was always something missing in my life.

I know now that God was calling me, but I didn't know how to discern His call. His creating a desire in me to want to be a minister was one of His calls.

His letting me be born into a family which instilled the desire to do the Lord's will and follow the teachings of Jesus was His blessing in preparation for that call.

The encouragement from family and friends was signals and signs that I did not read. The ease by which I got into college at a time when poor people didn't go to college was just a sign from God for me to "keep-on-keeping-on."

I know now that God uses other people and circumstances to convey His wishes to His people. I know that He won't physically tap a person on the shoulder to get His attention.

In retrospect I know that I complicated the issues in choosing and in pursuing my vocation for the rest of my life. It is clear now that I did not have my priorities in order and was running from a choice to become a minister.

Sometimes when you try to do "the right thing" for yourself and for your family, it might not be "the right thing" for God. My choice may have been different if I had held fast to the principals in a poem I learned long ago written by Henry Van Dyke entitled "Four Things:"

>Four things a man must learn to do,
>If he would keep his calling true,
>To think without confusion, clearly,
>To love his fellow-man sincerely,
>To act from honest motives purely,
>To trust in God and heaven securely."

Chapter 62

THE ONSLAUGHT OF WORLD WAR II

Our country was just coming out of the worst depression that its people had ever endured during its 165 year history. People were beginning to enjoy having plenty of food and jobs were more obtainable.

When President Franklin D. Roosevelt told the people, "You have nothing to fear but fear itself," they listened. People were becoming cautiously optimistic about the future.

Electrification of homes was spreading like wildfire. Cars, radios, and refrigerators, once considered obtainable only by the wealthy, were selling as fast as they came off the assembly lines.

This optimistic outlook soon began to fade when Germany and Italy began to terrorize their European neighbors. Rumors were surfacing about the inevitability of war.

On September 30, 1939, the German Nazis invaded Poland and divided it with Russia, with whom it had signed a non-aggression pact. On this same day, Great Britain and France declared war on Germany. Later that year in the month of November the Soviets attacked Finland.

The Nazis, determined to conquer the world, entered the Scandinavian countries in April of 1940, thus opening up a new front. That same year Winston Churchill was elected Prime Minister of Great Britain. He walked into the House of Commons and told them, "I have nothing to offer but blood, toil, tears, and sweat."

A new phase of the war began as Holland and Belgium surrendered to the Nazis in May of 1940. Then in June of the same year France surrendered and signed an armistice with the Nazis.

In July of 1940 the Nazis began an aerial blitz over Great Britain in an effort to bring it to its knees and end the war. In conjunction with the Blitz over England, the Nazis made a massive attack on Russia. With that maneuver the non-aggression pact the two countries had signed in 1939 was severed.

In September 1940 yet a new front opened up as Japan joined the Axis Pact, which previously consisted of Germany and Italy. Japan's first venture was into Indochina.

While this was going on in Europe, America still had not been drawn into the fighting. We were beginning to prepare physically for the eventuality of war, but we were not prepared mentally. We were supplying Great Britain and Russia with aid, but our day-to-day lives remained untouched.

The World's Fair opened in New York with a big splash in 1939. <u>The Wizard of Oz</u> premiered in August of that year. <u>Gone With The Wind</u> opened to loud acclaim in Atlanta with Clark Gable and Vivian Leigh starring in November of 1939.

The movie which depicted how bad things really were during the depression, <u>The Grapes of Wrath</u> starring Henry Fonda, opened in January 1940. The movie industry was experiencing great success and many, many more people were going to the theaters.

The war continued to engulf Europe, Asia, and Indochina. News became more gloomy each day. Then on December 7, 1941, the Japanese devastated the U. S. Base at Pearl Harbor. The nation was in shock!

Our own community was in shock as we knew men who were over there and had lost their lives. For many of us, we had never heard of Pearl Harbor and had no idea of where it was.

This was the beginning of the ever-shrinking world for me. On this fateful day I was with a friend, David Taylor, out in the woods climbing trees and playing Tarzan. Nellie, my sister, came out to the woods to tell us about the attack.

It was on a Sunday afternoon when we heard about it. Everyone was stunned and walked around like zombies. President Roosevelt got on the radio and said, "December 7, 1941 will live in infamy."

On Monday, December 8, 1941 the United States declared war on Japan, and a few days later war was declared on Germany and Italy. Then mobilization for war went in high gear. There were no more reservations of "if's," " but's," or "how" as we were in the war and were in it to win.

The war went badly for the United States in the beginning. The Philippines were captured in March of 1942. Roosevelt ordered MacArthur out of the islands. As he was leaving, he told the people defiantly, "I shall return."

In April Bataan was captured and in May Corregidor fell after being pounded with three hundred air attacks. The only bright spot for the U. S. during this period of tragic losses was in April of 1942 when the Doolittle Bombers hit Tokyo with a surprise raid. We paid them back a little for Pearl Harbor. The war in Europe was still going poorly for the Allied Forces, so Major General Dwight D. Eisenhower took command in Europe.

Almost every family had members of the immediate family in far away places fighting the war. Many families kept a big map on the wall to trace the progress of the battles and hopefully keep up with where their sons or brothers were.

We listened to the news on the radio every night, which was dominated by the commentators: Walter Winchell, Edward R. Murrow, H. V. Kaltenbarn, and Lowell Thomas. Some of the atrocities that these men related would make your hair stand up.

The first victory for the United States in the Pacific came in February of 1943, when Japan gave the Solomon Islands up after viciously defending them. This was a moral boost and a turning point in the war.

In July of 1943 Italy's fascist leader, Mussolini, was deposed. The real turn came in February 1944 when MacArthur began a drive through the Pacific Islands.

In March of 1944, U. S. planes bombed Berlin for the first time. On June 4 the Allied Forces entered the Eternal City of Rome. Two days later on June 6 Allied Forces landed in Normandy, which was called D-Day.

The Allied Forces had trained over 3,000,000 men in England for the invasion of Normandy. The Germans retaliated when they made their first hit on London with a V-1 Rocket on June 12 and again on September 8 when they hit London with the more deadly V-2 Rocket, which traveled at the speed of sound.

The tide continued to shift in favor of the Allied Forces in Europe which boosted the moral of the Allied countries. This coincided with General MacArthur's successes in re-capturing the Islands of the South Pacific and his return to the Philippines.

Roosevelt won his fourth term easily on November 7, 1944. Harry Truman was the Vice President.

The war now seemed to have shifted to the Allied Forces' advantage. Confident that Germany was about ready to surrender, the Allies prepared to cross the Rhine River. It was here that the Allies faced the most staunch resistance of the entire war.

Hitler personally planned the onslaught in the Ardennes Forest, which became known as the Battle of the Bulge. Germany hurled 38 divisions at the Allies along a fifty mile front on December 16, 1944.

Not until two months later on February 1, 1945 did the Allies recapture all the ground they had lost. The Germans had 100,000 casualties and lost over 100,000 prisoners.

Roosevelt, Churchill, and Stalin met at Yalta on February 11, 1945. It was here that they made agreements that shaped history for generations.

The preparedness of the United States at this point in time had reached a level that had been undreamed of. There were over 12,000,000 men in uniform, which was the largest fighting force ever assembled in the history of man.

The population of the United States was approximately 132,000,000, so this made the ratio of men in the fighting force about one to ten. All able-bodied young men were drafted for service. Women and older men were working in the defense factories.

The manufacturing of non-essential goods such as automobiles, refrigerators, and various types of machinery was halted until the end of the war. Everything was geared to manufacturing ships, submarines, airplanes, tanks, guns, and ammunition.

These goods were mass produced at rates no nation on earth or all the nations put together could match. Japan grudgingly admitted they had "awakened a sleeping giant."

Life for people on the home front was tough. Almost everything was scarce. Gasoline was rationed; people in non-essential work got an A stamp book, which allowed three gallons per week.

Farmers got a C stamp book, which allowed five gallons of gasoline per week. Speed limits were set at 35 miles per hour to conserve gas and tires. Tires were almost unobtainable, which was really a worse problem than the gas shortage.

Before the war was over, I had to take one tire and peel all the rubber off and use the liner to put in another tire to make an eight-ply tire. This was done for all four tires and made the car ride extremely rough, but it kept the car going for the duration.

Sugar, meat, lard, and canned goods were rationed -- allowing a given amount of each per week. About the only thing in food rationing that hurt the farmers was sugar. We never used all the other items that were allotted except sugar and, even with the tight allotment, the government did allow extra sugar for canning.

There was not a lot of good clothing or shoes available. If a lady wanted a nice dress, she had to sign an order at a store and wait for it to come in.

Good suits for men were extremely hard to get. If you ordered a white shirt, it might take six months to get it after you placed your order.

The hardest thing for ladies to get was nylon hose; it was almost impossible to find them. Nylon was used heavily in the war effort. The scarcity of nylon hose caused hose to get on what was called "the black market," and the price became extremely high.

The government did keep wages and prices frozen. This kept the cost of living under control.

Our country pulled together for the war purpose better than it had ever done so before and probably ever will again. People worked hard and made sacrifices without complaining.

If a person was seen doing something that was thought to be against the effort, he was reported. If a young, able-bodied man was seen and it was thought that he should be in service, investigations were made as to why he was not in uniform.

Men in uniform were looked up to, idolized, and almost worshipped. Any man between the ages of 18 and 48, who wasn't in uniform, was looked at with disdain. He had a tough life coping with the glares and snide remarks from people who weren't of draft age.

Men who didn't pass the physical examination were rejected from military service and were labeled as 4 F's. This was a title no one wanted as most people thought the 4 F's tried to flunk the examination to stay out of service. Girls did not want to date 4 F's as they didn't want to be called "4 F lovers." I'm sure this attitude forced a lot of people to enter service who could possibly have been deferred.

The most popular singers during this period were: Bing Crosby, Dennis Day, Tony Martin, Dinah Shore, Kate Smith, and Frances Langford.

During the war the most popular songs were songs of romance relating to men being away at war. Some of these were: "I'm Dreaming of a White Christmas," "Don't Fence Me In," "Deep in the Heart of Texas," "God Bless America," "Praise the Lord and Pass the Ammunition," and "Saturday Night is the Loneliest Night of the Week."

This period was the last hurrah for the Big-band with such band leaders as: Guy Lombardo, Kay Kyser, Fred Waring, Tommy Dorsey, and Glen Miller.

Some of the most popular Big-band tunes were: "Take the A Train," "Chattanooga Choo Choo," "Boogie Woogie Bugle Boy," "Rhapsody in Blue," and "When you Wish upon a Star."

Our country was saddened when Glen Miller was killed while flying in a plane over the English Channel. He was on his way to entertain our troops during World War II.

All cities were blacked-out at night because of possible air raids causing a song writer to pen the tune: "When the Lights Go On Again All over the World." Hearing this song would often bring tears to our eyes.

After the Battle of the Bulge, the war in Europe reverted back in favor of the Allies, and the Allied Forces crossed the Rhine in March of 1945. Then the whole allied world was saddened by the news of the death of President Franklin D. Roosevelt on April 12, 1945.

His death was a devastating blow to all of our Armed Forces when we learned that our Commander and Chief was dead. When we were told of his death, our troops broke rank and scattered all over the field — some were crying, some were praying, some were sitting, some were standing — but all were stunned.

The day President Roosevelt died is a day that will live forever with me. He had worked so hard to bring the war to a close and just missed it by a few months.

On April 28, 1945 Benito Mussolini was caught, tried, and executed; then in two days on April 30 Adolf Hitler committed suicide. On May 7, 1945 Germany surrendered unconditionally.

V.E. Day was declared and celebrated. With the war over in Europe, all of our attention was turned toward the defeat of Japan.

By June of 1945 most of the Islands were secured except Okinawa. The Japs were wagging a fierce battle trying to hold onto this island. They knew that if they lost this island the invasion of the mainland of Japan was inevitable.

The Japs dug into the rocks of Okinawa with thousands of gun emplacements and individual snipers. They had a tunnel network that was virtually impenetrable. The only way the Americans ever got them out was to burn them out with flame throwers.

Japan, in desperation, launched over 6,000 kamikazes. These were suicide planes piloted by live pilots. These suicide planes sank 36 ships and damaged 332 others.

The Japanese resistance ended on June 21, 1945 with Allied casualties at 40,000 and Japanese at well over 100,000. With Okinawa secured, the Allied Forces pulled back to the Philippines and other islands to regroup and train for the invasion of Japan.

For years there had been some very secretive work going on in the United States that most citizens were not even faintly aware of. This research into atoms became known as the Manhattan Project.

Proton was discovered in the late 1800's. By 1920 scientists realized the importance of the hydrogen nucleus in the atomic structure. Then in the early 1930's scientists discovered neutrons.

In 1938 German chemists started working on splitting the atom. In December 1942 the United States succeeded in atomic fission thus opening the way for the atomic bomb and nuclear energy.

The United States of America achieved the atomic fission ahead of other countries. The first atomic bomb was exploded July 16, 1945.

After the bomb was set off, the American people were told that there had been a large explosion in New Mexico. The American people still were not told that the United States had developed a very devastating bomb. After the war we learned that the explosion in New Mexico was an atomic bomb with power equal to 20,000 tons of T.N.T.

The United Nations was formed on July 26, 1945. President Truman announced to a cheering throng of people, "Oh, what a great day this can be in history!"

Late in July "The Big Three" met in Potsdam, Germany — "The Big Three" being Truman of the U.S.A., Stalin of Russia, and Winston Churchill of Great Britain. Churchill started the meeting, but Clement Attlee succeeded him as Prime Minister during the conference and went to Potsdam to conclude the conference.

The purpose of the meeting was to fix occupation zones, set up administrations for enemy territory, and arrange for peace treaties.

As we know now, it was a give away to Stalin as Russia secured control of all of Europe east of the Elbe River.

They did issue an ultimatum to Japan to surrender or face complete and utter destruction. The Japanese ignored the ultimatum but did try to negotiate a settlement through Russia. Russia, however, did not relay the information to the rest of the Allies.

On August 6, 1945 the United States dropped an atomic bomb on Hiroshima, Japan, which destroyed more than half of the city. Then on August 9, 1945 an atomic bomb was dropped on Nagasaki.

The two bombs killed more than 70,000 people and injured more than 100,000. On August 10, 1945 Japan offered to surrender, and on August 15 they did surrender. The war was finally over.

Historians have questioned the decision to use the atomic bomb with Japan so near to defeat already. Those who questioned this decision could not imagine what was facing us had we invaded Japan.

Japan didn't take the prospects of being invaded lightly. They had over 10,000 kamikaze pilots ready to launch a deadly attack at a moments notice. They had anti-aircraft guns, machine guns, and mortars placed everywhere imaginable.

Tunnels several miles long had been dug into the mountains that were wide enough for trucks to pass. The Japanese had stored guns and ammunition in these tunnels. I know all about this because I personally helped dismantle many of the weapons. It took months to complete the task.

I know that dropping the atomic bomb was an agonizing decision, but I think fewer lives were lost than would have been if Japan had been invaded. Only God knows for sure.

The war was finally over and the boys came home — except for the over 400,000 who gave their lives so that we might enjoy the freedom that we now cherish. The lights did come on again all over the world. We were at peace after a long, long struggle.

People at home worked hard, made sacrifices and set the tone for the victory. The greed and insanity of the likes of Adolf Hitler, Hirohito, Hideki Tojo, Benito Mussolini, and Joseph Stalin directly and indirectly caused more than 14,000,000 deaths. Let us hope and pray that all this bloodshed was not in vain.

Rationing during World War II

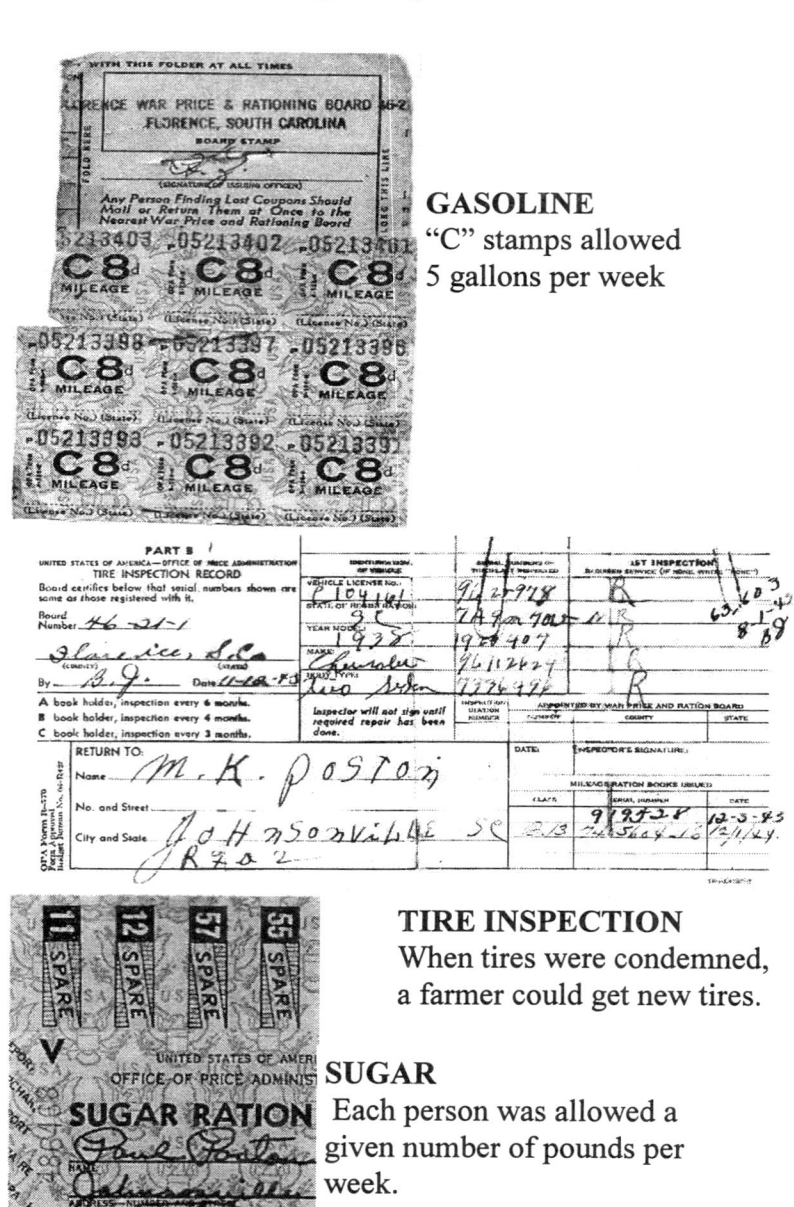

GASOLINE
"C" stamps allowed 5 gallons per week

TIRE INSPECTION
When tires were condemned, a farmer could get new tires.

SUGAR
Each person was allowed a given number of pounds per week.

Ration stamps and books
for canned goods and meats
during World War II.

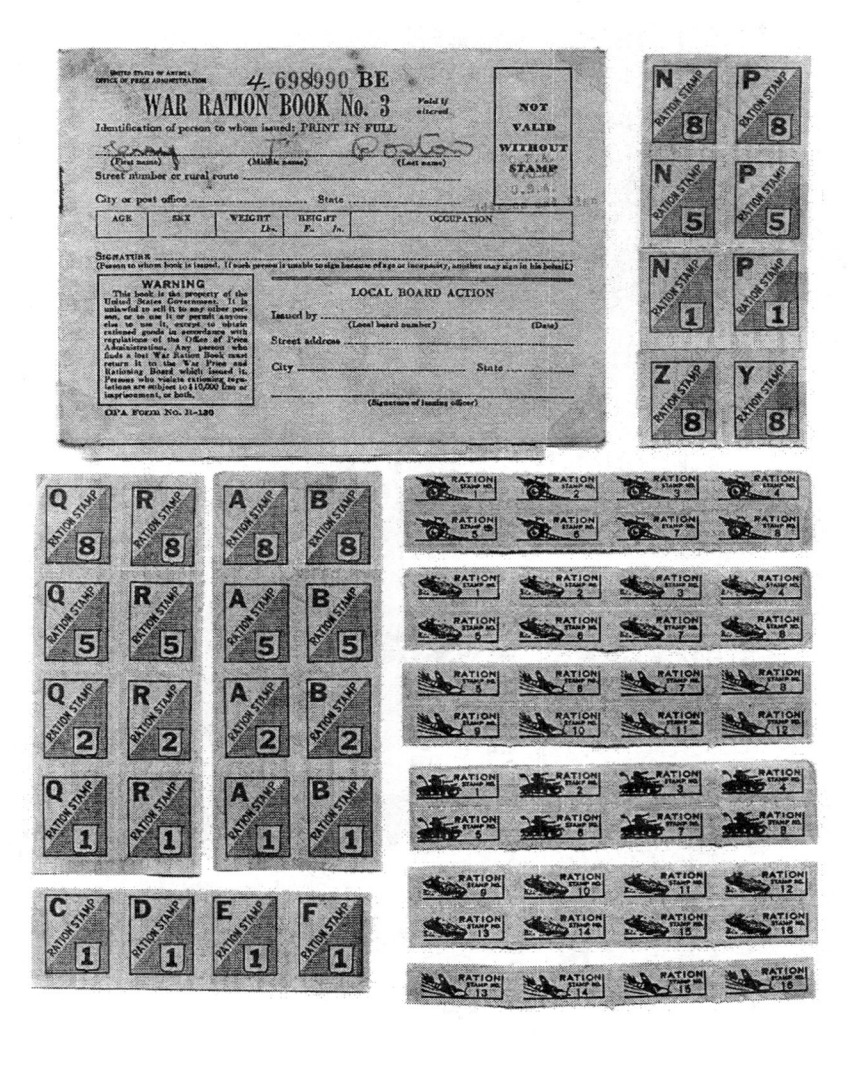

240

War Ration Book
Extra sugar was allowed for canning.

Chapter 63

ANSWERING MY COUNTRY'S CALL

On August 20, 1944 I had my eighteenth birthday and that made me subject to the draft into the Armed Forces of the United States of America. We affectionately called ourselves the "Forty-Eight" as there were only 48 states in the Union at that time.

The population of the country was about 140,000,000 and more than half of those people lived on farms. People who lived in cities generally thought the country folks were somewhat backwards. People in the country thought the same about city people, and in a way they were both right. During the war people put this pettiness aside and worked together to win the war.

During the afternoon of August 21, Dad and I went to Lake City to Local Board No. 34 of the Selective Service System. It was here that I registered for the draft.

I was scared but I knew this was something I had to do. I had been given one-day's grace because my birthday fell on Sunday.

Everything was quiet on my draft status until September 26, when I received a notice from the Draft Board that I had been classified in Class 1-A. This meant that I was in the top category to be drafted.

Nothing happened until December 19, 1944 when I received a greeting from the President of the U.S.A. This greeting meant that I had to report for a Pre-induction Physical Examination on January 13, 1945.

This greeting ruined my Christmas because I was getting more concerned each day as my inevitable entry into the Armed Forces approached.

Time just flew by until Thursday morning, January 13, 1945 when I reported to the Local Board in Lake City, S. C. The people running Local Board 34 were waiting for the new prospective inductees to arrive.

After checking us out, two bus loads of new inductees were shipped to Fort Jackson at Columbia, S.C. There we were greeted by a host of soldiers who were eager to tell us all about the army.

For an 18 year old kid, this pre-induction physical was a

totally new and shocking experience. We were stripped of all our worldly belongings and lined up in long lines going in several different directions.

All the buildings were poorly heated and I thought I was going to freeze to death. Under these circumstances, I think I'd have been cold even if it had been in the summertime.

The only thing we had was an examination form for each doctor to check. The single sheet of paper was the only thing we had to try to conceal our private parts.

We tried not to touch each other, but there were times when we got pushed together and this made matters even more humiliating. You could look down those long lines of human bodies and see all different sizes, shapes, forms, and colors. The one thing we had in common though was the fact that we were all cold and shaking.

This activity went on Thursday afternoon and all day Friday. I nearly completed my physical on Friday. I just needed to see one more doctor, who was a psychiatrist. So, I had to stay at Fort Jackson all weekend just to answer a few of his questions.

My weekend at Fort Jackson was terrible. The weather was cold and the barracks were poorly heated; and to make matters even worse, all of us who had to stay over were quarantined to a one block area. We were told that if we were caught out of that designated block we would be locked up.

This was a happy time for the soldiers who were stationed in this block. They couldn't wait to tell us all about the army.

First thing Saturday morning a couple of Non-Commissioned Officers came through the barracks. They wanted a list of names of anyone who would be interested in training for police work, if it would keep them in the states.

This sounded like a pretty good deal, as I didn't particularly want to go where the war was going on, so I signed up. In a few minutes the "Non-Coms" came back through and told us that all who had signed up to train for police work had been accepted and for us to fall out of the barracks.

They told us to gather in the field in front of the barracks. When we got there they said, "The police work we have in mind for you is policing and picking up all the cigarette butts and trash in the area; so stoop over and get started."

I knew then that I had been taken and these "Non-Coms"

were enjoying every minute of it. A lesson had been learned, but it certainly wouldn't be the last of these experiences.

As I mentioned earlier, we were quarantined and could not leave the area. Having grown up in the wide open country and being free to roam wherever I wanted made adjustment to these restrictions very difficult.

There was a Post Exchange in the block that sold about everything except alcoholic beverages. The jukebox was gorged with nickels all weekend. The tune that was played most was "Don't Fence Me In," which coupled with the quarantine, just ate my heart out.

I bought my first pack of cigarettes and started smoking. If they had been selling beer, I probably would have started drinking.

Monday morning finally came and everyone who hadn't finished his examination had to go back to the station where they left off on Friday. The psychiatrist asked me a few questions — mostly about girls and my relationship with them. I later figured out that he was trying to determine if I was heterosexual or homosexual.

The psychiatrist wrote across my papers: "Fit for general military service," so by my answers he must have determined I was straight. To have been turned down for military service would have been a disaster in my life.

To a young man classification as unfit for military duty was the worst thing that could happen to him. I had decided ahead of time, that if I did get turned down I was not going back home. I had no idea where I was going but it definitely was not home.

Those of us who passed were told that we would probably be called for induction within 90 days. My papers almost beat me back home.

On January 26 I received greetings from the President to report for induction on February 7, 1945. This was earth-shaking. I guessed some very big changes were about to occur in my life. It was a time when I had to "grow up and cut myself loose from my mother's apron string."

The Battle of the Bulge was in its darkest moments as I reported for induction on February 7. All draftees who were inducted in South Carolina went through Fort Jackson for this process.

As I was being processed, papers were given to me to fill out on my preference of service. I put Navy as my first preference,

Marines second, and Army third.

When I got to the end of the line, an officer asked me why I preferred the Navy. I told him that I had three brothers in the Navy; I told him that my feet had been damaged when I was a child; and I told him that I thought I could serve my country better in the Navy.

All the time I was talking, he was erasing my preferences and just stamped on my papers "Army." He said, "At least one in your family needs to see how it is to walk and not sail, and by the way the Infantry is getting everybody today." That pretty well signed and sealed my fate.

As I finished my processing, a soldier came over to where I was and started talking. His uniform had more medals, stars, stripes, insignias, bars, and hash marks than I had ever seen. I figured he must have been a general who had been through several battles and had about 30 years of service.

This soldier asked me all about my family, where I grew up, how much education I had, what my hobbies were, and what I wanted to do in the Army. He said that he really would like to have me work for him but that he'd have to ask the Officer of the Day.

It was my understanding that this would be a permanent job, so I readily agreed that I would do it. In a short while he came back and said the Officer of the Day had agreed for me to work for him.

He said that what he wanted me to do was answer the telephone for headquarters just for that night. I was boiling mad and figured I had learned another lesson because I had been taken again.

The next morning several bus loads of recruits shipped out to Fort Bragg, North Carolina, and I just happened to be one of them. After our arrival, we were given a battery of tests that lasted all day.

After each series of tests were given, the ones with the lower scores dropped out. The ones with the higher scores took another series of tests.

I must have done all right because I took tests until they closed the place up that night. They told me that I was qualified to try out for Officer's Candidate School, but at eighteen years of age I really wasn't interested.

A whole trainload of us were shipped out that night, but they wouldn't tell us where we were going. At about two A.M. the train stopped in Augusta, Georgia. We knew then that we'd spend the next few months at Fort Gordon.

There was a convoy of trucks waiting for us, which unloaded at our assigned barracks at about three A.M. It seemed that as soon as we got to bed, the lights were switched on and the bugle blew reveille at 6:00 A.M.

I stayed in bed for a few minutes and the C.Q. (Charge of Quarters) came through and put everyone who wasn't out of bed on K.P. (Kitchen Police). So, I peeled potatoes the first day I was assigned to a unit. This K.P. job helped me to get to know the cooks real well. Afterwards, they always put big servings on my tray when I went through the chow line. The next day I had all of my hair cut off and I looked like a "skint possum."

The company I joined at Fort Gordon, Georgia had four platoons with approximately 50 soldiers in each platoon. The first three platoons were filled with men from Fort Mead, Maryland and the fourth was filled with farm boys from Fort Jackson, South Carolina.

Our First Sergeant Elliott was from Florida, so it wasn't long before we were fighting the Civil War again. Sergeant Elliott called the 4th platoon his "Rebel Platoon." He really built us up at the expense of the three "Yankee Platoons."

This just made the rebel platoon soldiers work a little bit harder for him. When we got ready to go on a forced march, he would say, "Put the Rebel Platoon in front to lead the Yankees and put the meat wagon behind to pick up the Yankees that fall out."

Sergeant Elliott would get disgusted at the way the company looked while marching on the parade field. He would tell the three Yankee Platoons to stand at attention while he marched the Rebel Platoon by them so they could see what soldiers were supposed to look like.

This made us try just that much harder... and we were good! Sergeant Elliott would show us off at Battalion and Regiment levels.

Not all of Sergeant Elliott's Cadre were Southerners and some of them resented his belittling remarks about the Northern boys. Therefore, some of them made it hard on us farm boys.

The worst of the group was Buck Sergeant White from Chicago. I think I was one soldier that he disliked the most because I had tried so hard to be a model soldier for Sergeant Elliott.

He was always watching me, and if I missed one step, he would yell or rap my helmet with his baton. Of course, this would make me jump and my ears would ring for a long time. He seemed to really enjoy intimidating several of us.

One day we were disassembling and reassembling a machine gun. I had studied it and felt that I had a mechanical aptitude for this, so I was getting that gun back in operation. Sergeant White yelled, "Poston, that's not the way to do it." I responded, "Sergeant White, I thought it was."

He looked at me and said, "Poston, you are not paid to think; I'm paid to think for you." I knew that if I responded I'd be in deep trouble. This thought came to my mind: "The army is paying me only twenty-one dollars a month and this is not enough for me to have to listen and take this kind of junk."

During basic training at Fort Gordon, it was required that we camp out two weeks in pup tents. The weather was cold and it rained everyday during the two weeks I camped out. We didn't get dry or warm the entire time we were out there. We were so miserable!

The morale of the soldiers was at a very low point in our training. One morning there was a tragic incident while we were on the firing range doing target practicing with M-1 rifles.

One of the trainees from the north turned his M-1 to his head and blew the side of his head off. This happened only a few yards from where I was lying on the wet ground firing my M-1 rifle. The body was removed and we kept on firing.

It was a practice while on bivouac to stack rifles. Thus, each squad of eight men would hook their rifles together in the shape of an Indian tepee. Well, one evening we stacked rifles while we viewed an indoctrination film.

Sergeant White came along and inspected our rifles and found a little rust on some of them. You have to remember that it was raining all the time. He was fit to be tied in all of his glory. He just ate us alive, chewed us up, and spit us out. He finally said, "When we get back to the barracks you will scrub the latrine floor with your tooth brush until I tell you to stop."

Several days later, when we got back to the barracks, Sergeant White had not forgotten our punishment. We were told that as soon as we finished our evening chow we were to start scrubbing the latrine floor, and he would come by later to inspect and tell us when we could quit.

It was close to 6:30 P.M. when we started; we scrubbed and

scrubbed and no one came. Near midnight Sergeant Elliott happened to come through. He looked in the latrine and said, "What in the hell are you doing?"

We told him what had happened; his face turned red as a beet, and he said, "Get out of here; get in bed, and I'll see Sergeant White." That incident was never mentioned again, but we surely did have a clean latrine floor!

The remaining weeks of basic training were spent trying to stay ahead of Sergeant White. He was after a few of us and we knew it; so we tried to "soldier" to perfection. He managed to catch me off guard one more time.

We were having a full field inspection on Saturday morning. This is where you take everything you own and spread it out on shelter-half (half of a tent) in the open field. Then the Company Officers and Non-Commissioned Officers come around and inspect. They really wanted to see if we had everything that had been issued to us, and to see if everything was clean and in good condition.

When the group arrived at my station, I snapped to attention while the inspection was being done. All of my gear was in excellent shape, but I made one blunder. While I was at attention, I yawned. Who would notice that little yawn but Sergeant White. He said, "Poston, what's the matter? Are you sleepy?" My remark back to him was, "I didn't think I was." The good Sergeant then said, "Your weekend pass has been canceled; you will stay in bed the whole weekend, and only get up to go to chow."

By now I had about all of Sergeant White that I could take. When we were dismissed, I put up all my gear and made the decision to go home. I went to the orderly room and specifically asked Sergeant Elliott if I had a pass and he responded, "Sure, why not?" That was all I wanted to hear. I picked up my pass, left the base, and didn't return until check-in time Sunday night.

Monday morning I expected all hell to break loose. Yet, nothing happened; Sergeant White didn't show up all day. The situation was never mentioned, but I'm sure Sergeant Elliott had saved me.

The war was over in Europe before I completed basic training. All training was diverted to fighting and killing Japanese. Indoctrination films were shown everyday by the Army showing "Japs" raping and killing American women and children.

By the time we were through training, we were so full of hate that really it was difficult to wait until we could get over there to kill some "Japs." They made good soldiers out of us, and on our last hour before shipping out, Sergeant White came around and told us that all he was doing was trying to make good soldiers out of us and maybe save our lives. That's not the way I had perceived it, and he received very few handshakes as we shipped out.

After completing basic training, we were given a ten day delay in route before shipping out to the South Pacific. This happened in June, so when I got home my family was busy gathering tobacco. My vacation was spent cropping tobacco. When tobacco starts ripening, it will not wait; so I had little choice but to help gather tobacco -- if I wanted to be with the family.

While I was at home that week, an event did happen that changed my life forever. I was fortunate enough to meet my future bride. The days passed like lightning and before I knew it I was on a troop train heading west. There were no available pullman cars so we went by day coach.

The train was pulled by steam locomotives and the soot was awful. We boarded the train on Saturday night and arrived at Fort Ord in California the next Friday morning. It was a long week of just sitting.

There was no reason to change clothes because all that would happen would be just another set of sooty clothes. Some of us got off the train in Phoenix, Arizona and the Military Police ran us back on because we looked so bad. He said that we looked more like convicts than soldiers.

Training continued daily while we were in California; they didn't want us to get "out of shape." One Second Lieutenant said that we should go on a forced march in Death Valley to see how tough we were. It was the most awful heat I had ever experienced.

I think the only thing that saved me was that the Lieutenant passed out -- leaving us with no leader. We packed up and went back to the base since we didn't have a leader. In a few days we were shipped out of Fort Ord to Camp Stoneman, which was the Port of Debarkation on the Sacramento River. From here we shipped out for overseas.

On August 6, 1945 we boarded the U.S.S. Golden City, a ship that had been converted to a troop carrier from a merchant ship. It had big fans to circulate the air but no air conditioning. The compartments were small and it was crowded. The bunks were stacked about eighteen inches apart or just enough room to turn over. Our duffel bags were hanging on the ends of the bunks and stacked all over the floor.

At 7:30 A.M. on August 7, 1945 we slipped out under the Golden Gate Bridge (with no fanfare). The ship started a zigzag course to try to avoid the enemy subs. On the first day out, one of the engines died on us. With the remaining engine doing all the work, the ship traveled with a list that was something less than 45 degrees. The top speed was nine knots an hour, so we felt that we were sitting ducks for the "Japs."

Men started getting seasick after a day at sea; it was awesome. The latrines were full of soldiers, and those who couldn't get to the latrine were using their steel helmets to try to catch their vomit. The bunks were stacked so tightly that if a soldier on the upper deck got sick, it was not unusual for those on the lower decks to get sprayed good. One wise sailor told us that if something fuzzy came up while we were throwing-up to be sure and swallow it back down.

The disabled engine was repaired and started after several days. The ship leveled off and finally reached a speed of about eighteen knots an hour. It was thought that at this speed we had a better chance of escaping the Japanese torpedoes so we felt a little more secure.

As we approached the Central Pacific, near the Atolls, the wind began to blow and we were bounced around like we were in a tub. These rough seas just made it more foreboding for the seasick.

Living in this new and strange environment just made us edgy and quick to respond to the slightest impulse. By now we had been sailing six days and were being informed very little about what was going on in the world far removed from us.

On the sixth night of sailing, we sat on the top deck in total darkness for several hours before deciding to turn in for some sleep. The ship had to be in total darkness with no smoking at night to keep the Japanese from spotting us.

Everyone turned in and crowded in those tight bunks. If anyone above or below you turned over, you knew it. Remember the place was very dimly lit with only a single exit sign on. Apparently almost everyone went on off to sleep and was totally oblivious to what was taking place.

Sometime before daylight the men in the bottom bunks woke up and started hollering and screaming to the top of their lungs. Water had run into the compartment until it was about two feet deep. Those men in the bottom bunks were lying in the water. You can believe me, they woke up everyone.

Water was sloshing around, duffel bags were floating, and steel helmets were banging against the ship sides. All troops rolled out and headed for the escape. Somebody yelled that the "Japs" had torpedoed us and we were sinking.

All of our life jackets were on because we were required to sleep with them on. But the life jackets weren't going to do us any good unless we could get out of the hatch. Everyone was just scrambling and clamoring to get out of the single small hatch.

This was madness and the "Mutiny on the Bounty" would have been like a Sunday School picnic compared to these 200 plus men trying to get through this small hatch. Some of the men were hurt but none suffocated.

After we reached topside and the pandemonium subsided, anger set in as we realized we had been had again. The flushing system for the so-called commodes was designed to take water in from the front and flush it out at the back.

The toilet seats were boards run across a trough and water ran through the trough all the time the ship was moving. This was all installed at water level, which was one deck above our hold. The intake hole for the water was ten inches in diameter so a lot of water went through the system.

All raw sewage was discharged into the ocean. Well, someone got smart and plugged up the outlet hole, so we took in water all through the night. No one ever confessed to this dastardly crime. I always thought that it was the person who yelled that we had been hit by a torpedo, but nobody could pick him out.

There were no pumps to pump the water out. We had to dip with steel helmets and pour into garbage cans. Then the cans had to be carried by hand to the next deck to be dumped. It took several days to get all the water out and our gear dried.

After fourteen days at sea without seeing land, we sailed to the Marshall Islands. We embarked at Eniwetok Island to refuel. The troops were mostly eighteen year old soldiers who had just finished basic training.

We did have one company of men from "ECPC" (East Coast Prison Camp). These men were kept under guard at all times. While the refueling was going on, they let us go ashore for a few hours to get the feel of solid ground again. When we got ready to leave Eniwetok, one of the men from "ECPC" was missing. A group of us were sent back on the island to find him, but he completely eluded us. Later we heard that he had buried himself in the sand until we were gone.

Eniwetok was probably a mile square with no vegetation — just rocks, sand, a small Quonset hut, and some underground fuel tanks. The island was used as a testing ground for atomic and hydrogen bombs in the later 40's and early 50's. In fact the United States detonated a hydrogen bomb that released energy equal to 5,000,000 tons of T.N.T. That blast pretty well obliterated the island. I hope our man from "ECPC" made it off before then.

On the twenty-first day after sailing under the Golden Gate Bridge, we landed in the Philippine Islands at Leyte. This island, having been the sight of a devastating battle, was in ruins and wreaked of decaying flesh.

We went into the Fourth Replacement Depot where they weren't expecting us. It was customary to carry several days rations, but we didn't carry any to this Depot. For three days we had nothing to eat except bananas and coconuts, and we had to climb trees to get them. We ate mostly a banana diet because we found coconut trees too hard to climb. It took years for me to get back to eating bananas.

On the fourth day in Leyte, some of us shipped out to Cebu Island and joined the 77th Infantry Division. The 77th was a New York Division with the Statue of Liberty as its insignia. Cebu was supposed to have been a secured island for several months. The first morning that I was there over 5000 Japanese marched out of the hills and surrendered.

A few days earlier we were eating breakfast before daylight, when I heard a commotion in the line behind me. I went to see what was going on and there was a soldier on the ground who had been cut all to pieces.

Upon inquiring what was going on, I found that it was a Japanese in an American uniform. We had a company of Philippine soldiers who wore American uniforms and ate at the same mess hall that we did. While in line that morning a Philippine soldier determined that this guy was a "Jap" so he took his machete out and made mincemeat out of him.

The Filipinos had suffered intensely from the atrocities of the Japanese and had built up a great deal of hatred toward them. As it turned out, this Japanese had killed an American soldier, had taken his uniform, and was wearing it so he could get in the food line.

The 77th Division had just pulled back from the bloody battles of Okinawa to Cebu Island to rest. The purpose was to replace those who had been killed and to refit and train for the invasion of Japan.

Okinawa had been the worst of the five campaigns the division had gone through. Men in this division were quiet and withdrawn. Their eyes were bloodshot. A lot of them were having nightmares at night. They would just sit and stare into space.

During the battle of Okinawa this division alone had killed over 16,000 Japanese. They had seen over 1000 of their comrades die and over 3000 suffer wounds.

Some of the men I joined were with Ernie Pyle, the noted War Correspondent, when he was killed. One soldier told me about holding Pyle after he was shot. As he was telling about it, he couldn't hold back the tears.

The Division fought through five of the Island Campaigns: Guam, Leyte, Kerama Retto, Ie Shima, and Okinawa. Through all those campaigns the Division killed over 43,000 Japs and had over 3000 of its men killed.

It was a sad awakening for me to have to leave these fallen men on foreign enemy soil. I knew that they once had the same hopes, dreams, and love of family that I did.

Numerous ships formed a convoy and were fueled, loaded and readied to sail out of Cebu harbor. On September 26, 1945 we sailed toward our destination of the Island of Hokkaido, Japan.

Of course, the 'seasick' epidemic swept through the ship again. But this time we were not as crowded. We were traveling in a new troop transport, the USS Eastman, which was comfortable and had plenty of good food.

All was not well though as we ran into the worst typhoon of the century. The turbulent wind caused the ships to bounce around like tin tubs; we weren't permitted to go topside.

While peeping out of the portholes, I could see the Destroyer

Escort Ships, which were smaller than the Troop Ships, as they completely submerged. I would say, "Well, that one's gone," but in a short time it plowed back up. Then they rode the top of the mountainous waves and the whole ships looked to be out of the water.

Our ship bucked and tossed from stern to bow. When the rudders came out of the water, the vibration was so bad that the boat twisted and shook from port to starboard -- with a loud cracking sound.

My compartment was one deck below the water level in the bow of the ship. My bunk was in the middle in the very front of the ship where it was welded together. That welded seam was what was making the loud cracking noise. My biggest fear was that the ship was going to split and I was going to be the first one out.

When the ship arrived back in the states several months later, it was determined that it had been severely damaged and could have split at any moment. After hearing about the damaged ship, I couldn't help but be humble and give thanks to God for sparing me "one more time."

The convoy sailed on by the main Japanese Island of Honsho going through the Tsugaree Strait. It finally docked at the Port City of Hakodate on the 4th of October, 1945.

Hokodate is a city on the Island of Hokkaido, with a climate roughly equivalent to that of the state of Maine. Snow started falling in late October and kept on with no melting until spring. There were places on the northern tip of the Island where snow got up to twenty feet deep.

We guarded an Air Base at Chitose where the only incoming and outgoing transportation was ski planes; this situation went on for several weeks.

Our landing at Hakodate went smooth. Very few Japanese people were visible. You could just feel that they were peeping and wanting to see what was going on.

The first night that we were on the Island of Hokkaido we stayed in an old school building. Everyone was tense and jumpy as we settled in and ate our C-rations.

My lot was drawn to pull guard that first night. We were set up to walk from post to post in pairs. My buddy was from Georgia. He was probably as scared as I was but showed it more.

We were walking a line on an old tram road. The flashlights we had were so dim you could not distinguish an object fifty feet in front of you. As we were walking, we could hear something slowly approaching us. We yelled, "halt! halt!" The "thing" kept on coming toward us, so after it didn't halt we both cut loose with our M-1 rifles with several blasts.

The "thing" did halt and for good. When we were brave enough to check more closely, we found that we had killed someone's big bull. By this time all this shooting had alerted the Sergeant of the Guard, the Officer of the Day, and a lot of the sleeping troops. They thought we were being attacked. We were not exactly commended for our attack on the bull but were told that we were doing our job.

At every base, fort, camp, and outpost that I had ever been to, "Kilroy" had already been there. I felt sure that I was going to beat him to Japan. It didn't happen though because as we cleaned up the old school that was to be our home for the next several months, we found that "Ole Kilroy" had already been there.

The living conditions for us on Hokkaido were terrible. The weather was cold and we tried to heat those big high-ceiling classrooms with potbellied stoves. The Japanese coal was powdered with no lumps bigger than an egg.

Sometimes water would get into the coal and freeze so that you would get big pieces, but when you put them in the stove, the fire went out. We found out that those big pieces were held together by pieces of ice. It was the most miserable time of my entire life.

Something happened to the logistics of getting fresh food to Hokkaido. We had only C-rations (canned food) and K-rations (cardboard packaged food) from the first of October until Thanksgiving Day. Fresh vegetables, turkeys, and other supplies were shipped in for Thanksgiving dinner. We ate until our stomachs would hold no more!

The months of C-rations were quickly forgotten, but were we in for a surprise. Now remember that by Thanksgiving the snow was about three feet deep. We had it piled up everywhere because we tried to keep a path open to the dining room, the latrine, and the guard houses. Well, after our feast, Thanksgiving night was a nightmare.

Our stomachs were not conditioned for all this rich fresh food. Our latrine consisted of a shack that covered eight barrels with seats on them. That night there were so many sick soldiers that the latrine would not begin to hold us.

Men were scattered all over the place. They were in the latrine, in the paths, and in the snow, as we were flowing from both ends. We had to keep a check all night to be sure nobody stayed out too long and froze to death. This disease that we called "G.I.'s" lasted for several days and surprisingly most of us lived through it.

The news got around about the deplorable conditions that we were living in. Once when a chaplain came to inspect our living conditions, we were hovered around the potbellied stove trying to stay warm. Someone looked up and saw that an officer, the chaplain, had entered the room so he yelled, "Attention!"

All of us except one soldier jumped up and stood at attention. The soldier who didn't stand at attention had jumped up but fell over the coal bucket. His head hit the corner of a cot and he was knocked out cold.

The chaplain said, "I know you men must be having it rough because this soldier was too weak to stand up." There was a very critical write-up in Time Magazine about the dreadful circumstances we were living in. Congress did investigate and the situation slowly got better.

The decision was made to de-activate the 77th Infantry Division in March of 1946. All the men with enough points to be discharged from service were to return to the states with the Division. Those of us who didn't have enough points had to stay.

It happened that an Airborne Division was to take control of Hokkaido from the 77th Division. They told all of us who were in the acceptable range for height, weight, and physical condition that we could transfer to the Airborne.

All that was required for this transfer was to take two weeks of jump training, make two jumps, and we would start drawing jump pay. My reply to them was for them to find something else for me to do. I was not going to jump out of a good running plane. Also, I believed it would take more than one of them to push me out.

The "powers that be" apparently decided I was not a good candidate for the paratroopers. I was shipped to Tokyo, where I joined MacArthur's "pride and joy," The First Calvary. After a few days of processing, I was assigned to the famous "F Troop" of the First Calvary.

This duty was absolutely incredible without any reservations. It was a well-polished and strictly military division. The military discipline accommodated the preparation I had received in basic training.

By this time I had been promoted to Sergeant. The living quarters were clean and in excellent condition. The only thing that disturbed our sleep was the frequent earthquakes that woke us up -- with our bunks just bucking.

Our duties consisted of occupational control of the City of Kamakuri, Japan, which also included escorting dignitaries from Washington and other world leaders. Also we had to be prepared at a moments notice for military parades.

The largest and most important of these parades was to honor General Dwight D. Eisenhower, Chief of Staff. It was the largest show of United States military personnel ever put together in the Eastern Hemisphere. This performance to honor General Eisenhower caused him to cite the Division with a commendation for Military Perfection.

Our unit had the honor of escorting several members of the President's Cabinet around Tokyo and Yokohama. The most important world leader who we met and escorted was General Chaing Kai-Shek, the ruler of China at that time.

The troops had tremendous respect for General MacArthur, and we would have gone to the limits of our physical bodies for him. MacArthur was a strict military leader, but he was reachable, and we felt like he was our friend. He was not a good politician, which is why he was fired by President Truman.

I had been out of the military for several years when Truman fired MacArthur. I felt a deep hurt for General MacArthur and had some resentments toward President Truman.

It is my belief that if Truman had let MacArthur continue his progress in Korea, there would not be a North Korea and a South Korea. I believe MacArthur would have beaten the communist in North Korea and there would be one Korea today.

Tojo told all the young Japanese women to go back into the hills and hide, because the American soldiers would come in raping and killing them. He probably thought we would try to repay them for all the atrocities that the Japanese soldiers had done throughout the Islands which they had occupied.

We proved Tojo wrong. After several months, the young women came down from their hiding in the hills to join their families.

The relations with the Japanese were cordial and presented very few problems for the American Victors. We were not permitted any outward display of fraternization. Nor were we allowed to eat Japanese food. The Japanese customs were a lot different from ours; the most noticeable custom was not wearing shoes in a home. The Japanese would have a fit if you went in their home with your shoes on.

They had unisex rest rooms, which was an uncomfortable situation for us Americans. One thing that amazed the American men was the Turkish baths where all sexes of all ages bathed at the same time.

The tubs were about the size of a normal swimming pool; it was not unusual for twenty-five people to bathe at the same time. This was more of a curiosity than anything else for the American men. It was possibly the first time many of them had ever seen a nude woman.

While I was in Japan, I met one Christian family, and I visited them several times. However, Christianity had to go underground during the war so you had to look very hard for any signs of that faith.

Though the war was over, we worked diligently to try to win the peace. We had some difficult problems with some of our own people.

One night when I was Sergeant of the Guard, I received a call from a hotel that a marine was holding a girl at gun-point in his room. The excited voice on the telephone also said he was flashing a lot of money. I assembled eight of my best men and went to check the situation. When we got there, things were really in a stew. The marine was flashing his colt pistol and was holding two other people plus the girl as hostages in his room.

We talked to him (for what seemed like an eternity but was actually about an hour) before he gave up and came out. After he was disarmed and handcuffed, we searched the place and found a duffel bag that was full of money.

As it turned out, he had robbed a Japanese bank the day before and had over 600,000 yen in his duffel bag. I was most pleased to get this one behind us without firing a shot.

One Sunday afternoon I had another frightening event that

happened while I was Sergeant of the Guard. When we first went into Japan, a beer hall for U. S. Military Personnel was established.

The Navy men and Army men, thinking their respective branch of service won the war, began to fight each other. It got so bad that we established a beer hall for U. S. Navy and one for U. S. Army. We thought this solved the problem.

On this particular Sunday afternoon about an hour before the changing of the guard, it happened. A group of soldiers from Georgia were sitting in the parlor drinking beer. They probably already had more than they should have when several black soldiers from the Transportation Corps came in for a beer.

A couple of the white soldiers got up and, according to the guard on duty, fought rather viciously for a few minutes until the black soldiers left. The guard on duty said that the black soldiers said as they were leaving that they would be back.

The beer hall had no back door and one front door with a vestibule about four feet by four feet. This meant there was close quarters between the first set of doors and the second.

About the time I reached the door, two truck loads of black soldiers arrived and started piling off the trucks. They had shovels, axes, bottles, and sticks that were visible. I don't know if they had any concealed weapons or not.

These black soldiers were trying to get in the hall, and, of course, the whites were trying to get out. I think if there had been a back door the whites would have scrambled and gotten away from that place. They didn't really want to face the blacks and all those weapons -- they just wanted out.

The guard that I was escorting to relieve the one in the beer hall was a big soldier. He was a six-foot six-inches tall, broad-shouldered Indian from Oklahoma. He looked mighty good to me at that particular moment.

We both had carbines so I told him to put a round in the chamber and keep the whites in the hall. I threw a round in the chamber of my carbine and told the black soldiers that they weren't coming in under these circumstances.

I told them that if they went back to their base and dressed in full uniform and came back for the purpose of getting a beer, I would let them in. As it was, they were out of uniform and only wanted to get inside to fight. I was not going to let them in.

Several of them said, "We're coming in." I said, "I can't stop all of you, but I'm promising you I'm going to stop a pile of you." They kept looking at me and looking at the barrel of the carbine.

I was afraid to bat an eye for fear I would miss one of their moves; in fact, I'm not sure I was breathing.

After a while they started pulling back and getting on the trucks. The tail lights of those trucks was the best looking sight I had ever seen. The minute the trucks left, the white boys ran out of that beer hall and returned to their base with undue haste. The beer hall was closed after this incident until some new rules and procedures could be established.

The worst situation that I witnessed (or was involved in) as Sergeant of the Guard came one cold rainy evening. This young Chinese lad had joined the American Army. He had watched the Japanese torture and kill his parents and hated the Japanese with every ounce of emotions he could master.

He should never have been sent to Japan, and I should never have posted him at a railroad station. Of course, hindsight has 20/20 vision.

The Japanese trains were always crowded, as were the stations particularly just before the arrival of a train. On this momentous day the train was coming and the people started pushing toward the area where they were to board.

This young Chinese told them to back up, but they didn't pay attention to him. In his anger and confusion, he pulled his carbine and fired several rounds -- killing eight Japanese and wounding eight to ten more. It was awful -- just a devastating tragedy.

It was a scene that I'll never forget. This young fellow was court-martialed and was serving time in Manila when I completed my tour of duty.

After about eighteen months in Japan, things began to settle down to routine monotony. Soon my number came up to be shipped back home. I was most anxious to get back home.

Homesickness for my family was one thing, but something had happened back when I was on furlough before shipping overseas that I had not planned. I fell deeply and "unretrievably" in love with the girl who would become my bride and mate for life.

We wrote to each other often and that just made me miss her so much. My love for her had been growing all the time I was overseas. The longer I was overseas, the more I wanted to get home. A song came out that we would hear over the Armed Forces Network that didn't help any either. It was:

> I'll be overseas — always,
> Wearing my O.D.s — always;
> When the things we've planned
> Need a helping hand
> I'll be in Japan — always — always.
> When they count the score — always,
> I'll need just one more — always,
> Not for the duration
> Nor for de-mobilization
> But for occupation — always.

The long awaited day to return home finally came. We sailed out of Yokohama late one afternoon with the destination San Francisco.

On my first night at sea while sitting on the deck alone, I was so excited about going home and the happy faces I would see. Then it hit me. I thought of all the boys who would not experience this. I thought of the supreme sacrifice each of them had made.

The thought of leaving them on the Islands scattered all through the South Pacific was very emotional. I cried uncontrollably and unashamedly.

These soldiers had given all that their young lives had to give. They wanted so much to live and go home to their loved ones. I will never forget them, and I prayerfully hope that our country will never forget them.

The rest of the trip was uneventful. In three weeks I was at Fort Bragg being processed and discharged.

As I left Fort Bragg, I saluted the flag, which was rippling in the wind. I was proud of my country, proud of the U. S. Army, and proud of the job I had done. I felt very humble and grateful because my country had given me so many opportunities to broaden my horizon.

I had entered the Army as a boy, and now I was being discharged a man. I knew that my life would never be the same, and yet I didn't really want it to be. The experiences I had gained and the bigger world I had seen gave me the desire to reach out for more.

No longer would I be satisfied to stay on the farm and plow my mule Betty. In a way it was a little sad, but my restlessness for adventure was unstoppable at this point in my life.

Chapter 64

FOREVER

For three generations the men in my family had not rushed into marriage. My paternal grandfather, my Dad, and my three older brothers were all twenty-five years or older before they were married.

My maternal grandfather was over thirty-five before he took a bride. Mom's two older brothers were never married, and her two younger brothers were over thirty before they began their life of matrimony.

It was just expected that none of us would rush into anything as serious as taking on the responsibility of a wife. It was also expected that we would not lose control of our emotions and get caught-up in a shotgun situation.

Mom and Dad both discouraged dating before their sons were eighteen. They also cautioned that we should avoid serious relationships until we were mature and capable of supporting a wife and family.

The world had changed so much by the time I came along. It was difficult for my parents to closely monitor me.

However, on my going-away conference as I was leaving for college, Mom told me that I had been raised right. She ended her conversation by saying that she would be praying for me and was confident that I would do the right thing in all situations. So, I suppose with this "send-off," I really felt that I had more pressure to live within the bounds of my parents' teachings than my older brothers did.

At age seventeen, I went to Pfeiffer College, a co-educational college with a ratio of seven girls to one boy. Some serious courtships developed for some of the boys at Pfeiffer. My very best friend, J. W. Eaddy from Johnsonville, married the girl he met and dated during that year.

Of course, each of the boys cultivated friendships with particular girls. The girl that I dated most of the year was a beautiful blonde from Raleigh, N. C. Our relationship was more like buddies.

We tried to keep a certain distance between us and not get too emotionally attached. I had no desire to get emotionally involved at such a young age. This friendship was great. We were pals for the school year and said good-bye at the school year's end -- with a few tears but no hysteria.

In February of 1945 I was drafted into the Army just a few months after my eighteenth birthday. The Army sent me to Fort Gordon, Georgia for basic training.

After seventeen weeks of intense Infantry Combat Training, I was given a ten day leave to go home before being shipped overseas. Gasoline was rationed due to the war effort, so there was none available for any pleasure travel.

Consequently, my vacation plans were to stay at home and help the family gather tobacco. This is exactly what I did for the first several days. Since everyone in the area was busy gathering tobacco, the only chance my friends had to see me before I shipped out was to visit me at night.

I had a very close friend and neighbor, Bill Davis, who farmed and ran a service station in Johnsonville. Bill had a nice 1941 Ford and, with his service station connections, he had some extra gas.

Bill's brother-in-law, Jack, was visiting Bill and his wife, Dell. Jack was in the Army. He had just gone through several battles in Europe and was wounded. He was on a convalescent leave recovering from his injuries.

One of my high school pals, Howard Davis who was working at the shipyard at Charleston, came to be with me before I left for overseas. Bill told me that he would furnish the car and gas if Howard and I would take his brother-in-law Jack on a date.

This sounded exciting to us as Howard already had a date with Doris Spivey of Hemingway. He said that he would get Doris to get a date for Jack and me.

Immediately after dinner on Sunday, June 24, 1945 the three of us, Jack, Howard and I, took off in the shiny red 1941 Ford bound for Hemingway. We were met in Hemingway by Doris Spivey and a girl named Leta Mae Tanner, who was spending the day with Doris.

Howard, Doris, and Leta got off to the side and were doing some low talking. What they were doing was giving Leta the choice of Jack or me as her date. Well, to my extreme delight, she chose me.

After pairing Leta and me, then we went out in the country to Emma Lou Baxley's house and got her to date Jack. The six of us rode all over Hemingway and Johnsonville, just burning up that free gas Bill had so generously provided for us.

With six in a car, there just weren't many private conversations. Kissing on the first date was absolutely a "No-No" back then, and with six in the car it was somewhat overwhelming anyway.

Bill's red Ford was beautiful but it was not air conditioned. The weather outside was hot, and with four people in the back seat we were not only warm but crowded.

The girls were young, so we had to get them home by 10:00 P.M. So, we made sure to get them home on time as we didn't want to have their dad's waiting for us when we got there.

There was something about Leta that attracted me to her. She was beautiful with sparkling brown eyes; but it was more than that. For one thing, I couldn't figure out why she chose me as her date rather than Jack.

Jack was a tall handsome hero of several war battles. He had medals, bars, patches, and stars all over his chest. One of the medals was the purple heart. There I was only eighteen and a skinny 150 pounds trainee. I didn't even have a patch on my shoulder!

Before the evening was over, I just had a feeling that I wanted to see her again. When I walked her to the door, I asked her if I could see her again. She hesitated a little but agreed that I could come on Thursday night. Leta told me that she had a fairly serious romance going with a boyfriend who was not in service.

I helped gather tobacco everyday until Thursday. I couldn't wait for Thursday night to come! One of my buddies gave me a three gallon gas stamp to enable me to fulfill my Thursday night date with Leta.

When I arrived at Leta's house, she was ready. So off we rode into the future with a lot of faith and three gallons of gas.

It was a fun night. We discovered that we had a lot of common interests. Conversation was easy, and I began to have a curious inner feeling. Leta agreed with some less hesitation to see me again on Saturday afternoon.

Our Saturday date went even better than Thursday as we were more familiar with each other and less tense. There was also the realization that I had to catch a troop train at 12:00 midnight in Florence bound for California.

The trauma of leaving a new friend and going off into the

unknown was extremely stressful for an eighteen year old kid. Before the night was over, I felt that I had been hit by something, but I didn't know how hard. Only time would tell how tight a grip it had on me.

Leaving Leta that night was one of the toughest things I had ever encountered up to that time. As I was leaving, we embraced and kissed, and suddenly lights flashed, sparks flew, bells rang, and whistles blew.

Those moments left memories that will remain forever. We both shed tears unashamedly. This night would turn out to be a reference point for both of our lives in the future.

The rush was on now as I had stayed a lot longer than I had planned. There was only a few hours left to get home and head for Florence to catch the train.

When I got home, Mom was concerned since time was so short before I had to leave. I apologized to her for being away on my last night at home. I confessed to her that I might have been bitten by something.

I told her all about Leta and how I was afraid of what I felt. She said that she thought that it would sort of fade away after a while because both of us were so young. Mom had always been extremely wise and I was inclined to believe her, or at least I wanted to believe her.

Leaving home that night was another terrible experience which made two such struggles in the same day. Mom already had two sons in the Pacific and seeing the third one leave just overwhelmed her. She held her composure though until she saw me off.

Then, it was off to Florence, where I made it with just a few minutes to spare. As I was boarding the train, Dad grabbed me in his arms and through tears said, "Paul, remember, we'll be praying for you."

This was the first time since I was a child that my Dad had hugged me. Three times in one day was too many good-byes to have to endure. But knowing that I was loved eased some of the pain.

When I boarded the train in Florence, I selected a seat where I could be alone. I got a corner seat, sat back, and closed my eyes. My little overseas cap just fit my face as I leaned back and covered my face with it.

I stayed in that position for hours. I wanted all the soldiers around me to think that I was asleep. However, sleep was the farthest thing from my mind. What was I to do? What choices did I have? Leta already had a friend, who was not in service whom she had known for quite sometime. She made no effort to conceal that fact.

A little self pity crept in as I wondered: "Why do I have to be in the Army and he doesn't?" The thought came to me: "How am I going to compete with a rival who lives just a few miles from Leta? And he has his own car while I will be living in fox holes in the South Pacific?"

There was no oral commitment between us as I didn't think it would be fair to ask for one. We did promise to write to each other. My whole body just felt numb as my mind wondered.

Riding the train in a day coach all the way to California was an ordeal. I just moped around. I ate what was available, slept sitting up, and got more sooty by the hour.

After a week we arrived at Ford Ord, California. My new surroundings were beautiful but did little to cheer me up.

After debating with myself for a day, I built up the nerve to write Leta. My literary communicating skills were very limited thus making letter writing a real task. Anyway, I decided to write and the following was my first letter to my new friend:

Dear Leta,

I am going to try to write a few lines tonight even though it is a very hard thing for me to do. Usually I can't think of anything to say, and so often when I do it's the wrong thing at the wrong time.

It's my hope that I'm not rushing you because I've known you for such a short time. I can tell you that the three evenings we spent together were more enjoyable than any I have ever spent with a girl. I'm just sorry we didn't meet sooner or that somehow we couldn't have been together longer.

I'm remembering you as a very sweet girl, whose brown eyes sparkle, and one who has a beautiful smile. Those are a few of the things I'll never forget.

The ride out here was very long and tiresome. There were no pullman cars available, so we had a special day coach for six days and nights. Can you imagine how a fellow felt after not having been to bed for six nights? Last night right after supper I fell in the bed (did I say bed?--it was a bunk) and didn't wake up until revelry this morning.

Fort Ord isn't such a bad place after all. There are some beautiful scenes here. It's located on Monterey Bay right on the water. I can lie on my bunk and see what's happening on the Bay. Perhaps I'll see the ship coming in to take us for a long watery ride.

There isn't much to write about so I guess I better switch off. Will be looking forward for a letter from you.
Love,
Paul

The letter was mailed on July 7, 1945. I just kept waiting and hoping that I would get an answer before I had to ship out. Leta received the letter on July 10, which was excellent service, and she answered it that same day.

July 10, 1945

Hi-ya Paul!

Is that you? Well, don't be surprised cause this is me. I received your letter today and thought I'd try to say hello if nothing else. I haven't written any letters in about two weeks, so thought I'd write a few tonight. Out of nearly a dozen people, you seem to be the first one I'm writing to. I wonder why?

I really enjoyed your letter. I was about to think you weren't going to write at all. I appreciate all those things you said about me, but I'm very much afraid I don't deserve them. I could say all that about someone else, so may I return them to you? You deserve them.

I really enjoyed those three nights we were together. Remember that Sunday night when I told you I'd date you the following Thursday night? Well, afterwards I wondered why. I told you that I would and several times I started to write and tell you not to come. Just look how things worked out. I hated to see you go, but maybe you won't have to stay so long.

You know I told you about my brother in Germany. Well, last night we were all asleep and he came in. Boy! wasn't that a happy time? We sat up for about three hours. He's just on furlough - 30 days before going to the Pacific. He's really had a tough time, but he looks good and talks all about the war. Sure is interesting to listen to.

I have some film so I'll try to make some good pictures to send you. Did I say good? Well, anyway, a picture. Please have one made for me before you go over. I have received several compliments on your picture.

I know you're tired of this stuff so I'll sign off.
Love,
Leta
P.S.
I have a brother in the Pacific; he is on the Carrier U.S.S. Hancock. If you have a chance, look him up.

In the first letter I received from Leta was a poem that she had written the night we said good-bye.

> We had only met
> But we had to part
> Because he had to leave
> And Oh! it broke my heart.
> Those few hours together
> Were just so much fun
> He made me think
> I was the only one.
> He hated so bad to leave
> And so did I
> How very sad
> Was our last good-bye.
> But, he's coming back
> When this war is won
> And Boy! Don't forget
> We'll have heaps of fun.
>   With love,
>   Leta

In a few days after the exchange of those two letters, I shipped out to parts unknown. It was two months before my mail caught up with me. During that two months all my letters written to Leta were censored.

The long delay between sending and receiving letters and the censorship were detrimental to our relationship. Yet, it did nothing to abate the yearning that I had within me. I started my next letter off with a statement saying:

> *"The censorship of my letters is over and I can be a little more free with what I say. It has been tough trying to write someone I really like and have to worry about what the censor will cut out."*
>
> *"It has now been two months since I received any mail from you or from home. I think I'm going batty, or maybe I'm already there. Two months is just too long for a fellow to have to wait for a letter from his girl.*
>
> *Am in my tent trying to write and it's raining cats and dogs outside. My tent is leaking more on the inside than on the outside or so it seems. Everything I have is wet, but this red cross stationary. And it's getting there. If it will stop I might get to finish this letter.*
>
> *It rains everyday here in the Philippines. I'm going to send you a grass skirt from here; I hope you don't mind. They are pretty but somewhat suggestive.*
>
> *You know it's been almost three months since I have seen you. It still seems like a dream. I know I shouldn't say what I am about to and you'll just say "what a line". But here goes..."you're different from other girls I have met. You're just a girl a fellow can't forget, and Leta I really do mean it."*
>
> *I'm thinking of you,*
> *Paul*

I always closed my letters with "I'm thinking of you" or "My thoughts are about you." Next I wrote to Leta about receiving two long awaited and much appreciated letters from her:

> "Received the pictures you sent and do I remember? My! My! I would never forget you!" Leta, you said something in one of your letters that made a deep impression on me. You said that you were praying for me. There are no words that I know that can justly explain how this makes me feel. I have never had a girl to tell me she was praying for me before. Thank you very much; I need and appreciate your prayers and concerns. You just can't possibly know how that makes me feel and how much your letters mean to me."

In September of 1945 I sailed from the Philippines to Japan. This created another long delay before my mail caught up with me. This same month Leta left home for the first time and entered Winthrop College at Rock Hill, S. C. I could tell by the tone of her letters that she was having it pretty tough - being away from home for the first time. The college degree she was pursuing was most laborious and restrictions at the college were very unyielding. Uniforms were a requirement, which stripped away some of the individuality. The transition from a relatively carefree farmer's daughter situation to a strict relegated environment was making an impact on Leta's attitude.

Then, in December I was temporarily transferred to an Air Base at Chitose, Japan for several weeks. Snow was about ten feet deep and the only transportation was by ski planes or one train a day, which made the trip only occasionally. My mail was delayed for several weeks again. The pressures at Winthrop, the mixed-up mail, and I think some persuasion from my rival was causing Leta to have some serious questions.

Consequently, when I got back to my base at Hokadota, Japan in late January, I had a mild "Dear John" letter waiting for me. Leta asked in a letter if I didn't think we should fade out of each others lives. Of course, I was shocked, but I could understand her thinking. I had been a part of her life for only three days and had been gone for almost a year. I realized at that point that I had never really told Leta that I loved her. Answering her letter was difficult but went as follows:

> "Leta, your last letter sounded as if you were really worried. I don't have a lot of experience at offering advice. Don't get me wrong, as I am not mad that you wrote this letter. Not every girl would be as open and honest with me as

you have been. I know that I haven't known you for a long time and dated you only three times. It does seem that I have known you all my life, and I have to confess that I love you.

However, I am ten thousand miles away from you and have been gone a long time. If we could only see each other and talk, it would help so much; but, that's impossible. Only time is going to help us straighten things out."

In February of 1946 I was transferred to Kamakuri, Japan (a town near Tokyo) and the mail service improved greatly. We began getting letters within a week after they were written and this really helped. By this time we were back to writing each other about every two weeks. In one of my letters I went down memory lane and relived our last night together. I said, "I wanted to make a pretty speech that night but it just wouldn't come out."

Leta wrote back and said she read the letter, "and relived that last night and just cried." In my next letter I told her, "I'm sorry I had mentioned that last night because I'd rather say something to make her laugh than to make her cry."

By summer of 1946, according to the normal rotating schedule, the time was near for me to transfer back to the states. We were both getting excited about this possibility. Leta wrote, "that she was afraid that we would be like strangers when I got home." I wrote back and said, "I didn't think we would be like strangers, but if we were it surely wouldn't take long to get acquainted again."

The long separation had done nothing to weaken my love for Leta; if anything, it had grown stronger. Neither of us had asked for a commitment from the other, but I had absolutely no desire to date anyone else. Consequently, I palled around with married men who did have commitments and weren't always going out and looking for girls.

August came and when I was all set to go home, I was declared essential for 30 days, so I unpacked. Toward the end of September, I became eligible to go home. It wasn't to be though because of a Maritime strike on the west coast. That strike did not do a lot to enhance my love for the Maritime Union. I felt that the sacrifices that the men of the Armed Forces had made were considered less important than the selfishness and greed of the union.

I wrote Leta and told her all the bad news. I told her that I wanted to see her so badly. I reinforced that statement by telling her that writing to her and receiving her letters had helped me through the past long and lonely months. It had been difficult to maintain the relation with the occurrences of the various hitches and snags, but I felt good about where we were. The long waiting was coming to an end, I thought.

My last letter from overseas was written October 6, 1946: "My shipping orders came in today. Am so excited! I'm fluttering around like a chicken with his head cut off. Will leave at 2:00 P. M. today. It will take about a month to get home. Will try to let you know when I arrive at Fort Bragg, N. C."

The long awaited day finally came as I arrived at home on November 2, 1946. I sent Leta a telegram that said, "I arrived at home and could not see her the following weekend." As it turned out though, Leta had forgotten to sign in after going to the dentist with her roommate; she had received a "campus" for the weekend, which meant that she could not go away from the college for the entire weekend.

It was 140 miles from home to Winthrop. There were no cars in the family that were mechanically sound enough to make the trip to Rock Hill and back. I had saved enough money to buy a new car, so I went to the Ford dealer and signed up for a new Ford. As it turned out though, due to the shortages of new cars, I would learn later that I would not get a car from this dealership at all.

I wrote Leta the next week that I would catch a bus on Saturday, November 16 and see her sometime that evening. I told her that since she was afraid she wouldn't recognize me to be on the lookout for a stray male person bearing the following description: "Ht. 5'10", Wt. 160 lbs., eyes grey, hair dark brown and nose prominent. I disappeared 18 months ago with a "skint" head, but now have hair."

The bus arrived at Rock Hill in mid-afternoon. I was so nervous I really wasn't sure I knew what I was doing. When I arrived at Leta's dormitory, the nice little hostess was expecting me. She seated me in a small parlor and went to get Leta. Soon she brought Leta and for a few minutes that sweet hostess closed the parlor door and stood outside to keep anyone from coming in. I always loved her for that thoughtful act.

The moment I saw Leta, any doubts or hesitations vanished. We immediately picked up where we had left off that Saturday night long ago. The rules at Winthrop were so strict. Later, when we were walking on campus and stopped under the street light to talk, a police came by and said that we had to keep moving.

With all the restrictions and limitations of not having a car, we still had a wonderful time. Just being together after waiting so long was beyond description. When I returned back home, I was in some sort of daze as I just couldn't get Leta off my mind.

On November 27 Leta came home on her Thanksgiving break. Each date we had was always better than the one before as we discovered more about each other. This was the first time that I had the opportunity to meet all of Leta's family and their first chance to meet me.

I was impressed with her family and basically I think they approved of me. Of course, they had concerns about their sweet little daughter and sister as she was only eighteen at that time. They had some pretty strict rules such as how early to have Leta back home, etc. This one got me in more trouble than anything else as I was never prompt in getting her back home.

The whole weekend was just an unforgettable series of events. It was weird that our likes and dislikes were so similar. We thought alike on many issues as we had grown up in families with values that were closely aligned. The last Saturday night that we were together before Leta had to go back to Winthrop was just a dream come true. The physical restraints that I applied to myself that night were awesome.

When Leta returned to school, we started writing each other every two or three days. My folks were really beginning to wonder and worry about me. They couldn't understand why I just came home at night and did not go out. Mom was concerned that I didn't act like my usual self. She thought something had happened to me when I was in the Army and I wasn't telling her. Several people had parties and set me up with dates. I really tried to go and have a good time, but they all seemed so empty. I felt somewhat guilty when I went out with someone, yet Leta and I had not made or asked for a commitment. It just wasn't fun being out with someone else.

Leta wrote and asked if I didn't think we were moving too fast. I wrote back and said, "I don't know if we are moving too fast or not. Since Thanksgiving all I have been doing is going around in circles." I just couldn't get her off my mind. I thought I loved her all along, but I never dreamed it could reach this level. I confessed to her that she was my one and only dream girl and started using "I love you" in the closing of my letters.

The days and nights went so slowly between Thanksgiving and Christmas. We just couldn't wait for Leta to get home from Winthrop for the Christmas holidays. The two weeks that she was home were times of total joy. Leta didn't have books to worry about and I didn't have anything bothering me. This was the first time that we would be together for more than three dates. We became so engrossed in each other that we were oblivious to our surroundings.

The last night that we were together before Leta went back to Winthrop we were sitting in her living room with a big fire going. All the family had gone to bed. I looked at Leta, put my arms around her, held her tightly and said, "Leta, I want you to be my wife." It came out as natural as anything I have ever done. I had done a little pre-thinking about it but had not pre-planned when to ask her.

Leta let out a low squeal, but I don't believe she was totally surprised. She pretty well already had the answer, which was, "Yes, I want to be your wife, but we have to wait a while. We are going to have to keep our secret for now. For one thing, my parents say we're too young." The song that was popular about this time was fitting for the occasion: "They try to tell us we're too young to really be in love; they say that loves a word we've only heard but can't begin to know the meaning of. And yet we're not too young to know, love will last though years may go—and then some day they may recall, we were not too young at all."

We said our good-byes, and leaving Leta was so sad. It just opened up the old wounds of separation again. My feelings were all mingled. I was sad because Leta was leaving for Winthrop the next morning. Yet! I was elated by the results of what I had just done. It was as if I was walking on air. The drive home was a time for some soul searching, but I truly felt positive about the turn of events.

My jubilation was short-lived though because when I got home my Mom was having a heart attack. This surely took away all my sleep for that night and all the joy I had stored up. I wanted to tell Mom what I had done earlier that night, but I had committed to Leta that we would tell no one for the time being.

Mom's illness was a serious concern for the family for the next several days. Mom was only 52 at the time and this debilitating disease was extremely tough on her and the rest of the family. Seeing her struggle was inordinately stressful to me as I had never seen her suffer.

I had always thought of her as immortal.

There was another person who did not get any sleep that night after my proposal. When Leta arrived back at Winthrop, she sat down and wrote a long letter. To begin with she confessed that she did not sleep a wink the night before.

She said that her answer was still yes but we were going to have to wait a while. Her family had strained financially to send her to college; she honored this and was not going to let them down. She had a special love and a sense of gratitude for all of her family. Her biggest complaint was that her family loved her and did so much for her and she wasn't able to do anything in return.

My answer to her for that was that she gave to them just by loving them. In a plea she asked me to please don't ask her to quit school. As tough as it was, there was still no way that I was going to push Leta into doing something that would not have been fulfilling to her commitment to her family. I loved her too much for that.

We wrote each other everyday from then until school was out in June; that is, everyday except the days I was at Winthrop and the days Leta was at home. The separation was difficult for both of us. I think it was probably worse on Leta than it was on me because she was away from home, and she was carrying a heavy load of college courses. She remarked in one of her letters how "we each just seemed to fit into what the other said or did." I wrote back and said, "Leta, my dear heart, that's love." In the next letter she sent me there was a couple of verses of a poem:

> TO A FRIEND (author unknown)
> I love you,
> Not only for what you are,
> But for what I am
> When I am with you.
> I love you
> Because you have done
> More than any creed
> To make me good,
> And more than any fate
> Could have done
> To make me happy.

The poem just tore my heart out. I wanted to see her so badly.

Leta began to be a little less reserved with the expressing of her emotions. She began to ask, "What did I do to her?" My reply always was, "The same thing she did to me." We both felt differently toward each other than we had imagined possible. Leta asked: "Why must love be such a strange thing?" For this I didn't have a good answer. Another poem came in February:

> THE OLD STORY (author unknown)
> I try to think of things to say—
> And yet I said them yesterday.
> For only yesterday I told you
> How in my heart I always hold you.
> Now, if I said the same again,
> My words would be the same as then.
>
> I try to think of something new—
> And yet I never manage to.
> I told you yesterday (and this you
> still must remember) how I miss you.
> Today I miss you even more,
> But you have heard that all before.
> I try to think, yet not a word
> But I have said, and you have heard.
>
> For yesterday, while thinking of you,
> I know I told you how I love you.
> Yet all that I can think to say
> Is all I told you yesterday.

Time continued to pass so slowly. Each time I went to Winthrop or Leta came home, parting was that much worse. Mom still didn't realize what I was going through. One night we were having one of our little private conversations, and she told me that I should get out more at night. She said that I was acting like an old man. I confessed to her about how much I loved Leta and that I had no interest in going out with any other girls.

I finally told Mom that I hoped to marry Leta someday. All she said was, "Just be sure you know what you're doing" and the subject was never broached again until Leta and I announced our engagement.

After Leta came home in April and returned to Winthrop, she wrote one of her most forthright letters. She said, "I don't know how I'd get along without you. It seems like you have become a part of me or something. I'm rather glad we didn't know each other so well before you went overseas, or rather discover each other as we have now. I have found a person whom I know I'll always love and somehow just don't mind the whole world knowing it."

In May I went to Winthrop one weekend, and we had such a wonderful time. Leta wrote me that Sunday night after I left. She said, "I hated to see you leave so terribly bad and felt for you having to drive home alone. The more I see and be with you the worse it is for me to stay up here. Your coming up here means more to me than I can put in words. It seems that I've been knowing you for years. Do you appreciate me when I say 'It's wonderful to be in love?' Yes, I really mean it."

"Paul, when you were overseas and we were writing, I had to be so careful in what I said. I couldn't let you know that I cared for you. I really fell in love with you when you kissed me that night before you left. I thought I was in love with this boy I was dating, but when you kissed me, I had the craziest feeling and I knew then that I wasn't in love with him. So, I waited for you to come back -- I wanted to be sure.

When you returned home and came to Winthrop that first weekend, the moment I saw you and we touched, I was sure. Paul, it means so much to me to hear you say you love me and somehow I know it's true. I don't question or doubt a speck. I guess that's what love really means."

We continued to write each day through the month of May. Then on May 30 Leta graduated and what a happy day for both of us. I watched her get her diploma with a great deal of pride, and I felt that we both had made sacrifices to reach this goal. My sacrifice was one of waiting and missing her.

Leta came home and didn't go to work for several weeks. We saw each other at least every other day during this time. This togetherness just made the waiting for us more difficult. Leta still felt she should work a while before we got married. It was a fun summer though. It was our first opportunity to be together and not have to worry about the war, or the army for me, or college for Leta. It was a time when we learned more about each other and our love continued to grow.

In August Leta got a job in Kingstree, South Carolina. This was about 25 miles from Johnsonville; therefore this did separate us some. She would come home on weekends so consequently we were together on Friday night, Saturday night and Sunday night. Then I went to Kingstree on Wednesday nights. We wrote on the days we didn't see each other.

The carefree days of summer began to have a cloud. The Chinese government was about to be overthrown by the communist. The Soviet Union was causing serious problems in Germany thus causing the Berlin Air Lift and the creation of the Berlin Wall. When I was discharged from the army I joined the reserves for four years. Therefore, I became subject to recall into Active Duty. I was notified continuously of my status. It became very scary as it came within 30 days of my recall. This was just eating away at my whole being.

Leta was beginning to get concerned also. She listened to the news one evening and wrote the following: "Paul, have you heard the news lately? They are going to start drafting again. They can't do this to you and us. All our hopes and dreams would be gone and it would simply be terrible. You can't leave me now -- not for another long period of waiting. Why didn't we get married a long time ago? O.K., don't say it. Well, Paul, I'm ready now -- ready to be your wife. I've always dreamed of you -- you know your dream person who you want to marry. Well, you're my dream. I couldn't tell you these things for so long, but now I want you to know."

The status of my being recalled for Active Duty was very uncertain. I checked with the reserves to see if being married would change my status any and was advised that it wouldn't. We took our chances that I would not be recalled. We announced our engagement on Christmas Eve of 1947. Our wedding date was set for June 12, 1948. To get to this point I had reached another milestone by having asked Leta's Dad for her hand in marriage.

Mr. William E. "Mott" Tanner, Leta's Dad, was a tall, big man in his seventies, and I will admit that I was a little awed by him. Mr. "Mott" and I became good friends as I made a special effort to spend some time with him every time I visited Leta. He had a vast storehouse of knowledge and was a real joy to talk to.

Mr. "Mott" was born November 17, 1868 in the Marion

District on the west side of the Great Pee Dee River. He grew up as a farmer and lumberjack. He told me how he used to float logs down the Pee Dee River to Georgetown, and how he would ride the logs to try to prevent the logs from jamming. At times this was very treacherous and he talked about a number of times getting knocked off. He said that many times he went under and related how cold the Pee Dee water was.

Mr. "Mott" was my Paul Bunyan, the mythical lumberjack of the great Northwest. He got out of the lumber business and bought a big tract of farmland in Williamsburg County. He and his first wife had eight children. His first wife died very young leaving him with small children.

A few years later he married a beautiful young woman, Annie Poston, and they had eight children. Leta was the sixth child born to this union. She was twelve years old when her baby sister, Betty, was born. So she was really still "Daddy's little girl." I don't think he ever thought of her as anything other than his little girl. For this reason I knew I had to be careful and play my cards right.

When I got up enough nerve to ask him for Leta, I carried him for a ride one Sunday afternoon. While we were riding, I kept rehearsing mentally what I wanted to say. Finally I just said, "Mr. 'Mott', do you have any objections to my marrying Leta?" He thought for a moment and said, "Well, if I didn't think she was doing all right, I would object, but I think she's doing all right, so you both have my blessings." What a relief! I felt like shouting.

There were two more battles that I felt I had to win before the sailing would be smooth. These battles were to win Leta's older sister, Ora Lee, and Leta's mother.

Ora Lee was nine years older than Leta and really tended and took care of Leta when their mother worked in the fields. A bond grew between them more like a mother-daughter relationship than sisters.

Ora Lee was protective of Leta more out of pure love and she wanted the very best for her. I soon found out that I had absolutely no obstacles with her because we both loved the same person very much. She voluntarily took on the task of making Leta's wedding gown, which was made of white satin and lace. It was beautiful and her making it made the occasion even more meaningful.

The unusual part about this is that I grew the same bond of love for Ora Lee and her husband, Theron Cox, that Leta had. They are the two most care-giving people I have ever known. They have been brother, sister, mother, father, and mentors, but most of all friends to the two of us.

Leta's mother, Annie Poston Tanner, was born March 9, 1898 in the Blossom section of Florence County. She had a very difficult time while growing up and a hard life after she was married. Her eight children grew up during the depression years and life was a struggle.

Leta's Mom was an intelligent, thrifty, hard-working woman who loved her children very much. It was traumatic for her to have to give up one of her daughters in marriage. She had a real fear that her daughters would have some of the same hardships that she had endured.

However, by the time for our wedding, she was reconciled to it and was most supportive. She and I became very close friends. My mother died just a few months after Leta and I were married, and I think that I unknowingly adopted her as a surrogate mother. I honestly believe that the feeling was mutual, as she was a very special person in my life.

Leta's sister, Lois, was three years older than Leta. Lois came to Johnsonville High School to finish the eleventh grade, and this was the year I graduated -- so I knew her in school. But, I didn't know Leta. The two of them were close and shared a lot, so I'm sure that after I met Leta I must have been the topic of discussion for a few times. Lois was working and helped with the financing of Leta's college expenses, which strengthened the bond between them.

There was a popular song back then that said, "It's a long, long time from May to December." As it turned out, it was a very long time from December to June. Leta wanted a church wedding, so she kept busy making plans. I'm sure time didn't drag as slowly for her as it did for me.

My preference was to go to the preacher and get the job done. Leta thought since we'd waited this long that we should do it up right. During these months, she was working in Kingstree, South Carolina and I was working at Kingsburg, South Carolina. I kept the 25 mile stretch of road between these two towns warm.

Usually we dated three times a week, and then we had the weekends -- Leta always came home on weekends. We had a lot of time together, and we used this time to discuss and plan what we wanted our marriage to be. Sometimes we lived in a dream world and tried to visualize Utopia, but before we went too far we came back down to the real world. We talked about our likes and dislikes, our pet peeves, our religion, and our politics.

It turned out that we were both Democrats but that wasn't unusual as 90 per cent of the people in that area were Democrats at that time. Leta was a Baptist and I a Methodist, so Leta agreed to join the Methodist Church. She was working in Kingstree and I in Kingsburg, so I made the decision that after we were married I would get a job in Kingstree. These were the kinds of things that we talked about and compromised on. We discussed the things that we expected from each other after we became husband and wife.

The long awaited day of June 12, 1948 finally arrived. The little Midway Baptist Church, which was located just a few miles out of Hemingway, S. C., was decorated beautifully. The church was in the middle of a big corn field and the corn was up about five feet high -- just high enough to cut off all air movement.

The weather that typical June day was extremely hot. There was no air conditioning in the church and the ceiling was fairly low. This church would hold about 250 people and was filled to capacity with our families and friends. This was the first big wedding held in this sanctuary.

The wedding was at six p.m., the sun was still shining, and the temperature was very hot. When all the people got seated closely together, you felt like you were in an oven. The groom and groomsmen wore black wool suits and they were awesome. When I came inside the sanctuary from one of the back rooms, the Morris Funeral Home fans were flying back and forth all over the congregation. The candles wilted and drooped over. The drooped candles were replaced a few minutes before the ceremony, but even the replacement candles wilted and drooped.

Leta's four bridesmaids, her maid of honor, and two flower girls were beautiful, but I was too awed to notice them. Her attendants were: Lois (Leta's sister) - maid of honor; Virginia Poston (my sister), Wilhelmina Ivey (Leta's friend), Doris Spivey (Leta's friend), Elizabeth Lane (Leta's niece) - bridesmaids; Betty Tanner (Leta's sister) and Elaine Tanner (Leta's cousin)- flower girls.

But, even with all the heat, the wedding was still the most sacred experience of my life. It was well planned and a "once in a lifetime adventure." I had not seen Leta all day, and I had missed her.

As I stood at the altar and watched her come down the aisle, she was so beautiful and I loved her so much. As soon as she came close enough for our eyes to make contact, we each burst into a big smile.

This greeting somehow electrified the already warm congregation. Leta's mother said later that if there had ever been any doubts about how Leta and I felt about each other, those doubts were erased at that time.

My sister, Nellie, told us afterwards that she normally got emotional and shed tears at weddings. But, just to see us joined together after so long a wait, she felt so much happiness for us that she just wanted to shout it out.

The reception was held at Leta's home, which was a big white country home, beautifully decorated with flowers grown by Leta's mother. She had grown the white gladiolus that were used to decorate the church. All of this made the celebration of our wedding even more special.

With the wedding and reception now coming to a close, Leta and I had to try to make our escape. I had reserved a room at Pawley's Island as our planned destination. As a precaution, I hid my car at a friend's house in the country a few miles out of Hemingway.

My brother, Lance, had taken me from there to the church. In our scheme he was to carry Leta and me from the reception to my car. A number of our family and friends were doing some scheming also. They had looked everywhere imaginable for my car as they had some plans for it. When the schemers couldn't find my car, they became restless and maybe a wee bit mean-spirited.

As we left the reception, we were blasted with rice. At that point in time rice sold for about five cents per pound so there must have been a bushel thrown at us. We got into my brother Lance's car and everyone was giving us a happy "send-off."

Lance turned the ignition on and mashed the starter. Bomb! The car exploded. One of the perpetrators suspected that Lance's car would be the vehicle used for our escape, so consequently he had switched the spark plug wires causing the engine to backfire. This blew the muffler completely off.

So, I had to change the strategy for our departure. It was my belief that the schemers would guess that I would use another brother as a means for our disappearance. So, to outfox them, I asked my new brother-in-law, Theron Cox, to take us to my car.

The route to the car had some unexpected impediments that we had to overcome. The teasers had spotters located at most of the intersections and at the one red light in Hemingway. Theron had to do some astute maneuvering to evade the pranksters.

Finally, we reached my car safely and felt good about avoiding them. We did feel a little guilty for denying them the pleasure of plastering the car. However, they were not through with us yet.

When I pulled out in the highway going toward Georgetown, we were spotted. The 1942 Mercury I owned had a new 100 horse power engine in it, and it would literally fly. There was no way this group could catch me now. I was glad no patrolman came along when this speed chase was going on.

It was about twelve midnight when we arrived at our room at Pawley's Island. We unloaded the car, went in the room and cut the lights on. I think at that moment we were both stunned by the impact of what had really transpired on that day of June 12, 1948.

We fumbled around some and finally both of us just sat on the bed. For some reason neither of us could undress for bed. After a while we had to cut out the lights before we could dress for bed. We thought we had made a lot of plans, but we weren't quite prepared for this instance.

A new day dawned for us as we entered into a husband and wife relationship. The carefree days of teenage courtship were gone. Leta was twenty and I was twenty-one -- making me the youngest male in my family to get married in three generations. The wait for the wedding day had been long, but the education had been good. As we discovered each other, we found that not only did we love each other, but that we were best friends and real buddies. We had a lot of similar interests and liked doing things together. I even had a new fishing partner. Our growing-up during the depression made us more conservative in our expectations and more appreciative of our accomplishments.

From the beginning, we knew we had entered into a lifetime relationship. We both knew that we had been "raised right" and hoped we hadn't done anything that would disappoint our parents.

We also hoped we could pass along that heritage to our children.

We knew there would be some bumps and some disagreements at times but believed our love was strong enough to see us through the bad times. We cared for each other so greatly that it seemed our bodies were molded into another being. This other being is like a Siamese twin with one body, but with two heads and two hearts. I have felt, since the night I asked Leta to be my mate for life, that my love for her and my commitment to her were profound enough to last forever.

Leta at her home in 1945. She stole my heart.

Paul on his way to the South Pacific after having just left Leta and his family in 1945.

Leta's home at Midway - near Indiantown. 1945

Paul - stationed in Japan
1946

Paul a civilian again with his
first car - a 1942 Mercury -
taken in 1947

Paul's first girlfriend and
first car - taken in 1947

Paul and Leta on a Sunday
date - taken in 1947

The Day They Became One

Leta and Paul at wedding reception
June 12, 1948

Leta's Mother. Photo taken by Wayne in 1976

Leta Tanner in top right. Then clockwise, Genevieve Poston, sister Betty Tanner, Donnette Poston, Miriam Poston, brother Junior Tanner

Leta's parents at their farm taken about 1944
William Ebenezer Tanner 1868 - 1949
Annie Poston Tanner 1897 - 1983

A pleasant visit from Leta's family when we were at Wofford College in 1953   Back row- Betty, Leta, Leta's Mother, Lois, Ora Lee and Theron Front row - Wayne, Dale, and Tim

Chapter 65

PARABLES OF LIFE

Throughout my life I have experienced numerous events that have helped to mold me into the person that I have become. The ones that I am sharing are those that I consider to be parables, which made a dramatic impact in my thought and development process.

I fully realize that the reader may read them and perceive a different understanding from them than I did. With that rationalization, I have no qualms as we all know that each individual is unique and perceives signals differently.

Eye-Opening Experience With Prayer

When I was five years old, we had a severe epidemic of sore eyes (pink eyes). All of the smaller children in my family had them, and this always happened in the summer when there were many gnats around. The gnats passed the disease from child to child. There were no screens on the doors and windows, so there was just no way to protect children from the gnats and pink eye.

During this particular summer the disease was the worst that anyone could recollect. Some of the eyes of the children were decaying, and there was real concern by our own parents. My eyes had closed tightly and just would not open. By the time my eyes had remained shut for three days, everyone started doing everything they could think of to open them. Nothing seemed to do any good. I felt like my eyelids were glued together. With my five-year-old faith I just didn't believe that God wanted me to be this way, and I couldn't think that He wanted me to be blind.

I told everyone that I was going to pray for my eyes to open. As I can remember, I prayed out loud and asked the Lord to please help me open my eyes and don't let me go blind. I fretted a little but soon dropped off to sleep. In a few hours I woke up and I could open my eyes.

Yes, I believe prayers of five-year-old children are answered. This experience helped build a foundation of faith that has been a rock of strength through all of my life.

Autumn Colors Bloomed

Winter used to be so harsh for us as we were growing up during the depression. The houses we lived in were open and impossible to heat. Our clothes were not adequate to keep us warm. It was a real chore to keep enough wood cut to keep the fires burning in the fireplaces. The severity of suffering during these months was such that I abhorred anything that reminded me of winter.

Autumn with all its color just reminded me of the cold, cold months that followed. I looked at all the different colors of the leaves as the dying of summer. I thought the colors really looked sick in the final days before falling off. For those reasons I could see nothing positive or glowing about anything that autumn had to offer.

My conception about autumn all changed one day when I was twelve years old. At Trinity United Methodist Church we had a minister by the name of Rev. Jones, who had a son a few years older than I. We lived in "Powell's Corner" at the time. Rev. Jones liked to squirrel hunt in this area.

One morning Rev. Jones and his son came to our house to go hunting with my Dad. Dad had other plans and could not go, so he told me to go as a guide to keep them from getting lost. We reached the area about sunrise -- where I thought the squirrels would be plentiful.

When the sun began to shine on all the colored leaves, Preacher Jones (that's what I called him) became so engrossed that he forgot about hunting. He was amazed at all the different hues that glittered in the sunlight. He said, "Just look at what God has done! No one but God could create all this beauty."

He wanted to stop and praise the Lord for all His handiwork. He took out his little Bible and read the third chapter of Ecclesiastes, which reads as follows:

To everything there is a season,
A time for every purpose under heaven:
A time to be born,
And a time to die;
A time to plant,
And a time to pluck what is planted;
A time to kill,
And a time to heal;
A time to break down,

And a time to build up;
A time to weep,
And a time to laugh;
A time to mourn,
And a time to dance;
A time to cast away stones,
And a time to gather stones;
A time to embrace,
And a time to refrain from embracing;
A time to gain,
And a time to lose;
A time to keep,
And a time to throw away;
A time to tear,
And a time to sew;
A time to keep silence,
And a time to speak;
A time to love,
And a time to hate;
A time of war,
And a time of peace.

Then Preacher Jones asked us to recite the 23rd Psalm:

The Lord is my Shepherd; I shall not want.
He makes me to lie down in green pastures;
He leads me beside the still waters.
He restores my soul;
He leads me in the paths of righteousness
For His name's sake.
Yea, though I walk through the valley of the shadow of death,
I will fear no evil;
For You are with me;
Your rod and Your staff, they comfort me.
You prepare a table before me in the presence of my enemies;
You anoint my head with oil;
My cup runs over.
Surely goodness and mercy shall follow me

All the days of my life;
And I will dwell in the house of the Lord
Forever.

Then Preacher Jones knelt by a big tree and prayed. He prayed something about thanks for all the beauty around us, for the different seasons, and for letting us enjoy them.

It dawned on me at that moment that all of this world was God's creation. I realized that these leaves weren't dying - they were just entering a new life. My belief was reinforced that when we leave this earth we just enter another stage. Yes, from the day I was a guide for Preacher Jones, I see beauty in the autumn colors.

One of My Mentors
When I had my fourteenth birthday, I received my social security card. This was in 1940 just before the Second World War. I began working part-time at Bernie Poston's Service Station and General Store.

Bernie's father, Mr. Charlie Poston, was a prominent merchant and farmer who died in 1920. Bernie's mother, Mrs. Emily, was in her seventies and lived with Bernie and his family. Mrs. Emily's health was bad; she had to be taken to the doctor quite often. When she had an appointment, Bernie would ask me to take her. He didn't have the patience to wait on her at the doctor's office. Mrs. Emily was well-educated, well-read, and a devout Christian Lady. It was both an educational and a religious experience just to listen to her. During the times we were traveling together and at the doctor's office, we became very close friends.

Helping this dear little lady was one of the most satisfying experiences of my young life. She would cook different things and bring them to me at the store. Out of her meager sustenance, she would give me Christmas presents. She wrote me regularly after I was drafted in the Army and kept me up-to-date on what was going on in Kingsburg. A bond grew between us that lasted as long as she lived.

Mrs. "M" taught me so much about life and how fleeting it is. Her life was a living example of the glow a person has when she allows the living Christ to reside in her heart. I will always value the influence that she impacted on my young life. Without question or reservation, I know I'll see Mrs. "M" again. Somehow I believe she has watched me all these years.

A Gift From A Friend

After completing basic training, I was given a ten day furlough before being shipped to the South Pacific. War was still raging in that area and I will admit that I was scared.

On the Friday night before I was to leave, I was alone at the tobacco barn curing tobacco. One of my black friends, William Williams, came by to see me before I left for overseas. Willie was a very fine person and I was fond of him. He was a lay preacher and was aspiring to enter the ministry full-time. Willie asked me how I felt about leaving and going off into the unknown. I told him that I thought the Army had trained me to be prepared, but admittedly I still had some fears. One of my concerns was that I might crack in the heat of battle and cause some of my comrades to be killed.

Willie said, "Paul, we've been knowing each other for a long time, and I know you're going to be okay. I have something I want to give you, and I want you to promise me that you'll take it with you everywhere you go. I want to give you the thirty-first verse of the fortieth chapter of Isaiah which reads like this:

"But they who wait for the Lord shall renew their strength,
They shall mount up with wings like eagles,
They shall run and not be weary,
They shall walk and not faint."

We chatted on for a while and as he was leaving he said, "Paul, don't worry now; You gonna be all right." This scripture and Willie's confidence in me was a faith builder at one of the most anxious times of my young life.

Three Cans of Beer

During World War Two I sailed to the South Pacific in an old merchant ship that had been converted to a troop transport ship. The ship had no air conditioning -- just fans to remove the stale air out of the compartments.

The ship was small and was carrying 1400 troops, so it was crowded. Food was terrible and there were no luxuries such as cold soft drinks.

To make matters even worse, one of the motors on the ship shut down. The ship's speed was cut in half to about 8 knots an hour while the motor was being repaired. Because of Japanese submarines, the ship had to zigzag to try to avoid being hit by a torpedo. We sailed for about three weeks before we saw land.

Our first stop was at one of the Carolina Islands, Mog Mog, for refueling and R and R (rest and recuperation) for the troops. Before we docked, we were told that there would be three ice cold drinks for each man. We had to pay ahead of time and order either cokes or beer. My order was for cokes, as I didn't drink beer.

As we walked down the gang plank, there were men on the island handing out the drinks to us. When I got to where the drinks were, they had run out of cokes and had only beer left. I took my three cans of beer and went to the shade of a palm tree and sat down on a log.

The weather was hot and I had not had a cold drink since I left San Francisco. I opened the first can of beer and tried to take a drink, but my right elbow just would not bend. Then I put the can in my left hand but with the same results. The left elbow would not bend. I tried just closing my eyes and taking a sip -- but nothing happened.

As I sat there, the memory of my Dad telling me that he would be praying for me everyday flashed in my mind. The memory of Mom telling me I had been "raised right" and that she had confidence in me that I would not waver came to me.

Convinced that I wasn't going to drink the beer, I gave them to my buddies. To quench my thirst, I went over to a "lister" bag that was filled with water, and I drank until I was satisfied.

For some reason this was the most satisfying water that I'd ever drunk. It was like holy water or living water from Jacob's Well, which had to be the answer to a lot of prayers. As an 18 year old kid, I was never again tempted to drink while I was in the army.

A Message from Mom

Mom loved her children so much and was very close to each one of us. She was always there to counsel and lead us through good times and bad times. For some reason I always looked on her as immortal. At age fifty-two she developed a serious heart condition, which caused her an appalling amount of suffering until her death at age fifty-four.

Until her death there had not been a death in our immediate family. I could see her suffer, but I could not prepare myself for her death. Therefore, when she died, I was in shock and could not accept her death. I really became bitter at God for letting such a good person die.

I grieved for months, which was affecting my health and my whole being. I couldn't sleep at night and this was taking its toll on my attitude.

Then one night Mom appeared to me; I don't know whether I was asleep or awake. I don't know if it was a dream or a vision. In either case, it was real and she got a message to me. Mom said, "Paul, I want you to stop worrying about me. I'm so much better now and I don't hurt anymore. Now, you just get on with your life." She was beautiful and looked just like she did before she became sick.

From that very moment I released her. No longer did I grieve or have any remorse over her death. She seemed so happy that somehow I felt happy for her. I just thanked God for letting it be possible for me to get this message.

A Young Man Who Didn't Want to Supervise

During my first Plant Manager's job at Laurinburg, NC, I was in the process of trying to organize and train a management team. There was a nice looking, well-mannered young man with a high school education working for me, and I thought he would do well in this management training program.

I asked him to come to my office so that we could talk. When I approached him about becoming a management trainee, he said, "No!" He didn't bat an eye or even think twice about it. He told me that he was a Christian and didn't feel that a Christian could be a supervisor.

This set me back and made me speechless for a moment. My first impulse was to say, "What do you think I am?" But before I said anything, I thought for a minute and decided that I must not be much of a Christian if he couldn't see it in me.

Right then and there I made the decision to try to live my life and conduct my affairs in a way that would be consistent with Christ's teachings. I wanted this to be visible in my everyday life -

not by what I said but by what I did.

This incident is one of the lessons of life that I learned at an unexpected time from an unexpected source. It helped me to realize that we just have to be open to the signals from the messenger and then react accordingly.

An Employee Who Wouldn't Work Regularly

Several years ago I was managing a large textile plant in a rural area of North Carolina. Unemployment in the county was very low, and it was a big issue to keep the plant staffed.

Absenteeism was a problem, so we initiated a policy whereby the first time an employee was out without a legitimate excuse, his supervisor counseled with him. The second time he was out, his department manager counseled with him. The third time he was out, the Plant Manager counseled with him, and after the fourth time, he was terminated.

There was a particular young man who had already been counseled with twice, and he was out a third time; so, now it was time for me to talk with him.

His supervisor brought him to my office and we began to talk. He wouldn't look at me while I was talking to him, so I felt I wasn't getting anywhere with him. I got mad and told the supervisor to fire him because he didn't seem the least bit interested in improving his attendance.

Then I got my composure and calmed down. I said to him, "Look, all we are trying to do is help you; tell me what your problems are." This was all he needed -- just a chance to vent his frustrations -- and he began to cry.

It turned out that he was an illegitimate child and his mother had abandoned him. His grandmother had raised him but really didn't want him. He had been kicked off the high school ball team, and he had been expelled from school. He was just waiting for us to fire him as he felt nobody cared what happened to him.

I told him that we didn't want to fire him and that we really wanted to help him. I asked him if he would work with us and give us a chance to help him. He said that he would, and he did.

This young man developed into a model employee. He worked regularly and was promoted to high-skilled jobs. I never went through the plant while he was working that he didn't speak and tell me how he was getting along. He gained a lot of self-esteem.

I gained assurance that if you use patience to analyze problems, you can better solve them. I also learned that everybody has worth, and it is up to us to help them find it. As stewards of God's love, He expects us to try to bring the best out of all who pass our way.

Corporate Vice President's Advice

Several years ago I was hired by a company to manage a plant that was performing very poorly. The efficiency of the plant was very low and the fabric quality was low.

A few days after I began working in this plant, I was visited by a Vice President of the company. As we were going through each department, he began pointing out to me the supervisory people that he thought I would have to fire before I got the plant started up.

By the time he named three people (who he felt had to go) I stopped him. I said, "Mr. H., you have brought me in to try to get the plant running. Please don't plant any seeds about who will or won't work out. Please let me evaluate and determine who I can get to run his job." Mr. H. said, "O.K., but I only want to help."

Well, the plant did turn around and started performing beautifully. As it turned out, the people who Mr. H. thought should be fired turned out to be my best performers.

I learned from this experience that each of us perceives the value of other people differently. Just because the past manager couldn't get these men to perform didn't mean that I couldn't get them motivated. I also learned that one of the most important ingredients between a plant manager and his management team is the chemistry mixture between them.

It was not long, after I began the rebuilding of this management team, that I discovered that all these people really wanted was an opportunity to run their job. I gave them that opportunity and, with God's help, it worked.

Wanting Recognition

Once I was hired to manage a plant where the moral was very low. There was a union organizing effort going full blast, and they were about ready to ask for a vote. There were three or four insiders who were really mobilizing the campaign, and there was a battery of outsiders.

It had always been my belief that management created the atmosphere whereby the employees felt the need for a union. I knew that a campaign such as this was just a reaction to something that management had or had not done.

So, I began searching for what management had done to cause all the grief for the employees. When I discovered a complaint, I corrected it or explained to the employees why I couldn't correct it.

Much time was spent in the plant learning the employees. I tried to find out what their hurts were; I talked to them about their families, hobbies, gardens, flowers, religion, etc.

After spending several months with these people, I got to know them in a different way. I felt a kinship and an appreciation for them. The employees let the union know that they weren't interested in having a union in their plant.

One of the main disgruntled employees, who had spearheaded the drive, raised exotic birds. This was a topic of much conversation between us as I loved birds also. I visited his home to see his birds.

Before the decision was made to drop the organizing effort, this man told the union that he was no longer interested in helping with the drive. Another employee asked this once disgruntled employee why he no longer wanted a union. He said, "Look, all I wanted was recognition and now I'm getting it."

This man developed into an excellent employee and a good friend. He taught me a very valuable lesson about the importance of cultivating relationships – relationships that bring out the best in a person and make him or her feel good about themselves.

An Experience When I Felt the Presence of Christ

In 1979 I was having an annual physical examination, which was required by my employer. Everything was fine until I was put on the treadmill. After 4 minutes, the doctor took me off and told me to dress and see him in his office.

When I entered his office and sat down, he said, "I know you just came prepared for a routine physical and then return to your job. You didn't come prepared for bad news. But, there are indications that you have serious blockages in the arteries supplying blood to your heart. After only 4 minutes of exercise, your heart was screaming for blood."

After gulping several times, I said, "What does that mean?" He said, "You could have a serious or fatal heart attack at any moment." He then went over my options and then left the office for me to ponder alone.

I thought -- how am I going to tell Leta? What am I going to do? I wanted to get out of there and just run and run, but there was no place to go. I closed my eyes and said, "Lord, don't dump this on me now! I can't handle it." But I got the feeling that He didn't like that statement too well.

For, He surely hadn't dumped on me all the mashed potatoes and gravy I had eaten through the years, nor the french fries, nor T-bone steaks, nor the banana pudding. He had not forced me to smoke all the cigarettes and cigars I had smoked. I didn't think I was getting anywhere with Him, so I just asked Him, "Don't leave me -- please be with me through this ordeal."

With His help I was able to get my composure back and tell Leta of my problems on a positive note. By the time I got to Emory for surgery, I gave my pastor and doctor a pep talk. The whole process went extremely well.

God didn't desert me. I found Him to be faithful to his promise as stated in Hebrews 13:5 where He said, "I will never leave you nor forsake you." This scripture came alive for me.

Chapter 66

FAMILY HISTORY

Poston Genealogy

The first Poston on record to come to America immigrated from England to Chester County in Pennsylvania. His name was John Hamill Poston I, and it is believed that he sailed from Liverpool, England on the 26th day of April 1703. It has been concluded that he came from Shropshire, England.

During a genealogy search by Erma Poston Landers, she discovered other Postons in England — all living in Shropshire. So, we assume that Shropshire is the ancestral home of the Postons.

John I was a farmer and lived the remaining years of his life in Pennsylvania. He died in 1747 leaving four children; Robert, John II, Anthony, and Ann.

According to John I's will, the estate was left to the oldest son, Robert. Sons John II and Anthony received livestock and cash, but for some reason daughter Ann was cut out of the will. John II and Anthony migrated to the Carolinas about 1766. John II married in Pennsylvania prior to moving to the Carolinas.

John III was born about 1755, and migrated to the Carolinas with his parents at age 11. John III settled in the Marion District of South Carolina on the west side of the Great Pee Dee River. He had eight children.

The third son born to John III was named Francis "Frank" Poston IV and he was born in 1790 in the Marion District. Francis IV was our ancestor, as we now know. He had three sons and three daughters. His first son, Josiah R. Poston V, was born in 1817 and he was my great grandfather.

Josiah V had four sons and four daughters. The third son, Edward P. Poston VI, was born in 1847 and was my grandfather. Edward VI married Emily Ann Creel, who was born in 1852. This union brought forth nine children as follows:

Name	Date of Birth
1. Zack	about 1869
2. Ansel	about 1873
3. Missouri	1877

4. Tula	1879
5. Luvenia	1881
6. Cornelius	about 1884
7. Mack Kenzie	1888
8. Bertha	1894
9. Rozela	1897

Mack Kenzie Poston VII (Edward VI, Josiah V, Frank IV, John III, John II, and John I) born in 1888 in Florence County was my father. Mack married Carrie Yulee Greenwood, who was born in 1894. From this union seven boys and three girls were born as follows:

Name	Date of Birth
Merrill Willard	November 17, 1914
Lance Edward	December 15, 1916
Daltrum Holmes "Bunkus"	May 30, 1919
Nellie Yulee	October 7, 1921
Rowena Byrd	November 27, 1923
John Paul "Peenbung"	August 20, 1926
David Milton "Peenywinkus"	November 1, 1928
Max Lefay "That Boy"	November 16, 1931
Virginia Ann "Sis"	November 18, 1933
Jerry Travis	July 1, 1937

The writer of this book is John Paul Poston VIII, the sixth child of Mack K. and Yulee G. Poston. Without the Christian love, dedication of beliefs, and strong family values given by my parents, the writing of this book would not have happened. As far as we can determine from past records, none of our ancestors owned slaves. We certainly hope and believe that this is true.

The genealogy prior to my grandfather, Edward P. Poston VI, came from a book entitled <u>A Poston Family of South Carolina</u> by Erma Poston Landers.

Biographies of Immediate Family:

The following facts about the immediate family are given to enable the reader to relate the particular person to the various incidents that I have attempted to describe. These events happened to us during the span of time that this book covers from the mid-1920's to the mid-1940's.

There is nothing unusual about any of the people being written about in this book. They were mostly very poor, honest, hard-working, dirt farmers. They had a strong faith in their Christian beliefs.

FATHER
Mack Kenzie Poston
Born December 25, 1888 and died December 28, 1954.

Mack was born into a family of nine children. His father owned a farm, but late in life during sickness and several poor crop years, he lost the farm due to indebtedness. This left the family struggling for survival.

Mack was not able to go to school until he was thirteen years old, and then he had to work for money to buy his first book. He finished the third grade before he had to quit to help support the family. He had an older brother, Zack, but even at a young age, Mack had to assume a lot of the responsibilities for the family.

As a young man he worked in Lake Helen, Florida in the orange groves in an effort to better his lot in life. In that era a young man's ego status was concentrated around his horse and buggy as his means to travel about and "sport" the girls; this ego status changed to cars in the 20's, 30's, and 40's.

Mack bought his first buggy when he was nineteen years old for fifty-five dollars on December 21, 1907. The buggy was a fancy one with red running gears, black body, a buggy harness set, and a lap robe. He signed a note and got his brother-in-law, McKeever Poston, to co-sign the note.

Mack, my father, fell in love with Carrie Yulee Greenwood and they were married on December 25, 1913 - on his twenty-fifth birthday. He was born late in the family or about twenty years after Uncle Zack was born. The girls of the family just spoiled him in looking after his every need, and he never got that out of his system.

My mother started where the sisters stopped and continued during their life together. She saw to it that his every need and desire was taken care of.

He could never eat large meals and would have to eat something between meals. When he worked in the fields, Mom would send him a snack between breakfast and dinner and another between dinner and supper.

Mack was physically a very strong man particularly in his young life. It was told that once when ginning cotton someone bet him a bale of cotton that he couldn't lift it. It was said that he backed up to the bale that was on the dock and gave it a hump and carried it to his wagon.

He was also a very handsome man; he was six feet tall and weighed about 175 pounds. He loved to walk better than anyone I've ever known. He maintained good health until he was 64 years old, when it was concluded that he had cancer.

Mack always wore clean, neat, and fitted clothes. He always had one good dress suit, which he kept clean and pressed. When he dressed in that suit with white shirt and tie he looked as distinguished as any lawyer, preacher, or politician that came along.

He read constantly anything that he could get his hands on. He could discuss intelligently most any subject that came up. He was a very effective public speaker. Some people called him "the college professor with a third grade education."

When he was young, he played a fiddle with a group that entertained at various functions. After his wedding, he quit the fiddle; but he would set us children on his knees and sing some of the songs that he remembered from his earlier days.

Mack had a spiritual conversion experience in his young adult life, and this changed his direction forever. From that day on there was never any doubt where he stood with his Lord. As far as any of the family knew, he never varied or backslid from that conviction.

He was a devoted Methodist and strongly supported the Trinity Methodist Church until he moved to Possum Fork in 1945. He then joined the Johnsonville Methodist church, and -- if the doors of the church were open, he was there. This was the kind of life he tried to show and teach his children.

He was strongly opinionated on some subjects but none more than politics. He was very active in local, county and state politics. He was not bashful when it came to trying to persuade someone to vote for a person or an issue that he believed in.

By the very strongest terms, he was a democrat. After the depression, which by the way he blamed on Hoover, he looked on Republicans with the same affection as with communist, or the

Germans, and Japanese during the Second World War.

Everything that Mack did, he tried to do it to the best of his ability. If he plowed the fields, he plowed the straightest rows that I have ever seen. If he built a barn, or a mule stable, or anything, you could bet that it would be the best. He was strict on us children and always had enough work delegated to keep us busy and "out of trouble."

Mack had a Model T Ford and drove it and several other Model T cars and trucks. When he bought a Chevrolet with shift gears in 1938, he never even tried to drive it. We never understood his reason.

He never really worked hard; he would get things set-up and show us what he wanted done and then take off. He would then go do something that was less strenuous, or go hunting or fishing, or just go and sit and read. He was a good "delegator" -- he would show, tell, and follow-up. He would have been an excellent Mill Manager, if he had been given the opportunity.

Mack spent his whole life helping people out that had fallen on hard times. He would deprive himself to help someone out. Note attached copies of doctor bills that he paid for his father. Also note doctor bills he paid for various black people who had no means for paying their bills, but who needed to see a doctor.

Mack died of cancer at age 66 in 1954, which was six years after my mother died. He was a person who never really showed his emotions and always presented a strong and positive image. Yet, he never got over my mother's death -- he was never really the same after she passed away.

MOTHER
Carrie Yulee Greenwood Poston,
Born August 25, 1894, died September 25, 1948.

Yulee, my mother, was born into the family of John Travis and Adelia Virginia Marsh Greenwood. There were six children born to this couple, who lived to adulthood. Yulee was the third child and the first girl born into this family.

John Travis and Adelia were either married later in life than normal for that era, or they didn't have children for several years. Adelia was thirty years old when their first child was born and John was forty-two. This length of time without children probably gave them some time to accumulate a little wealth. It seemed that they got along a little better than the average family in that area and time.

Yulee finished the seventh grade in school and, from information obtained, she was an excellent student. She was in various school plays and sang songs with different groups.

Mom would tell us children about the parts that she had played, and she could still recite the words and phrases that she had learned. She had learned a number of songs and sang them constantly for us. The song that stands out in my memory was an Indian love song. It went something like this:

"Now, the moon shines tonight on pretty Red Wing.
the breeze is sighing—the night bird's crying,
For afar 'neath his star her brave is sleeping,
While Red Wing's weeping—her heart away."

She had learned a lot of short stories and was a very good storyteller. Often at night before her children were put to bed, the small ones gathered around her and listened to stories.

Yulee was an excellent reader and would read to her children what she thought they would enjoy. One article that I can remember most vividly was a retelling of the story of the Titanic. This article was written in the Progressive Farmer in 1932 on the Twentieth Anniversary of the sinking of the big ship, the Titanic.

Yulee was the most unselfish, care-giving, self-sacrificing person that God ever made. She was beautiful but her pride was not in herself; it was in her husband and her children. This was really her downfall because there wasn't a member of the family that didn't take advantage of this generosity.

She did not have any discipline problems as the children usually obeyed her wishes. The problem was that she just didn't require enough of the children. She did not delegate enough things for the children to do, and they usually didn't volunteer to do a lot. So what happened is that she did the chores that the children should have done. She also did a lot of things that her husband should have done.

Yulee was an excellent cook and, of course, this brought meal guests from far and near. Very few weeks went by that the Methodist preacher and his family didn't visit and have a meal with us. Most every Sunday we had at least one family of relatives to visit and eat Sunday dinner with us.

Mack did a lot of hunting and fishing, which often required her to get up early and fix breakfast for several of his friends. Usually on the farm several extra people would be working and they were always fed dinner.

Yulee could sew well and, when she had time, she made a lot of the clothes that she and the girls wore. Along with a shortage of time, there was also a shortage of money to buy fabrics. She made some shirts and underwear for the boys. Her sewing machine was a New Home pedal-type, and I can still remember the harmonic sounds coming from the sewing machine when it was going full speed.

My mother developed high blood pressure and a heart condition while in her forties. At that time there just wasn't any medication to relieve or abate these conditions. With these medical problems, nervous energy, and love of family, she burned herself out and died at the age of fifty-four.

Yulee gave all she had to the ones she loved. She was truly one of God's Chosen Saints. Her life everyday was lived as an example of the teachings of Christ. She carried the Living Christ in her heart and the Living Christ was seen in her not only by what she said but by what she did.

Biographies of Siblings:

Biographies of the siblings will be short and cover only the period starting in the mid 1920's through the Second World War in the mid 1940's.

Merrill Willard Poston

Born November 17, 1914 and died March 1, 1974.

Merrill was the first child born in the union between Mack and Yulee. He was also the first grandchild on the Greenwood side. I am sure this made him special.

He was special for a number of other reasons – but, being the oldest child, we all looked up to him and tried to follow the standards he set. This created problems for all of us as Merrill was an extremely strong student.

He made high grades all through school on all subjects, and the teachers, other students, and (I am sure our parents) expected all of us to do the same. We were not all equipped mentally as well as Merrill and some of us did have some disappointments.

When Merrill finished high school, he wanted to study law. Dad and Uncle Furman, mom's brother, wanted to get him into college. This was during the depth of the depression, and they just couldn't swing it. He stayed on the farm and helped with the farm duties.

In 1936 Trinity School bought a second school bus. During this time Uncle John Marsh, grandma Greenwood's brother, was a trustee, so Merrill got the job of driving the second bus.

We didn't have a car, so Merrill bought a bicycle to ride from the schoolhouse back home. He worked on the farm until time to take the children home in the evening. Then he rode the bicycle back to school to get the bus and leave the bicycle at school overnight. This bicycle was taken home on weekends as this was our only transportation — other than mules and wagon. This bicycle was ridden by all the children and we just wore it out.

Merrill never gave our parents any problems; he was always there "like a rock." He helped in supporting the family all that he could during those difficult times. He had no interest in hunting and fishing; he enjoyed reading much more.

Merrill loved singing and was in the Trinity choir as long as I can remember. It is my belief that our parents never forgot to thank God many times for sending them such a fine son. Merrill married Nellie Hope Furches in 1938, and they moved to Joe King's Farm to become sharecroppers.

This union brought forth four children: Robert Hope, Henry Mack, Merrinell, and James Willard.

Lance Edward Poston

Born December 15, 1916 and died September 17, 1961.

Lance was the second son and was born two years after Merrill. This had to be a difficult situation to be put in – following such a gifted brother.

Lance had a little more devilment in him than the rest of the family. He got more pleasure out of pulling a prank or a joke on someone than anyone I have ever known.

Lance was not a weak student, but studying his text books was not his first priority. The availability of so many library books overwhelmed him to the point that he lived in the library.

After Lance finished high school, he started a course with a correspondence school. The money to pay for it was hard to come by and nothing developed from it as it was the wrong thing at the wrong time. Lance had no interest in hunting and fishing; these activities were not his thing. He did buy a 22 caliber single-shot ranger rifle. He made the money by painting part-time for Mr. L. B. Rogers, who was the local paint contractor. He never really used the rifle, but the brothers who loved to hunt wore the rifle out.

Lance tried a number of different jobs while he was growing up to try to supplement our strained economic condition. He painted some for Mr. Rogers, he sold the Grit paper, and he sold the Blair Home products.

When he was about eighteen, he got a job at Mrs. Jessie Rawlings General Store. The store was a log store about 20' x 24', which was built in the heart of Poston. This job paid about a dollar a day, which was a big help for him and for the family.

Lance started smoking early at about thirteen or fourteen years old. He would buy a five cent bag of Golden Grain tobacco and hide it. Later he would slip off and make a cigarette by putting the loose tobacco in a thin piece of paper. He had to lick the pre-glued place and pinch the end so the tobacco wouldn't fall out.

When he was ready to light his cigarette, he watched cautiously for Mom and Dad. If either of them had caught him, they would have cured his desire for nicotine – at least for a while.

In the late 30's economic conditions began to improve. The rumbling of war was being heard throughout the world. Lance was drafted into the Navy during World War II.

Lance married Hannah Mae Evans in 1940 and this union brought forth four children: Harriett Ann, Gail Maxine, Lance Joyce, and Hannah Theresa.

Daltrum Holmes "Bunkus" Poston

Born May 30, 1919 and died August 2, 1970.

Daltrum, "Bunkus," was the first child in our family to take on and keep a nickname, which was given by our father. He was the third son, and the oldest was just five years old when he was born. So, I'm sure our mother had her hands full by this time.

"Bunkus" grew into the child with the bubbly personality. He just didn't seem to take things as seriously as the rest of the children when we were growing up. But he had a knack for getting into a little more trouble than the rest of the family. He even tried to make wine out of plums. This experiment really didn't turn out so well.

When "Bunkus" was about twelve years old, he started smoking. He didn't have money to buy his five cent bags of Golden Grain, so somehow he would just find a couple of chicken eggs, take them to the store, and trade them for tobacco.

Sometimes our sister, Rowena, would help "Bunkus" find the eggs. I think he would bring her some candy for aiding and abetting him in this scheme.

Eggs were the best thing on the farm for bartering as the price for chicken eggs was around fifty cents a dozen during the tough times. Guinea and duck eggs were not worth as much as chicken eggs -- usually about thirty-five cents a dozen.

This smoking habit that "Bunkus" had got him into trouble several times by getting caught by our parents. They didn't take too lightly to children smoking. I used to try to shame him and tell him I was never going to smoke until I was man enough to do it in front of Daddy. However, he paid no attention to me.

As "Bunkus" was growing up, it seemed that all of life was an adventure. He made pleasure out of everything he had to do and let it fit into that philosophy.

He was a real hunting and fishing enthusiast and used both to improve his economic situation. He kept some fish traps in the Pee Dee River or the Lynches River and would sell any fish we did not need to eat.

He did the same thing with his hunting of squirrels and birds. He usually had a little extra money, which helped the family and himself.

"Bunkus" had no problems in school other than having a lot of projects going on that weren't school related. Studying, particularly in high school, was not on top of his priority list, but later he graduated from college and became a Methodist minister.

In 1939 he and his best friend, Joseph Furches, joined the Navy for six years. He did well in the Navy; he had a few close calls during the war, but he completed his six years in 1945 and by this time the war was over.

He met Grace Helen Nunn when he was stationed in Houston, Texas, and they were married in 1944. From this union there were four children: Karry Sue, Lynda Anne, Clara Jo, and Daltrum Holmes, Jr. He always had a smile for everyone he met.

Nellie Yulee Poston

Born October 7, 1921 and died March 14, 1992.

Nellie was the fourth child born in my family but she was the first girl. She must have been a joy to our parents after having three boys.

My parents lived in a house about two hundred yards from our grandparents, the Greenwoods, for several years after Nellie was born. She quickly became "their pick of the litter" and that never changed. She would walk over to their house and start calling for Grandpa to "Oh doe Grandpa" before she got there. They would keep her for long periods during her growing years due to the bond that had developed.

Nellie always seemed like a grown adult to the younger children of the family. She set standards and values for her life and she never wavered from them.

To us young siblings it seemed that she was wise beyond her years because at times it appeared that she knew us better than we knew ourselves. One time we were sitting around talking about how bad things were and what little we had. Nellie came up with her famous words of wisdom: "You better be glad you is got what you is got." Friends that she made were true friends and were friends for life.

Nellie did not relish the idea of working in the fields, chopping cotton, succoring tobacco, worming tobacco, etc. These really weren't her favorite things in life. She was deathly afraid of the big green-horn tobacco worms. My older brothers kept her running and screaming as they attempted to put worms on her. This pestering her continued until one of our parents stepped-in and put a stop to it.

Also, Nellie was not too crazy about washing all the dishes needed to feed twelve people. One time she was washing and drying the dishes. She had about twelve plates stacked and was carrying them into the pantry. Her elbow hit the door and she dropped and broke all the plates. This about wiped us out until some more plates could be bought. We children told her she meant to do it because she was mad; I'm sure that was not the case.

Nellie had no serious problems in school. She did love to

read, and she read everything she could get out of the school library.

One Sunday afternoon Lance left his Model A Coupe at the house. Nellie who was 16 years old decided that she was going to drive it. She had never driven before nor had she ever even attempted to drive.

She started backing it out of the yard and got it hung-up in the fence. To make matters even worse, she got out and left the wheels spinning. The car bogged down deep in the sand.

There were just some of the small children at home no adults. We had a time getting the car out of the bog and loose from the fence.

Then we tried to destroy the evidence. The fence had to be patched, the holes in the sand covered, the tire tracks erased, and the scratches on Lance's shiny Model A covered with black shoe polish. We apparently did a good job because this is the first revelation that this ever happened.

Nellie got a job with the Atlantic Seaboard Railway as a depot agent in Gresham. This was in the heyday of the railroads and a lot of freight was being shipped in and out of Gresham. This also helped to improve the economic strife for Nellie and the family.

While working at Gresham, Nellie met Mr. Ed Whaley, who asked her to write his son Dan, who was in the Navy. She did write Dan, they corresponded for a while, and then in 1943 they were married. From this union three children were born: Carol Ann, Nellie Jean, and Daniel Edward, III.

Rowena Byrd Poston
Born November 27, 1923.

Rowena was the fifth child born into the family within nine years. Having five small children with the economic conditions as they were had to be real stressful for our parents. But, you would have never known it.

Rowena was born with a serious handicap as some of her organs had not developed in the correct places. There was nothing medically that could be done at that time. The doctors gave her only a few days to live, but she showed them.

Then they said she would live not more than a few months. Again she showed them. Then they said she surely couldn't live more than seven years and again she proved them wrong.

The next prediction was that she couldn't live past thirteen, but they still didn't know Rowena nor did they know the power of the many prayers being "sent-up" for her. There were no further predictions made after this last one was proven wrong.

After World War II, medical knowledge had improved, so she went to Duke Hospital in Durham, North Carolina. Here they did some corrective surgery, which improved her condition somewhat.

Rowena had a very keen mind. She did not attend regular school because of her handicap, but she learned right along with those of us who did go to school. The county started a tutoring program in the mid-thirties for handicapped children and hired Norvel Bragdon to tutor her. She did exceptionally well in this program, but after a couple of years the county quit funding it. We were all sad because she was doing so well.

When we were growing up Rowena had some connections that the rest of us didn't have. She would overhear different people talking and pass that information on to us.

Just before Christmas when I was in the first grade in school, she learned a status on Santa Claus that we small children had never heard of. It shocked me and I wanted to find out for sure if the new findings were correct. I would say to her, "I'm going to ask Mom."

She would beg, plead, and cry to get me not to approach Mom on the subject. For a long time I used this to get my way just by saying, "I'm going to tell Mom." She would always know where everything was hidden at Christmas.

When we were very small, Rowena was the leader in getting us to try various uses of tobacco. First we tried to smoke rabbit tobacco; then we tried dead grape vine stems that were about a quarter of an inch in diameter; and then we tried dried tobacco leaves. None of this worked too well so we tried chewing some of the regular leaf. Well, this did us in as all of us got sick.

We built play houses out of tobacco sticks. Daddy didn't take too kindly to this because invariably we broke a stick or two. Rowena might have lacked in formal education, but she held her own and made up for it with savvy.

From young adulthood, Rowena had a very deep faith in Christ and lived that faith. She was helpful to Mom during her critical illness and until her death. She was also a big support to Dad after Mom's death and until his death.

Rowena married Fred McPhatter in 1962 and from this union they had one son: Frederick Franklin, Jr.

David Milton "Peenywinkus" Poston
Born November 1, 1928.

David was the seventh child and the fifth boy born in this family. At the time of his birth we were living on a farm in Salem, South Carolina. The name David was given by our Dad as he wanted another son with a Biblical name. The nickname "Peenywinkus" was also given by Dad but it did not stick -- and was later forgotten.

David as a child had a God-given talent, which caused adults to like him. When he was about four, we had a friend, Arthur Junior Poston, who was my age. He came to our house to play almost everyday.

Andrew Prosser, an adult neighbor, would come by with empty 200 lb. fertilizer bags. He would catch me and Arthur Junior and tie us up in these bags. He would let us roll around, yell, and scream. For some reason he wouldn't do this to David; they were big buddies.

David was a little shyer than the rest of the family; also, he would not venture off very far from home. Once he and I went to the Greenwoods to spend several days. The first night some of the Marshes, cousins of the Greenwoods, came in and David got so upset that they took both of us home.

When David started to school, he had not quite gotten out of all his shyness. He was young as he wasn't six until November, so his adjustment to school was difficult. After that he got the idea of what school was all about so he breezed through the rest of school. He had grades near to what Merrill had made during his school years.

Some of the students ribbed us about our grades. They would say, "If you wanted to make good grades, you needed to have Mack Poston and Yulee Greenwood for parents."

David never expressed any desire to go to college; he certainly had all the credentials needed for college work. He joined the Navy shortly after graduation from high school for four years.

David, being the seventh child, had to be a lot of relief and pleasure to our parents. He was one who never gave them any problems of any kind. He always tried to do things the way they wanted them done. He established a moral and Christian code of ethics early in life and lived by them.

David was never much of a smoker when he was a boy, but he did learn to chew tobacco. He never developed any interest in hunting and fishing so he did very little of either.

The friendships that David developed were deep and remained strong for a long time. He did not have any serious girl friends until he returned from the Navy. When he came out of the Navy, he met Lura Belle Hardee. They were married in 1954 and from this union two children were born: Virginia Dale and David Mack.

Max Lefay "That Boy" Poston
Born November 16, 1931 and died June 6, 1977.

We were living on Joe King's Farm when Max was born. He was the eighth child and was born three years after David, so our parents had a little break between them.

Max, we thought, was the prettiest baby we had ever seen, but I'm sure we were prejudiced. The older children were growing up and he came along at a time when we all just spoiled him. The children were up big enough, particularly the girls, to help Mom take care of him.

His name being Max and Dad's being Mack made Dad reluctant to call him Max, so he started calling him "That Boy." This name did not stick after he got into school.

Max got a lot of attention from everyone and probably got into more trouble than the children before him. He kept his good looks, had a smile for everyone, and grew to be about 6' 4", looking more like our Dad than any of the other children.

He was the first Poston child born after our Mother's brothers, Mack and Jessie Greenwood, got married and started having children. Mack had a son, Norman, born before Max so all the attention that the Poston children had been getting from the Greenwoods was now diverted to the Greenwood grandchildren. This, of course, hurt us Poston children and our relationship with Grandma, Uncle "Bubba" and Aunt Alma was never the same. We began to feel somewhat like outsiders.

Uncle Furman "Pum" never seemed to change. We remained close until his death. So Max never shared the bonding experiences as a child with the Greenwoods that the older children had.

Max developed asthma very early and this held him back some from the normal growing-up boy activities. We used to feel so sorry for him -- seeing him struggling to breathe when he had an attack. We children would cry and pray for him, and I'm sure our parents were doing the same. There was so little that the doctors could do for asthma back then.

Max was a very strong student and breezed through school with no problems. He expressed no interest in going to college--that I know of. He loved hunting, fishing and camping-out. Camping-out was one of his real joys, but this usually caused problems with his asthma.

Max had an outgoing personality and made a lot of friends. He seemed to possess more leadership than most of our siblings. This showed up early in Max's endeavors in the business world. He had the ability to become anything that he wanted to be: an architect, Certified Public Accountant, lawyer, or doctor had he so desired.

Max married Jean Turner in 1952 and from this union two children were born: Max Lefay, Jr. and Kimberlyn Marie. He went in business for himself shortly after their marriage.

Virginia Ann "Sis" Poston
Born November 11, 1933.

Virginia Ann was the ninth child born to our parents. The name "Ann" came from our Grandmother Poston and "Virginia" came from our Grandmother Greenwood. The name Ann was used four times for children of our brothers and sisters.

We were living on Joe King's place when Virginia was born. Most of the children were born bald or with just a little light fuzz, but Virginia had a head full of black hair. She was so little and pretty and was a pleasant change after three boys. Max was just two years old and just starting to talk. He couldn't say Virginia, so "Sis" came naturally and has stuck forever.

Growing up with older brothers, "Sis" had a tough struggle. She was small, but she stood her ground. She was both tough and feisty.

When "Sis" was born, Rowena was ten years old and couldn't work in the fields. Mom worked in the fields and Rowena tended to "Sis," and was really like a mother to her. This created a close bond between them that will last forever.

Mom was sick about five years before she died in 1948. I feel that "Sis" missed a lot of what the other children had gotten from Mom. She was only fifteen when Mom died. Rowena tried to step-in and take Mom's place and did a remarkable job.

A discipline problem would have been a fairly normal thing by "Sis" missing so much of Mom's guidance and being near the last of a large family. This absolutely was not the case as "Sis" grew up to be a lady of the first order and a beautiful person.

She was another Poston who was a strong student and just breezed through school with no problems. She even made a good cotton picker! Mom wrote me while I was in service that "Sis", Rowena, and David had picked all the cotton because she couldn't get Max and Jerry to pick.

Like Max ahead of her she did not have the Greenwood affection as it was being channeled to the Greenwood grandchildren. Nellie stepped-in and gave her a lot of love and guidance. "Sis" went on several long trips with Nellie and stayed with Nellie for extended periods.

"Sis" attended Columbia College and completed a two year secretarial course. The family was extremely happy that she was afforded the opportunity. She met Bennie Chinnis from Hemingway and they were Married in 1954.

Jerry Travis Poston
Born July 1, 1937.

Jerry was the tenth child and was born four years after "Sis". Mom was forty-five when he was born and Dad was fifty-one. One thing that made him special was that he was so big and strong.

When he was born, he weighed twelve pounds and he jerked Aunt "Culia's" glasses off the first day he arrived. The women at our church had given Mom a baby shower, but the only things she could use were the diapers, blankets, etc. All the clothes were too small.

I remember Mrs. Lucille Cornwell, our landlord's wife, saying that she thought the breed ran out as the parents got older. She further stated that she believed that the reverse was the case with Jerry. He was big and strong enough right off for all of us to hold him, so he really got held a lot and spoiled a little.

We lived in "Powell's Corner" on the Woodberry place when

Jerry was born. The economy had improved. Our move to the Woodberry farm had been a good move, so our lifestyle had improved. Rowena continued as the daytime baby-sitter for "Sis" and took Jerry on as a bonus. Her mothering of Jerry was the same as with "Sis" and this created a bond that will last forever.

Rowena was fourteen when Jerry was born and had gained strength so she could run after Jerry better than she could "Sis" -- when she first started keeping her. Mom continued to work in the fields, plus cook, can, wash, etc.

Our parents, having grown older, seemed to be more protective of Jerry than they had been with the other children. I remember once when we lived in "The Backwoods" in a house with a tin top roof that we had a terrible hail storm. The hail was golf-ball size and in that tin roof it was so loud that you could hear nothing other than that loud roar. I looked at Dad and he had Jerry up in his arms—trying to comfort him, which was an unusual show of emotions for him.

Jerry had the usual childhood diseases, but in 1943 he contacted scarlet fever. There wasn't much that could be done about it back then. It could leave you as an invalid or kill you. This created a great deal of strain and concern for the whole family, but this crisis actually brought us all closer together.

Our family was quarantined for several weeks. No one could leave the house and no one could visit except Doctor Poston. Merrill was living on Joe King's place, and I can remember that occasionally he would slip around and visit Jerry without anyone knowing about it.

All of the school-age children in the family had to stay out for several weeks. It was an emotional time for all of us. There were a couple of weeks when we didn't know whether Jerry was going to live through this.

Jerry was only eleven years old when Mom died and only seventeen when Dad died. He had no problems in school, but I am sure he missed the discipline and direction of our parents. Studying was not a high priority.

Rowena stepped-in and was Mother and Father for Jerry. Jerry's lack of having his parents guidance and training did not hurt him much. He established positive values, principles, and a lifestyle to live by early and didn't waver from them.

For some reason Jerry never did develop a love for picking cotton. It was hard for him to develop any enthusiasm about this chore.

After graduating from high school, Jerry visited some friends in Columbia. Shortly thereafter he got a good job with Southern Bell where he continued to work until retirement. He and Amelia Stone were married in 1962, and they had one son, Jerry Travis, Jr.

John Paul "Peenbung" Poston, Author

Born August 20, 1926.

Paul was the sixth child in twelve years born to his parents. He was named by his father as he wanted a son with a Biblical name. The nickname of "Peenbung" given by my father lasted only a few years and did not stick.

There was about a three year span between Rowena and Paul. Paul was always considered by our father as the first of the second group of children. Dad thought that he and Mom had done a better job of raising the first group than they did with the second group. He would make a statement saying, "We raised the first group and the second group was jerked-up."

Paul, knowing that his Dad felt this way, made concerted efforts to do good and prove him wrong. He may have given his parents more anxieties than the rest of the children because he had a little more temper and determination.

Paul was driven to work at as many jobs as possible to help in the economic strife the family was in. By the time he was nine years old, he was selling magazines, the Grit paper, feeding hogs for Pete Cornwell, killing squirrels and selling them, and catching fish and selling them.

When he was fourteen, he got a job at Bernie Poston's Store working for $1.50 per day, which was very good for those days. He had a Sunday paper route for the State paper to supplement his income.

Paul had to miss a lot of school because of work on the farm. The older boys in the family were either getting married and moving out or were going into service, so he had to fill in where they left off.

Paul could only go to school the number of days required to get a report card. All other days he had to work on the farm. It was hard to keep up but somehow he managed. By the way, he didn't start smoking until he went to the Army.

Paul never slept a lot. At night he stayed awake and tried to think of some kind of invention to make a work process more efficient. Perpetual motion was always on his mind. Even at a young age, he made a bed, a boat, a small log cabin, and numerous other things.

He loved hunting and fishing and spent a right good bit of time doing both. He had a few close friends, but he didn't take the time to cultivate a lot of friendships. He didn't develop a serious girlfriend until he was in service. His best friend was Christmas Brown, a black man who lived on the farm. They worked together, hunted and fished together, and were inseparable for several years.

There were only eleven grades in school so Paul finished high school a few months before his seventeenth birthday. The war had already started, so every able-bodied male eighteen and over was being drafted. So he had a year to do something before he was drafted.

He was needed on the farm but decided to go to Pfeiffer Junior College in Misenheimer, North Carolina. Pfeiffer had a work program on a farm, so Paul took the money he had saved from working at Bernie Poston's store and went to Pfeiffer.

He thought at that time that he was being called into the ministry. He worked so much at Pfeiffer that at the end of the school year they actually owed him money. Though he did not go into the ministry, he endeavored to maintain a personal relationship with Christ his Lord.

On February 8, 1945 Paul answered the call of his country for military duty. He was drafted into the Infantry and trained at Camp Gordon, Georgia. Time was spent in the Philippines and Japan before being discharged in January 1947.

When he returned from service, he went back to work at Bernie Poston's store. In 1951 he went to Wofford College on the G.I. Bill of Rights and finished in 1953. While at Wofford he worked at Beaumont Mill store every hour they would let him, but he still stayed on the Dean's List.

When Paul finished college he had more money in the bank than when he started. After graduation, he went to work in textiles, which was about the only industry in the South at that time.

On June 12, 1948 he married Leta Mae Tanner, a girl from Hemingway. He met her on a blind date while on furlough in June 1945. From this union three children were born: John Wayne, Leta Anne, and Stanley Ray.

Typical Sunday evening gathering of the Postons in Possum Fork in 1958.
L-to-R - Leta, Joyce, Stan, Danny, Wayne, Gail, Terry, Carol, Lance, Jean, Hanna Mae, Rowena, David, Lura, Max, Anne, and Nellie.

Poston house in Possum Fork
where children and grandchildren visited often.